PRISON DIARIES

From the Concrete Coffin

Charles Bronson

Foreword by Chris Cowlin
Introduction by Mark Peterson

Hardback first published in 2011
This edition published in 2014 by
Apex Publishing Ltd

12A St. John's Road, Clacton on Sea
Essex, CO15 4BP, United Kingdom
www.apexpublishing.co.uk

Paperback layout by
Andrews UK Limited
www.andrewsuk.com

Cover Design: Siobhan Smith
Production: Chris Cowlin and Kane Wingfield

Publishers Note: The views and opinions expressed in this
publication are those of the author and are not necessarily those of
Apex Publishing Ltd or Andrews UK Limited.

Copyright: Every attempt has been made to contact the relevant
copyright holders, Apex Publishing Ltd would be grateful if the
appropriate people contact us on: 01255 428500 or
mail@apexpublishing.co.uk

"I Dedicate This Book To The Queen —
— Of The Country "
     MY LANDLADY!!   ELiZaBeTH
She Has Given Me A Bed, Clothes, And Food,
For Almost 40 Years.
And Not CHARGed Me A Single Penny

    Long Live our Gracious Queen
                                        X
                                   2011

Foreword

I have met Charlie twice and visited him in September 2007 and then again in August 2010. Both visits were at Wakefield Prison, Yorkshire, also known as Monster Mansion.

I first came in contact with Charlie mid way through 2007 after publishing a book titled 'The Loose Screw' for former prison officer Jim Dawkins, and later 'Left Hooks and Dangerous Crooks' for Charlie's good friend Tel Currie.

Daunting isn't the word when I arrived at Wakefield Prison, my first ever visit to a prison. I went through 16 doors after the security process (fingerprints, searches, dog sniffing, etc, etc). I then went through the canteen, which is the room where other prisoners were, I didn't want to look up, but did; I remember seeing Ian Huntley and other high profile criminals, all famous for the wrong reasons - rape, murder, etc. One strange thing, I found the prison officers seemed to really like Charlie and appeared to respect him unlike other prisoners in Wakefield, which of course was full of murderers and sex-offenders.

Both times I have met with Charlie were good visits; we spoke about a lot of things, his books, his film, how he feels and what the future holds for him. He told me how he is looking forward to the day his film hits terrestrial television, so he can watch it for himself as he has been told so much about it and read so many reviews. People who have visited him will know how entertaining he is during your visit, as he does like to entertain you, telling you stories, jokes, etc, if I were allowed I would sit there for hours listening to him, he has so many stories to tell and is still desperate to be free, but he is realistic and knows there is a long way to go.

Charlie has told me stories about officers going to his cell door asking him to sign books and DVD covers, how can this be when we are meant to have a tight security system?

Charlie has never understood how I got passed to visit him, once maybe and when I arrived at Wakefield for the second time, his words were "How the fuck they let a publisher in here is beyond me - silly fuckers." You will read the first few pages of the book as though Charlie is writing letters to me, it had to be done this way for various reasons, the letters then stopped as the prison system thought Charlie was writing a book! There is a bit of a gap and then the book continues! I had the idea for the book whilst driving to see him in August 2010, he agreed but knew it may be hard with security being tight after he release of his film 'Bronson'. You will notice the book is in a diary style from August 2010 until March 2011, I asked Charlie to give us the facts written down, his thoughts, his mental state, funny stories, who visits him, who writes to him, who he speaks to, who he likes, who he doesn't like, what he eats, what he drinks and what he does 24/7 - he loved it and said "I love it Chris, yes, we will call it 'Prison Diaries: From The Concrete Coffin', and it will sell more copies than the fucking bible."

When I published Charlie's best selling book Loonylogy back in June 2008, I arranged a visit for a journalist from the Independent to visit Charlie to give the book good coverage in the national paper, I honestly didn't think the visit would go ahead especially when Bronson is such a high profile criminal and is not allowed much contact with the outside world, and thought it was a bad move when the journalist sent his letter on letter headed paper and an 'Independent' marked envelope. The prison authorities didn't do much checking and passed him and the feature on Charlie and his book ended up in the paper the following Monday morning.

One thing I have found with Charlie, he falls out with a lot of people. I really do think it's because he expects things from them and they don't deliver, and they don't understand his position - how could they, how could any of us imagine being locked up for nearly 35 years, especially is solitary. I have met Charlie's mother, Eira, and Charlie's brother, Mark, both of which I have a lot of time and respect for, Mark is actually one of the nicest people you would ever meet and some people would never think he is the brother of the infamous criminal Charles Bronson.

One thing I love about Charlie is his artwork - you think they are such simple drawings until you look at them closely and then found yourself looking at them in different ways, trying to get into his mind, trying to think what his thoughts were when he was putting pen to paper.

All of Charlie's books have been entertaining, Loonyology more than most I think as all of those words are his, no ghost writers, it was straight from his cell and then typed up at my office. This book, however, is much more - no editing, no typing, this is the REAL Charlie in his HANDWRITING. This has never been done before and I doubt will ever be done again. You will read humorous things like his love for the X Factor and Coronation Street, also his feelings about the prison system, it is a good mix of Charlie's day to day activities and thoughts.

We have had our ups and downs but I have really enjoyed working with Charlie. I don't believe things that have been printed in the papers about him, as I know the truth and hopefully within these pages you will realise that. Don't get me wrong, I don't condone anything Charlie has done in the past but I do think he should be given hope, a date of release and things to be fair.

I have always found his letters and books entertaining, one warning - there is a lot of swearing within these pages; I hope you enjoy reading this book. To keep up-to-date with Charlie's views, opinions, letters and reports please visit: www.freebronson.co.uk

Best wishes
Chris Cowlin

Introduction

Charlie has asked me to write the Introduction to his latest book - what an honour and where do I begin...?

When Charlie was sent down in 1974 in his early twenties I was only 13 and our folks kind of kept me in the dark, probably fearing I would go down the same road as him. They needn't have worried - I'd already had a clip round the ear off the local bobby for apple scrumping and I'd decided that a life of crime was not for me. I wanted to follow in my dad's and elder brother John's footsteps and join the armed forces, which I later did.

We all thought Charlie would be freed after a few years, but sadly that wasn't to be. He decided to fight a vicious, cruel prison regime and ended up in Broadmoor, drugged up on 'liquid cosh'. Visiting him there was soul destroying and we used to leave the 'hospital' in bits.

In 1981 I was summoned to see my commanding officer on HMS Osprey. The prison authorities had requested my attendance at Broadmoor to help resolve a 'problem'. On arrival I met my dad and we were asked if we could talk Charlie down off the roof. On being led to the exercise yard it looked as if a bomb had gone off - slates and pieces of roof everywhere. I was shown the drainpipe he'd gone up and thought, no way: it was encased with barbed wire and greased up. He had a point to prove and boy did he do it! He was the first prisoner in Broadmoor's evil history to get up on the roof - max respect, brother! Anyway, we managed to talk him down after an hour. Part of the deal was that he would be allowed a 30-min chat with me and our dad, which was granted, and he didn't stop eating throughout. He commented on how smart I scrubbed up in my navy uniform. He was then led away and beaten and hospitalised by the 'nurses'. Not long after, he was placed back in mainstream prison with a 'sane' certificate - job done, for if he'd stayed within the mental institutions I truly feel they would've killed him.

Charlie has had some bad press over the years. That idiot John Stalker (ex Greater Manchester Police Chief Constable) once listed the 'Top 20' UK murderers in a Sunday paper and included Charlie. This sort of 'paint job' rubs off on the general public. I've lost count of the number of people who've approached me saying it must be terrible having a murderer for a brother. Believe me, it gives me great pleasure putting them right. Charlie will be the first to say he's been a nasty bastard over the years, but that's history and he's more than served his time. He was given a life sentence in 1999 for the last person he took hostage, Phil Danielson, even though he never harmed the guy, but with a tariff of three years - and he's still in. As I'm writing this I've just established that Charlie has had yet another parole knock-back. His next chance will be in another two years, by which time he'll be 60 years old. Talk about gross miscarriage of justice! I feel there are only two ways that Charlie will ever get out of prison: either in a box or on human rights grounds. And his human rights have been well breached.

People ask me what Charlie is like, expecting me to say he's bitter and twisted, but that couldn't be further from the truth. The Charlie I know and love is warm, generous, funny and very talented. One thing that 37 years of 'bird' have given him is a self-education, and he's a tremendous artist, writer and poet. He even has diplomas for singing, though I've heard him sing and Wagner would put him to shame - but don't tell him I told you so.

I know for a fact that Charlie is no danger to the public. He would never have to return to a life of crime, as he would make a comfortable living as an artist, writer and after-dinner speaker. He and Dave Courtney have spoken about teaming up on the circuit: Chaz and Dave - hey, that's got a ring to it.

I've met some pretty amazing people through my brother (though some are somewhat shady). He has an amazing fan/ well-wisher base and some good people behind his cause for freedom. It's gonna be some party when he comes home! I even met my girlfriend Amanda through Charlie. She felt compelled to write to him after watching the Bronson movie and seeing his art on the

London Underground. So there you go - not only a top brother but also a matchmaker. Respect.

We've not always been as tight as we are now and we've had our ups and downs over the years. He wasn't too impressed with me being a military policeman and was even less happy when I tried to join the civvy police on leaving the Royal Navy in 1994. As you might have guessed, I wasn't successful. It was all going great till the vetting of my family. But it probably worked out for the best. I'm now working offshore in the oil industry, earning more than a policeman and only working six months a year. And I don't have to wear a stab vest or work for misinformed idiots like John Stalker.

I have plenty of contact with journalists; in fact I was banned from visiting Charlie last year due to 'media involvement'. Whatever happened to the freedom of speech our great country once enjoyed? Anyway, I appealed against the ban and it was overturned, but it's still in force for the other 12 people also banned at the time. It's as though they're trying their best to cut Charlie off from everyone on the outside. Who will it be next - our 80-year-old mother?

Charlie was banged up when our dad died in 1994 and when our brother John died in 2001, and he was unable even to attend their funerals, so I pray he's out before another loved one is lost. It is soul destroying for him not to be able to pay his respects at such sad times.

Charlie told me that this is going to be his last book whilst serving time, so sit back, strap yourself in and enjoy, as it's bound to be another roller-coaster ride, and join me in hoping that his next book, as a free man, is just over the horizon.

Maximum respect to you, brother. I love you, man.

Best wishes
Mark Peterson

PRISON DIARIES

" SATURDAY "
21. 8. 2010

I'M OFF.

CHRIS

GREAT VISIT TODAY BUDDY
CANT BELIEVE IT'S BEEN 3 YEARS oo
~

HOW TIME FLIES WHEN YOUR HAVING FUN.
{ARE YOU SURE IT'S BEEN 3YRS}?

ANYWAY. YOU LOOK FIT & WELL.
    ONLY SORRY OUR VISIT HAS GOTTA BE UNDER
THESE CONDITIONS.. "A FUCKING ZOO"
    I DON'T ENJOY SEEING GOOD HONEST PEOPLE THROUGH A
SET OF BARS. BUT THATS HOW IT WORKS HERE INSIDE
THE CONCRETE COFFIN.
    I REALLY DON'T GIVE A TOSS ABOUT MYSELF. OR
HOW THE JAIL TREATS ME.. BUT IT ALWAYS SICKENS ME
WHEN IT AFFECTS MY FAMILY AND FRIENDS.
        CAN YOU BELIEVE MY OLD DUCHESS HAS BEEN
VISITING ME FOR 36 YEARS ALL OVER ENGLAND?
    AS FAR AWAY AS THE ISLE OF WIGHT. ALL THE WAY
UP NORTH TO DURHAM. {THATS LOYALTY AT ITS BEST}
        SHE'S 80 NOW.. I'LL BE LOST WITHOUT HER.
IT'S NOW ODDS ON I'LL LOSE HER WHILST IM INSIDE.
        THATS HOW IT ALL ENDS UP CHRIS
            A FUCKING BIG BLACK EMPTY HOLE.

NOT THAT IM MOANING.. LIFE TO ME IS WHAT
IT IS.. "A JOURNEY OF MADNESS" :')

1

Yep! I Fucked up Big Time When I Moved Away From Here Last Year.
   I Just Lost The Plot.
 I even Had A Fight With An Alsation.
      You Cant Make it up.
   My Whole World is a Giant Insane Bubble.
      I Just Float Away on it.
 I Had 13 Months Away From Here.
      7 Months in Longlartin Seg Block in A High Control cell With Fuck All.
     And 6 Months at Woodhill C-S-C Unit.
       I even Chinned The N°1 Governor There!
         Nothing ever Changes.

So in A Strange Way.. IM HAPPY To Be Back Here.
      or Should I Say   Contented.
    (HAPPY is my Institutionalised Word) which im not
              Nor ever Will Be.
 Its Crazy To even Say IM Contented Being on A Max Secure Isolation Unit!
 IM Locked in A Double.Door Cage.
       Not Allowed To Mix
        Closed Visits.
      But its Become Normal To Me.
 I've Spent 32 Years in Solitary out of 36 Yrs inside
         (So How Can I Be Normal)?

    IM Just HAPPY in My own Little World. ☺
         CRAZY or WHAT?

    It's Been A Great Day Today.
      18 Letters. Thats A Total of 49 Letters I've Had Sent in This Week. Some Cons Dont Get That

MANY IN A YEAR. SOME DONT GET ANY. SOME DONT DESERVE ANY!
OBVIOUSLY I CANT REPLY THEM ALL.
ID NEED TO DO ANOTHER POST OFFICE TO REPLY ALL
THEM.
ITS EVERY WEEK I GET A SACK FULL.
PLENTY OF LOONIES TOO
YOUR BE AMAZED AT HOW MANY LOONS CONFIDE IN ME
IM LIKE A FUCKING AGONY UNCLE FOR THE INSANE ☺

I GOT ONE THE OTHER WEEK FROM A NUT IN
BRAODMOOR WHO WANTS ME TO ADOPT HIM "☺" AS MY SON..
AND HE WROTE DAD "0,0"

HEY. CHEERS FOR THE BANANA MILKY SHAKES
AND CHOCS. 'LOVELY. JUBBLY'

IM ON THE PHONE TOMORROW SO ILL TELL MY BROTHER
MARK YOU VISITED ME, I HOPE YOU CAN MAKE IT
TO THE BOXING SHOW AT BRIGHTON ON 11TH SEPT-
MY BUDDY IAN FROST IS PUTTING IT ON.
THERE'S 3 BRONZE BRONSON STATUES FOR THE BEST 3 FIGHTERS
'GONNA BE A GREAT NIGHT'
MARKS THERE TO REPRESENT ME.
HE DOES ME PROUD. A GOOD BROTHER.

"I CANT MAKE IT - IM TO BUSY ☺   (,
BIZZ BEFORE PLEASURE I ALWAYS SAY .

YEP! IM SERIOUS IN WHAT I TOLD YOU CHRIS
"I COULD WELL NEVER GO FREE."

LETS FACE FACTS.. IM UPSET TO MANY PRISON

OFFICIALS OVER THE YEARS,

You ADD it ALL UP. THE DAMAGE. THE COMPENSATION.
THE VIOLENCE. THE ROOFS. THE HOSTAGES. THE MADNESS.
"WHY WOULD THEY LET ME GO?"

AND AT 58TH OF AGE THEY STILL CONSIDER ME A DANGER
TO THE PUBLIC.
"FUCK ME". I CANT EVEN BE ALLOWED TO MIX
WITH PEOPLE INSIDE, SO. WHY WOULD THEY TRUST ME OUTSIDE?

WHO KNOWS WHAT LAYS AHEAD FOR ANY OF US.
BUT ILL BE TRUTHFUL WITH YOU NOW.

I ACTUALLY BELIEVE MY MOVIE BURIED ME.
I TRUELY BELIEVE THAT
I STILL HAVNT SEEN IT!"

ANYWAY IM OFF... X-FACTOR HAS JUST STARTED
I FUCKING LOVE IT.
I WOULD WIN THAT IF THE GOVERNOR ALLOWED
ME ON THERE. VIA UIDEO LINK (WHY NOT)?

IM NOT JOKING YOU... I MEAN IT
"MY WAY". SINATRA.
ID BLOW THAT SIMON AWAY.

STAY STRONG MY FRIEND.
ILL BE IN TOUCH.
MY VERY BEST TO ALL OUT THERE.
APART FROM THE PARASITES WHO SUCK ON MY NAME.
AND TELL ROBIN BARRAT IM STILL STUDIED OVER HIS DECISION
TO GET THAT TOE RAG INVILVED IN MY PROJECT, BUT IM PLEASD
HE SAW SENSE AND PUT IT RIGHT. HE MADE A FUCT UP AND KNEW IT
SO NO HARD FEELINGS ON IT. "MOVE ON"

"ADIOS AMIGO

BRONSON A8076AG
C.S.C. UNIT
H.M.P. WAKEFIELD
W.YORKS WF2-9AG

MY LITTLE BUDDY IFTY IFTKHAR WAS UP TODAY.
He GOT me 4 MILKSHAKES, 2 CAKES, AND 6 BARS OF CHOCOLATE.
    "BLOODY DELICIOUS"
 I'LL BE WORKING THAT LOT OFF TOMORROW.
IFTY'S A TOP GEEZER, A TRUE BROTHER, A MAN I TRUST
WITH MY LIFE. SO IT WAS GREAT TO SEE HIM.

    I ALSO GOT A GREAT BOOK SENT IN FROM MY BARRISTER
"FLO KLAUSS"   "JAIL HOUSE LAWYERS"
                    BY
            MUMIA ABU-JAMAL.

            MUMIA is ON DEATH-ROW - U.S.A.
            AND HAS BEEN FOR THE LAST 25 YEARS.
            "WE SALUTE YOU BROTHER"

            I DO LOVE A GOOD BOOK.
            YOU CANT BEAT A READ.
            GET INTO A GOOD BOOK AND YOUR NOT EVEN
            IN JAIL. IT TAKES YOU ON A JOURNEY.

        ALSO RECEIVED 7 LETTERS.
        1 OFF SANDRA GARDNER MY LOVELY FRIEND. FROM,
    LEEDS, AND THE OTHERS FROM WELL WISHERS
        3 WAS FROM THE GIRLS IN EASTWOOD PARK PRISON
    DOWN IN GLOUCESTERSHIRE WHO HAVE JUST READ ONE
    OF MY BOOKS AND ENJOYED IT.
        GET ON THIS - YOU WONT BELIEVE IT.
    ONE GOT VERY RANDY AND HAD TO FINGER
    HERSELF. (IM NOT MAKING IT UP)
    NOW SEE WHAT AFFECT I HAVE ON PEOPLE?

Come on ... wake up and smell the shit Chris.
This is the Bronson web of madness ..
It dont get any madder.
        Birds playing with themselfs reading my books."
        "Eat your heart out Jeffrey Archer" ☺

        I see that "Abdel. Baset - Al - Megrahi" is celebrating
his one year of freedom.
   He blows up a plane, kills 270 innocent people. Serves a
poxy 8 year, and they release him on compassionate grounds over
prostrate cancer.
        What about me? Why cant I be released? (?)
   Ive not killed 270 people.
   Ive not killed a single person but I'm serving life? ☺☺

        I had a nice bowl of veg soup for dinner
and 6 bread rolls. "Lovely"
   Liver caserole for tea.
        Big lumps of liver to.
        Plenty of iron in liver
        "Does you good"
   My mum does a nice liver and onions. with gravy
and mash and veg.
        I dont arf miss my mums grub
   "Even after all these years I still miss it"
   Her apple pie and custard is 2nd to none..
   Fudt Gordon Ramsey ... my mums the real deal. ☺

   Its been a magic day. Thats my LAST visit this
month.. ☺
        Thats the big difference with me and the zoo animals.
   "They get visits every day from thousands of visitors.
        Ludti Bastards. ☺

6

When writing to Members of Parliament please give your previous home address in order to avoid delay in your case being taken up by the M.P.

In replying to this letter, please write on the envelope:

Number A8076AG   Name BRONSON

Wing C.S.C. UNIT. CAGE.

26/8/2010

CHRIS

GREAT TO HEAR AND YOU ENJOYED THE VISIT. SO IT WAS 3 YRS SINCE OUR LAST VISIT... FUCK ME THAT LONG. LIFE'S A SLASH IN THE SNOW.

I GOT MY CANTEEN TODAY. 24 FRESH EGGS. I EAT THEM RAW. "GOOD PROTEIN." I GOT SOME NUTS, AND CHEESE, AND MILK. I DONT DO BAD HERE... ONE MUSNT GRUMBLE. BUT IT NEVER LASTS WITH ME. SOMETHING ALWAYS GOES WRONG; SOMEONE ALWAYS SPOILS IT. THATS WHY I ENJOY THE LITTLE LUXURIES WHILST I GET THEM... COZ IT CAN ALL CHANGE FROM DAY TO DAY.

7

I SAW THE GOVERNOR TODAY. MISS RAVEN.
AS GOVERNORS GO SHE IS ONE OF THE BEST.
I LIKE HER COZ SHE IS ALWAYS FARE AND HONEST
TO ME. NOT LIKE ALOT OF THEM I'VE COME ACROSS.
THE SNAKED EYED SLIPPERY REPTILIANS.
THERE ALOT LIKE OUR M/Ps.. GUTLESS.. SPINELESS..

I'VE ASKED THE GOVERNOR IF I CAN GO ON NEXT
YEARS X.FACTOR VIA VIDEO LINK.
IF YOU DONT ASK YOU DONT GET ""

ID WIN IT. FOR SURE..
MY VERSION OF "MY WAY" WOULD BLOW
THEM AWAY.
AND TO DO IT ON VIDEO LINK THERE IS NO
DANGER OF ME CHINNING SIMON COWELL...

ABIT OF SAD NEWS... I'VE FUCKED DEE
MORRIS OFF.. (NEVER THOUGHT I COULD OR WOULD
EVER DO THAT.)
DEE'S A LOVELY SOUL, AND BEEN SO
NICE TO ME FOR MANY YEARS
SHE'S ORGANIZED PROTESTS FOR ME.
MY MUM IDOLIZES HER.
BUT... SHE KNOWS WHY.
IT'S MY LOSS.
I'll MISS HER SMILE AND SUPPORT
BUT NOBODY ON THIS PLANET TAKES MY

KINDNESS FOR WEAKNESS.
Dee KNOWS WHY.. So THATS ALL THAT NEEDS
To KNOW.. "GOODBYE I SAY"
Some ACTUALLY Believed We Were AN ITEM.
"Lovers"
"I WISH".. MY DREAM. No We Were JUST
FRIENDS. THATS ALL.
ANYWAY SHe's OUT OF MY WORLD NOW.
I WISH Her Well..
I Never Did GET To EAT Her PUSSY
IT Would of Been Nice,
"NOT To Be"
MOVE ON AND Never LOOK BACK I SAY.
MARCH ON To GLORY.
(DONT ASK WHAT SHe DONE WRONG) off!

I HAD A Veg CURRY FOR TEA.
Bloody Delicious.
IT Was either THAT or CHeese FLAN AND
MASH POTATO.
I Hope THAT Abdel BAset Al MEGRAHi
HURRY UP AND Dies.
WHY SHould He Be FREE AND NOT Me.
"Hey" DID You KNOW ELVIS DIED 33 yrs
AGo? I Was IN THe BLOCK IN WANDSWORTH
AT THe TIME. I CAN even Remember THe

SCREW WHO UNLOCKED ME TO SLOP OUT AND
TELLING ME HE HAD DIED.
I ACTUALLY SAID "GOOD" WHO GIVES A FLYING
FUCK; BUT I WAS JUST A NASTY BASTARD THEM
DAYS.
33 YEARS AGO 😠 WHERE'S IT ALL GONE?

OH.. A BIG CROW WOKE ME UP AT
6.AM TODAY, IT WAS SITTING & SQUAWKING OUT
SIDE MY CAGED WINDOW ONTO OF THE EXERCISE
YARD. A FUCKING BIG ONE TOO.. CHEEKY SOD.
IT SEEMED TO BE DELIBERATLY DOING IT TO WIND
ME UP.. "I THOUGHT TO MYSELF IS THERE NO
PEACE FOR THE WICKED.

ANYWAY.. IM OFF.. BUT ILL LEAVE YOU
WITH A FACT OF LIFE.
"LEMONS HAVE MORE SUGAR
THAN ORANGES"

So Go SUCK A LEMON.

YOUR OLD CHINA.

LET
IT
BLEED!

THE MAN WHO
LIVES INSIDE A CONCRETE
COFFIN.

10

28/8/2010

BRONSON A8076AG
C.S.C. UNIT
H.M.P. WAKEFIELD.

" CHRIS "

Got a pile of Mail Today! Not Bad for
a Saturday. Nice card from The Chaps in The Peacock
Boxing Gym at Canning Town.

Tony + Chris Bowers own That Gaff... They Never Forget me!

Saturday Here we Have a "Fry up" for Dinner.

Beans, Sausage. Tomatoes. egg. Fried Bread, it's Fucking Magic.
I Just Love an old Fashion Fry up. with a Pint of Sweet Tea To
Wash it Down. "Lovelly Jubbley."

"Yeh" I Know you get all Them Health Freaks Saying it's
Bad for you. Fuck Them. So is Swimming in The Ocean.
or Walking Across a Mine Field.

A Fry up is a Mans Desire...

Oh. I Got a Right Muggy Letter from a "Nutter"
in Lindholme Prison. a J.M. Edmundson. Telling me
God Loves me. And for me To Rise To The Lords Crap.

"Do me a Favour."

And Come To Think of it... Why is Edmundson in Jail?
Whose He To Preach To me?

I Went on The Yard After Dinner To Work
My Fry up off. "Well Two Hours Later" I Had
a Little Kip First...

Before I Started My Work-out I Noticed a
spiders web in The Corner of The Yard.
with a Fly Stuck in it, Trying To get out.
it Must Have Just Got Stuck in There. Coz
it was Flapping Like a Demented Insect on
Speed. Then "Bang" a Fucking Big Spider

11

RAN DOWN THE WEB AND POUNCED ON IT.
"LUNCH IS SERVED"
YOU CAN ACTUALLY SEE THE SPIDERS BODY FILLING UP WITH THE
FLYS BLOOD AND GUTS,
COZ THATS WHAT A SPIDER DOES, IT SUCKS OUT THE
INSIDES OF ITS PREY.
"NATURE LESSON OVER" I GOT ON WITH MY WORK OUT.
PISSING OF RAIN. WINDY. AND FRESH. I LOVE IT.
IM ACTUALLY AT MY HAPPIEST WHEN IM OUT ON THE YARD.
(I CALL IT MY ONE HOUR OF FREEDOM).

I HAVE A NICE HOT SHOWER WHEN I COME BACK IN.
THATS MY ROUTINE. (ITS NOT BAD REALLY).
SUCH A SHAME ALL JAILS CANT TREAT ME THIS WAY.
ATLEAST HERE IM IN A NICE REGIME. AND TIME PASSES PEACEFULLY.
"WELL MOST DAYS!"
EVEN HEAVEN MUST HAVE ITS BAD DAYS ?

I HAD A PORKY PIE FOR TEA. WITH SOME SALAD AND EGGS
ILL HAVE TO SAY.. WITH $\frac{1}{2}$ A LOAF OF BREAD.
IM JUST CHILLING OUT NOW WAITING FOR. X-FACTOR.
I FUCKING LOVE IT.
COZ $\frac{1}{2}$ THE ACTS ARE LOONIES..... THEY ACTUALLY BELIEVE
THEY CAN SING "GO" ALL THEY DO IS GIVE US ALL A LAUGH.
YEH. A GREAT DAY IN ALL ... I CANT GRUMBLE.
I SEE THEY EXECUTED RONNIE LEE GARDNER IN UTAH —
— STATE PRISON. U.S.A. AFTER BEING ON DEATH ROW FOR 26 YRS
HIS FINAL WORDS WERE TO HIS DAUGHTER BRANDIE.
QUOTE — " DONT MOURN MY DEATH
CELEBRATE MY FREEDOM. "

HOW POWERFUL IS THAT? WORDS OF WISDOM.
IMAGINE SPENDING 26 YEARS INSIDE A CONCRETE TOMB.
THEN THE STATE PULLS YOU OUT AND KILLS YOU?
THATS THE U.S.A. FOR YOU ... "WICKED FUCKERS".

12

Sometimes I think about it all, and convince myself
this world is one Big Giant Lunatic Asylum.
"It's Fucking CRAZY"...

Well that's my Saturday almost at an end.
Only wish I had a few beers in for
·X·Factor

Hey! Did you know there's 12,000 Curry
Restaurants in Britain?
    Veeraswamy Restaurant in Londons Regent Street
is the Nº1 Place to eat.
    It's been there since 1926.
            AND
Chicken Tikka is now Britains National Dish.
"Yeh"..'Not Mine'
    Good old British Roast Beef is mine.
    With Yorkshire Pudding· Roast Spuds, and Veg.
    With Thick Gravy..
            Yummy Yummy·

    Stay Strong·· Stay Focused·
            Adios-Amigo

    Ps. Christmas Card enclosed..   ?
            'I bet it's your first this year'
            (I like to be 1st in all z a)

13

In replying to this letter, please write on the envelope:

Number A8076AG   Name BRONSON

Wing C.S.C. UNIT

HM PRISON
5 LOVE LANE
WAKEFIELD
WF2 9AG

2.9.2010

CHRIS

HAD A GREAT DAY TODAY.

SUNS OUT TOO.

I HAD A LOVELLY HOUR ON THE YARD.

I FELT THE SUN RAYS ON MY HEAD.

it's ONE OF THOSE DAYS iT FEELS GOOD.

To BE ALIVE... WHICH AINT BAD iS iT.

CONSIDERING iM LOCKED UP.

I GOT MY CANTEEN. 24 eggs.

THAT'S MY PROTEIN SORTED FOR ANOTHER WEEK.

I ALSO COPPED 17 LETTERS TODAY..

UNFORTUNTLY ONE WAS STOPPED AND PUT INTO

MY BOX IN RECEPTION BY SECURITY

iT WAS FROM NEIL BUDFLEY iN STOKE ON TRENT

WRITING ABOUT 'BIZZ DEALS' ect..

PEOPLE JUST DONT REALIZE OR UNDERSTAND HOW

PRISON WORKS. ITS NOT NEILS FAULT, He MEANS—

— Well.

BUT I'M NOT A RED COAT IN BUTLINS..
    I'M IN A MAX SECURE UNIT IN A COFFIN
NOT ALLOWED TO RUN A BIZZ...
    SO ALL YOU FREE SOULS "THINK" WHAT YOU
WRITE TO ME.... OTHERWISE YOUR LETTERS WILL
NOT EVEN GET TO ME..
    'FUCK ME' IT'S NOT ROCKET SCIENCE IS IT?
    OR IS IT?
WHAT IT REALLY IS... ANOTHER WORLD

    I GOT SOME SMASHING PHOTOS SENT IN FROM
MY BUDDY REDD MENZIES OF HIS HOLIDAY AT
ABERYSTWYTH AT MY MUMS PLACE -
        AND
    STEVE SWATTON POSTED ME IN SOME OF MY
XMAS POSTCARDS. "I MOSTLY CREATE MY OWN"
I SEND THE ORIGINAL TO HIM AND HE GETS THEM
    PRINTED UP FOR ME.
    A TOP GEEZER IS STEVE.
        A SOLID MATE.
    "
    DID YOU KNOW JOHN WAYNE USED TO SMOKE
60 FAGS A DAY? "
    I SEE MICHAEL DOUGLAS NOW HAS LUNG
CANCER. "THAT'S FAGS FOR YOU" IT ALL CREEPS
UP ON YOU IN THE END.
HIS OLD MAN KIRK MUST BE KNICKTING ON NOW
    WHAT A GREAT ACTOR HE WAS IN THE

Vikings with Tony Curtis... WHAT A FILM.
Those Old Actors HAD Something About Them..
   Burt Lancaster... Jack Palance. James Cagney.
Lee Marvin, Tely Savalas.
   "Now".. Tom Fucking Cruise ☺ HA.,
Brad Shit ☺ HA.!.
            "Do me A Favour"
Wake me up When its Home Time .... //
                    "I Wish" ..

I Called my Brother Tonight at 6·31pm
When I Use the Phone, I Have the extention
   Line Put under my Cage Door..
"Sounds Crazy" But its Actually Ace
   Its Like Calling From my Office ☺
We Always Have A Good Laugh.
   my Brother Marks A Good Guy. The Best
And He Does Alot For me.
      His Loyalty is Second To Nobody.

   I Also Called Mal Vango..
      So All in All A Double Bubble Job.

   Im Just About To Have A Jug of Tea
With 2 spoons of Honey in ☺ And A Few
   Fig Rolls..
(I know how To Celebrate)   ⌢⌢
                               ○○
   Who needs Champaign..   ⌣
                               ·.·

17

Well.. MY LOVELLY FRIEND SANDRA GARDNER IS
FLYING OUT TO Beijing, CHINA FRI 24TH SEPT.
TO TREK THE GREAT WALL OF CHINA
(ALL FOR CHARITY)

    DAY 1 26TH SEPT MUTIANYU A
4 HOUR WALK

    DAY 2 BLACK DRAGON PAW PARK 7 HOUR WALK
    DAY 5 Gubeikou 6 HOUR WALK
    DAY 6 JINSHANLING 7 HOUR WALK
    DAY 7 JUYONGGUAN 4 HOUR WALK
THIS PART OF THE GREAT WALL WAS BUILT IN 1368
"Fuckt me" - ITS AS OLD AS BRUCE FORSYTH ☺

    SAT 2ND OCTOBER SHE FLIES BACK HOME.
"A PROUD WOMAN"

OH. SHE'S UP TO SEE ME THE 19TH OCTOBER
BEFORE SHE STARTS HER TREK.

SANDRA.. WATCH OUT FOR THE DINNER PLATE SPIDERS ☺

YEP. A MAGICAL DAY TODAY..
EVERYDAYS A BIRTHDAY FOR ME.
  A BIRTHDAY WITHOUT A CAKE..

EGGS HAVE RIGHTS

ADIOS. AMIGO

"ENJOY THE SUNSHINE"

18

5/9/2010

BRONSON A8076AG.
C.S.C. UNIT
H.M.P. WAKEFIELD
W. YORKS
WF2.9AG

CHRIS!

' GREAT TO HEAR.. YEH YOUR SPOT-ON ITS SAD
I'VE HAD TO LET Dee GO.. BUT LIFE GOES ON BUDDY.
NOBODY ALIVE OR DEAD GETS TWO SHOTS AT ME.
I ALWAYS TELL PEOPLE THIS BEFORE THEY ENTER INTO
MY WORLD. ONE SHOT IS ALL YOUR EVER HAVE.
    I'M NOBODYS DOOR MAT. " END OF SUBJECT"

NOT SURE IF YOU KNOW ABOUT "MARK WILLIAMS
    THE TATTOOIST FROM WORCESTER, A REAL GIFTED CHAP,
HE ALSO CREATES SCULPTURES. HE'S DONE A SET OF 3 ON ME.
    THERE COLLECTORS ITEMS, WHICH WILL BE WORTH THOUSANDS IN
10 YEARS FROM NOW, HE'S ALREADY SORTED A SET OUT FOR MY MOTHER
AND BROTHER, IT'S THE DOGS BOLLOCKS.
    ANYBODY WHO WANTS TO ORDER A SET CALL HIM UP 07990602294.
    YOU WON'T BE DISAPOINTED.. THERE FUCKING AMAZING.

I CALLED UP JOHNNY GRIFFITHS TODAY. HE ALWAYS CHEERS ME UP.
    ONE GOOD BLOKE TO HAVE IN YOUR CORNER... HE WAS TELLING ME
ABOUT OUR OLD BUDDY HARRY ROBERTS WHO'S NOW INTO HIS 45TH YEAR OF
HIS LIFE SENTENCE. "FORTY FIVE YEARS" "QO " POOR OLD SOD.
I LAST SAW HARRY IN GARTREE JAIL BACK IN 1987.
    THE MANS A LIVING LEGEND. A TRUE SURVIVOR.   ?
    IMAGINE SERVING 45 YEARS' AND STILL NO HOPE OF RELEASE.

    I SEE BIG FAT MAN CYRIL SMITH M.P DIED THIS WEEK.
I ALWAYS LIKED HIM. HE SPOKE HIS MIND. HE HAD SOME GOOD
QUALITIES. THE YOUNG M.P's COULD TAKE A NOTE
OUT OF OLD CYRILS BOOK.

HEY. DID YOU KNOW WHEN ALCATRAZ OPENED UP
IN 1934 FOR U.S.A' INCORRIGIBLE CONVICTS, THE GOVERNOR MR JAMES
JOHNSTON HAD THEM WORKING IN WORK SHOPS MAKING HAUFMANS NOOSES.

ALCAPONE BECAME A GOOD COBBLER THERE.
AND ALVIN KARPIS AN ACCOMPLISHED MAT MAKER
(NOT ALOT OF PEOPLE NO THAT). WELL YOU DO NOW!

SUNDAY ROAST TODAY... NOT BAD EITHER. INFACT IT WAS LOVELY.
I'VE HAD A NICE RELAXING DAY...

I NEVER TRAIN ON A SUNDAY... MY ONE DAY OF REST.
GOT A NICE CARD FROM LEANNE MAYERS YESTERDAY FROM EASTWOOD PARK
JAIL. SHE'S HAD ALOT OF BAD LUCK IN LIFE - ALWAYS BEING USED AND
ABUSED AND ENDS UP IN JAIL ☹

SO I TRY TO HELP HER OUT AS MUCH AS I CAN.
  I'M LIKE A BLEEDING SOCIAL WORKER... "ONLY BETTER". COZ I SORT
ABIT OF DOSH OUT FOR PEOPLE.
  PEOPLE LIKE LEANNE HAVN'T GOT FUCK ALL.
  THEY NEED ABIT OF SUPPORT. A HELPING HAND.

I JUST TELL HER "DON'T BUY DRUGS.." "DON'T MUG ME OFF"
  AND SHE KNOWS NOT TO ABUSE MY KINDNESS OR FRIENDSHIP.

OH WELL. A NEW WEEK TOMORROW — I'M FEELING LUCKY.

  EARLY NIGHT FOR ME.

I'LL LEAVE YOU WITH A CRAZY FACT OF LIFE..
  ON THE 6TH DECEMBER 1952 AS I LEFT MY MOTHERS BODY,
ERIC NORCLIFFE WAS HUNG AT LINCOLN PRISON.
MANY YEARS LATER I WOULD BE LOCKED UP IN THAT VERY PRISON.
  STORIES LIKE THAT MAKE MY TASH CURL.
FROM 1903 RIGHT UP TO 1961 LINCOLN HAD 17 MEN EXECUTED
ON ITS GALLOWS..
  WASYL. GNYPIUK WAS THE LAST MAN TO
HANK THERE ON 27TH JAN 1961 (OFFICIALLY)
  ALTHOUGH THE DEATH PENALTY IS LONG GONE..
BUT SUICIDAL HANGINGS WILL ALWAYS CONTINUE.
  SAD. BUT. TRUE

HAVE A LUCKY WEEK AHEAD"

STAY STRONG!

When writing to Members of Parliament please give your previous home
address in order to avoid delay in your case being taken up by the M.P.

In replying to this letter, please write on the envelope:

Number A8076AG Name BRONSON

Wing C.S.C. (F WING)

F.V.N. 3
HM PRISON
5 LOVE LANE
WAKEFIELD
WF2 9AG

7.9.2010

"CHRIS"

GREAT VISIT TODAY FROM Joe + SANDRA
JONES. A RIGHT SMASHING COUPLE.
Joe RECENTLY HAD 3 HEART ATTACKS IN
ONE DAY 'OO' Yep. '3' THIS GUY is
— SUPERMAN.
I HAD TWO BANANA MILK SHAKES ON VISIT
WITH ½ A DOZEN CHOC BARS AND A CAKE.

GOT ME SOME WORKING OFF TO DO
TOMORROW ☺ I Fucking Love iT..

Hey! HOW FAT WOULD I BE iF I NEVER
WORKED iT ALL OFF?
I WOULD HAVE SIX CHINS AND A BELLY
LiKE A HIPPO. 40 STONE OR MORE

THE DAY I STOP WORKING OUT IS THE DAY
I'M FUCKED... (IT WONT HAPPEN) "BET ON IT.

I've HAD A GREAT DAY TODAY.. I WAS UP AT
6AM.. STRIP WASHED AND DRESSED BY 6.30 AM.
I DONE 10 x 50 PRESS UPS, AND 10 x 50 SIT-UPS
"THATS HOW TO START THE DAY.

A MAN'S GOTTA HAVE INSIGHT AND FOCUS IN
LIFE, even INSIDE A COFFIN..
ONCE A MAN GIVES UP ON HIS DREAM He
BURNS OUT AND DIES.
    A GOOD BRUSH of THE HAMPSTEAD HEATH.
DID YOU KNOW THE FIRST ever TOOTHBRUSH WAS
INVENTED BACK IN 1498 (NOT ALOT OF PEOPLE NO THAT)

                    well You Do NOW!

I See THEY ARRESTED ANGEL ALVAREZ IN
HARLEM, U.S.A ON A GANGLAND MURDER.
THE COPS SHOT HIM 21 TIMES
        TWENTY ONE TIMES.. AND ANGEL SURVIVED.
"THATS WHAT A REAL LEGEND IS MADE OF."
        UN FUCKIN BELIEVABLE...
    THATS AMERICA FOR YOU.

I CALLED MY BUDDY UP TONIGHT AT 6.30pm.

"DAVE TAYLOR". HE DOES ME PROUD OUT THERE.
A GOOD MAN. "SOLID".

I GOT SEVEN LETTERS.
  SO I'VE HAD A NICE DAY...

← NOT SURE ABOUT HIM ?

IT'S TWO FACED TED !

LAUGH AND THE WORLD LAUGHS
    WITH YOU —
Weep AND YOU Weep ALONE. "

I REMEMBER A LOONY IN RAMPTON ASYLUM
    BACK IN 1978.
ALL HE EVER DID WAS Weep... AND FEEL SO
SORRY FOR HIMSELF.
WHEN I FOUND OUT WHAT HE WAS IN FOR.
"A KIDDY FIDDLER". I GAVE HIM SOMETHING
TO CRY FOR... "CUNT".
    WHATS THE SENSE IN CRYING ?
LIFES A BLESSING.
HOW LUCKY ARE WE TO BE BREATHING ? ?
  "LIFE IS PRICELESS". (ENJOY)

I GOT A LETTER FROM EMMA TODAY.
SHES ONLY 18 yrs OLD. MY MATES DAUGHTER

23

She Beat Cancer... So shes my Hero..

Also copped a letter from a guy called
Peter Rose... He's beat Heroin..
And my books helped him through it.
"Yeh" my books helped cure a junkie.

We salute you Peter.. Well done my son.
Stay focused and go on and win.
And thanks for letting me know..
"I Respect a Fighter"

Yeh.. Not a bad month up to now..
Wish you was here

only joking.
(You really dont want to be in my world)

Right... That's the end to my day.
I'm ready for lights out.

I'm having a night in.

ps

Did you know Ben Hurr had 10,000 extras..
What a classic movie.

When writing to Members of Parliament please give your previous home address in order to avoid delay in your case being taken up by the M.P.

In replying to this letter, please write on the envelope:

Number A8076AG   Name Bronson

Wing C.S.C. UNIT

10/9/2010

F WING
HM PRISON
5 LOVE LANE
WAKEFIELD
WF2 9AG

CHRIS

Your card in.. Cheers.
A bit of sad news today. Angie Nicos got
a knock back off security to go on my
cat. A. approved visit list.
"Fucking crazy." It don't add up,
Roy Shaw can visit me, and other infamous
gangsters, but Angie cant.
     its just a total farce.
     Whose next out of my life?
I got a self portrait sent in off
Lorraine of me.
     Its a cracker... she's done it for my
mother, what a talented gift she's got
     Do you know Ive never known of any
woman called Lorraine who isnt gifted.
     Its a very lucky name... I knew one

Lorraine →

VF004 Printed for the Prison Service at HMP Norwich

FROM LUTON WHO COULD SMOKE
A FAG WITH HER JACK AND DANNY.
IT WAS MENTAL TO WATCH.
BUT MAGICAL.
CRAZY MEMORIES.

MARK SHARMAN SENT ME IN A
150 QUID.. A NICE TREAT.
THAT'S MY CANTEEN SORTED FOR THE NEXT
COUPLE OF MONTHS.
THE CHAPS NEVER FORGET THERE OLD BUDDY.
I GOT 19 LETTERS TODAY.
SADLY I CANT REPLY THEM ALL.
"ITS TO MUCH"
I'VE NOT GOT TIME 😊 I WOULD NEED
ANOTHER 20 YEAR SENTENCE TO REPLY ALL MY MAIL.

"HARRIETT MATHER" MY LAWYER ALSO WROTE
(I CANT SAY ALOT) BUT WATCH THIS SPACE.

MY BOXING SHOW IN BRIGHTON IS TOMORROW.
IAN FROST IS PUTTING IT ON.
MY BROTHER WILL BE REPRESENTING ME.
DID YOU KNOW, I'VE NOW BEEN INVOLVED IN A
DOZEN OR MORE SHOWS TO RAISE SOME DOSH
FOR KIDS.. (NASTY BASTARDS DO THAT) BUT THE
MEDIA DONT COVER IT, COZ IT DONT SELL LIKE BAD
NEWS. WE CANT WIN AS VILLAINS. ☹

26

"SHERI NEALE" WROTE ME.. OUT OF THE BLUE... IT TURNS OUT SHES BRAD ALLARDYCE's NIECE, IVE WROTE BACK TO TELL HER "NEVER EVER" SAY HIS NAME TO ME.

IF YOU NEED TO KNOW WHY, ITS ALL IN MY BOOK "THE KRAYS AND ME" BY BLAKES.

IM NOT A PARROTT SO ILL LEAVE IT THERE.

ID SOONER HAVE A SNAKE IN MY SPACE, THAN ALLARDYCE.

MY OLD MATE AL-RAYMENT JUST COPPED AN OFFICIAL LETTER FROM THE GOVERNOR HERE, SAYING HE IS STILL BANNED FROM VISITING ME.

HE STILL DONT EVEN NO WHAT HES EVER DONE WRONG, NOR DO I!

HE GOT STRUCK OFF MY VISIT LIST SOON AFTER MY FILM COME OUT. (ALONG WITH 6 MORE).

BUT HE WAS NOTHING TO DO WITH IT.

"CRAZY PEOPLE."

I SEE "MARK CHAPMAN" HAS JUST HAD HIS CHANCES OF PAROLE STOPPED "GOOD"

HE SHOT JOHN LENNON BACK IN 1980,

THEY SHOULD OF STUCK HIM IN THE CHAIR AND FRIED HIS BRAIN.

LETS FACE IT.. WHY LET A "THING" LIKE HIM OUT.

WHO CARES?

"THINGS" LIKE THAT.. LET EM ROT IN HELL..

27

FISH-N-CHIPS TODAY. LOVELY BIT OF FISH TOO.
MUSHY PEAS WITH IT. TOMATO SAUCE. VINEGAR
SALT. PEPPER. AND ½ A LOAF OF BREAD

I WAS IN MY APPLE CART.
½ A PINT OF SWEET TEA TO WASH IT DOWN
LOVELLY JUBBLEY ☺

WHAT ABOUT OLD PASTOR TERRY JONES OUT IN
FLORIDA WHOSE GONNA BURN THE KORAN ON THE
ANNIVERSARY OF 9/11 ?
I'VE ALWAYS SAID RELIGION WILL ONE DAY DESTROY
THE PLANET.
THERE ALL A BUNCH OF MUPPETTS.
CLOCK HIS NAME.
TERRY JONES... SUMS IT ALL UP TO ME.
MONTY PYTHONS FLYING CIRCUS ☺

LIFE'S
A
BITCH
FOR
EGGS

I'M GONNA HAVE A NICE MUG OF
DRINKING CHOCOLATE NOW.
WITH 6 FIG ROLLS.
IT'S BEEN A GREAT DAY
LOADS OF MAIL. NEWS.
GOOD WISHES. MY BOXING SHOW
TOMORROW. SOME CASH. AND
I'M AS FIT AS A BUTCHERS DOG.
WHO SAYS I'M NOT ON TOP OF IT?

28

BRONSON A8076AG
C.S.C. UNIT
H.M.P. WAKEFIELD

"12.9.2010"

Hi. CHRIS. "I RECEIVED YOUR CARD. CHEERS.

JUST CALLED MY BROTHER MARK.
AND STEVIE SWATTON.
LAST NIGHTS BOXING SHOW IN BRIGHTON WAS A
CORKER. EVERYBODY ENJOYED IT. AND WE'VE GOT
A NICE 1½K TO GIVE DARREN GODFREY'S LITTLE BOY.
SO ALL IN ALL A GREAT NIGHTS WORK.
A BIG "RESPECT" TO "IAN FROST" THE ORGANIZER.

WHAT MADE ME LAUGH. WHEN STEVE SWATTON WALKED
IN. ALL WENT SILENT. "WHISPERS". FUCK ME ITS CHARLIE BRONSON.
CHARLIES IN THE BUILDING.
THATS HOW MUCH HE LOOKS LIKE ME". TOP GEEZER.
I WOKE UP AT 5 AM TODAY. JUST LAY THERE "THINKING"
"WHAT EXACTLY AM I DOING SERVING "LIFE".?
IF ANYBODY KNOWS... LET ME KNOW. COZ I'VE NOT A CLUE".

ITS LOVELLY AND PEACEFUL SO EARLY. LIKE LIVING IN A
CONCRETE TOMB.. IT FEELS SO SERENE
ITS LIKE WAKING UP ON THE MOON.

NEW WEEK TOMORROW.. LOVE IT ☺
YOU JUST NEVER KNOW WHATS GONNA HAPPEN ON A MAX—
— SECURE UNIT. ITS LIKE BLIND MANS BUFF IN A MINE FIELD.

DID YOU READ ABOUT 90 YEAR OLD JOHN BUNZ IN NEW YORK
GETTING SENTENCED TO 17 YEARS FOR KILLING HIS 89 YEAR OLD WIFE
WITH A HAMMER "99".
THEY WAS MARRIED FOR 68 YEARS.
OH WELL. HE WONT BE FREED TILL HE'S 107 👓

I WAS ONLY READING ABOUT BRITAIN'S OLDEST WOMAN DYING -
"EUNICE BOWMAN", ONE MONTH AWAY FROM HER 112th BIRTHDAY.
SHE WAS BORN THE SAME YEAR AS GRACIE FIELDS IN 1898.
THERE A SPECIAL BREED OUR OLD FOLK ... "DON'T YOU LOVE EM?
WHAT A STORY EUNICE HAD EH?
<u>GOD BLESS HER</u> x

I SEE AUDLEY HARRISON IS FIGHTING "DAVID HAYE IN NOVEMBER
AND ITS 18 TO 1 FOR A WIN FOR HARRISON.
IVE JUST PUT A BULLSEYE ON IT.
HE COULD DO IT... LETS FACE IT. HE'S DONE FUCK ALL SINCE HE WON
THE OLYMPIC GOLD YEARS AGO. SO THIS CAN BE HIS LUCKY SHOT.
ONE GOOD HOOK ON HAYES CHIN AND LIGHTS OUT.

DO YOU KNOW ITS SO LONG SINCE I HAD 'TOAST' I CANT REMEMBER.
WHAT A FUCKING LIBERTY EH?
I LOVE CHEESE ON TOAST WITH A MUG OF ROSY LEA.
ITS SIMPLE THINGS LIKE THAT I MISS THE MOST.
WITH ME FOREVER BEING IN SOLITARY I CANT GET TO MAKE IT.
YOU LUCKY BASTARDS OUT THERE.. HAVE ONE FOR ME. ☺

I HAD A READ OF THE SUNDAY PAPERS TODAY.
I BUY MY OWN.. THE SPORT, PEOPLE, N.O.W. AND STAR.
I LOVE THE SPORT.
ITS THE FUNNIEST PAPER ON THE PLANET.
FULL OF FREAKY FUCKERS. CRAZY STORIES.
I ONLY GET IT FOR A LAUGH... IT ALSO PASSES MY DAY.
I HAD ROAST BEEF FOR TEA.. WITH ROAST SPUDS AND VEG.
"LOVELY".
THE GRAVY WAS GOOD TOO.
WE EAT ON PLASTIC PLATES WITH PLASTIC CUTLERY.
THIS IS THE PLASTICATED WORLD OF THE INSANE.
WELCOME TO PLANET PLASTIC. OO

I FINISHED MY TEA OFF WITH A CHOC-ICE.
I LOVE ICE CREAM, ESPECIALLY ON A BIRDS BODY.
I COULD LICK IT UP FOREVER.
I SPENT 4 HOURS ON A PIECE OF ART TODAY
BLACK + WHITE, INK + PENCIL, A4 WHITE CARD
ITS A LUNATIC STRAPPED UP IN A STRAW JACKET.
I CALLED IT ..... "SCREAMING ALL THE WAY TO THE CREMATORIUM.

30

Did You Know. The U.K "Adder" snake (Proper name Viper Berus) has only ever killed 14 People since 1876.

"Not Alot of People Know That."

Thats How Dangerous That Fucker is!

We Dont Know How Lucky We Are in This Country.

Apart From MAN. What other Dangerous Animals Have we Got? A Soppy old Fox. or A Man eating Badger. OO Ha!

Thats Why its A Soft Place To Live.

I Think We Should All Be Forced To Survive 6 Mths in The Borneo Jungle To Toughen us up A Bit.

Why Not? Do us All Good.

"Well". I've Had A Smashing Lazy. Chilled out Day.

I Love My Sunday Rest Day.

I've Drunk 8 Pints of Water Today To Flush out All The Toxics.

Sure You Piss Alot. But Its Worth it.

It Makes me Laugh With All These Pratts Who Buy Bottled Water? What For?

I've been Drinking Tap Water For 58 Years its Done Me No Harm.. Thats With The old Lead Pipes Too...

So Why Aint I Dead? {For am I?}

I Gave My Head A Shave Today.

its Glowing Like A Snooker Ball.

I Just Feel Good. And Ready For A Fresh Week..

It's 9 PM Now. I'll Just Have A Strip Wash and Brush my Teeth And Im off To Bed For A Good Kip.

What Would it Be Like To Go To Bed With A Nice Hot Sexy Chick... even To Wake up With one.

"Now That Would Be Something Special."

"one Day"... OO

"Adios-Amigo"

BRONSON A8076AF. C.S.C.
H·M·P· WAKEFIELD
W· YORKS. WF2·9AF

Hi CHRIS

Your CARD iN - "CHeeRs"

AL RAYMENT Posted Me iN MY <u>NEW eDiTiON</u> BOOK TODAY (VIA BLAKES
BRONSON - UP ON THE RooF! OFFICE)

GUESS WHAT? I CANT HAVE IT - ITS BEEN PUT iNTO STORED PROP.
How PETTY iS THAT? I <u>CANT</u> eveN CHeck OUT MY OWN BOOK.

ILL SLAM iN AN APPLICATION TO THE GOVERNOR TOMORROW TO See iF I CANT
HAVE A BUTCHERS OF iT - THEN DONATE iT TO THE LIBRARY.

FUCK Me - iT iS MY BOOK. MY CREATION, AM I NOT eNTITLED
So See MY OWN WORK? 00' WHATS THERE PROBLEM?

NOW See THE PROBLEMS I GET?

McALLISTER COMe TODAY.. He's No1 BOSS OF ALL THE MAX-SECURE
C·S·C·UNITS iN ENGLAND.. So I ASKED HiM.. WHY AM I HeRe
AND DO YOU KNOW WHY IM eveN SERVING A LiFe SENTENCE, AND WHY
AM I FOREVER iN ISOLATED CONDITIONS"

He SAID... QUOTE - IM KEEPiNG AN eYe ON iT 0.

So THATS iT THeN! THE BOSS AS SPOKEN! PROBLEM SOLVED
I MAY AS WELL OF ASKED MY TOOTHBRUSH..

I CALLED IAN FROST LAST NIGHT. He WAS WELL HAPPY OVER
His BRIGHTON BRONSON BOXiNG NIGHT.

I Tell YOU NOW.. THeRe iS NOT A VENUE BiG·ENOUGH
TO PUT MY SHOW ON WHEN <u>IM OUT</u>.

THE NIGHT I CLiMB THROUGH THE ROPES AND
PUT MY GLOVES BACK ON, I WILL eARN ONe
MILLION BUCKS. (DONT DOUBT MY WORDS)

I HAD MUSHROOM SOUP FOR DINNER.. WiTH 4
MUSHROOMS iN iT, AND 8 BREAD ROLLS. "I LOVE A ROLL"

We HAVE AN eARLY DINNER HeRe.. So I WATCH TRISHA AS I
eAT iT.. YeH IM A TRISHA FAN' I ONLY WATCH iT TO LAUGH

AT THE CLOWNS ON IT. WHAT A BUNCH OF HOBITS... THERE EITHER DRUGGIES
ALCHOHOLICS, POOFTERS OR RETARDS... TAKE YOUR PICK.
BUT IT ALL MAKES ME FEEL LUCKY TO BE WHAT
   I AM... A NORMAL HUMAN

DO YOU KNOW IT TOOK ME 30 YEARS OF JAIL
   AND ASYLUMS TO GET A T.V. SET.

BUT EVEN NOW I DONT WATCH IT ALL THE TIME
   I DONT WANT TO TURN INTO SOMETHING I DESPISE
               A BRAIN DEAD PRISON ZOMBIE

   I DO LOVE A BIT OF CORRIE THOUGH... 50 YEARS THE STREET AS BEEN
GOING. I GO BACK TO THE ENA SHARPLES AND ELSIE TANNER DAYS
NOW ITS ALL DOLLY BIRDS AND LOTS OF SHAGGING.

         ENA + ELSIE WOULD BE TURNING IN THER GRAVES EH?

HOW TIMES HAVE CHANGED.

   WHAT ABOUT THE PUSSY IN HOLLYOAKS. HAVE YOU SEEN IT?
THERES SOME SERIOUS TALENT IN THAT SOAP.

      NATURE SHOCKS ON TONIGHT AT 8PM. RAT INVASION
ILL BE WATCHING THAT.

      THE BIGGEST RAT I EVER SEE WAS SITTING ON MY WINDOW BARS
AT RISLEY JAIL IN 1971. IT WAS LIKE A CAT.
   IT SHRUGGD ITS SHOULDERS AND TWITCHED ITS NOSE AND STARED AT
ME FOR A GOOD 30 SECONDS. THEN LEAPT OFF INTO THE DARK.
      I SHUT MY WINDOW AFTER THAT. NASTY FUCKERS RATS.

I HAD CURRY FOR TEA... NICE LUMPS OF CHICKEN IN IT TOO.
   THEY DO A GOOD CURRY HERE... PLENTY OF IT TO.
I CREATED AN A4 ART. TOOK ME 3½ HOURS. PASSED THE DAY.
   ILL SEND IT TO MY PAL MARK WILLIAMS.
THEY ACTUALLY STOPPED ME POSTING MY ART OUT FOR A GOOD YEAR
   WHY? (LET ME KNOW IF YOU EVER FIND OUT).

HEY... DID YOU KNOW A MOLE CAN DIG A TUNNEL 300 FEET IN
ONE NIGHT... FUCK ME I WISH I COULD... STRAIGHT TO THE
FISH N CHIP SHOP OUTSIDE THIS JAIL. IM STARVING.

WELL... ITS NOT BEEN A GOOD DAY FOR GEORGE MICHAEL.
   HES JUST BEEN SENT DOWN FOR 8 WEEKS.
   IMAGINE THIS. TOMORROW HE WAKES UP ON A WING WITH
200 CONVICTS ALL SINGING ♪ WAKE ME UP BEFORE YOU GO GO ♪ ☺
            ♪   ♪   ♪   ♪

I WOULD GUESS ITS THE SCRUBBS HE WENT TO.
DO HIM GOOD. (SEE HOW THE OTHER HALF LIVE)

WELL ITS 7.45PM. THAT RAT DOCUMENTRY IS ON SOON SO ILL
FUCK OFF. I MAY COME BACK. I MAY NOT.
ADIOS AMIGO

9.10 PM
I'M BACK. THOSE RATS ARE FEARLESS.
ONE DAY THERE GONNA TAKE OVER THE PLANET OO
FOR REAL!

I GOT A NICE CARD FROM MY LOVELLY FRIEND DENISE BRIERLEY FROM
WALLSEND. SHES A GOOD SOUL.
AND A BUDDY IN MALTA JAIL CORADINO CORRECTIONAL FACILITY
MARK BUCKLEY IS ON REMAND THERE
HE SAYS ITS FULL OF SMACK HEADS.
IT LOOKS LIKE THE DRUG CRIME IS ALL OVER OUR PLANET.
90% OF CRIME NOW IS DRUG RELATED.

DID YOU READ ABOUT THE 28YR OLD POLISH TWINS WHO KILLED
EACH OTHER? PASHA AND JANUCH WORSELT WERE JUST PLAYING
ABOUT HAVING A WRESTLE AND THEY STRANGLED EACH OTHER.
HOW MAD IS THAT?

WHAT ABOUT DEREK WOOLTON FROM NORTH LONDON. HE JUST COPPED
150 HOURS COMMUNITY WORK FOR BASHING HIS MEAT WATCHING
HOLLY WILLOUGHBY ON T.V RIGHT IN HIS WINDOW SO PASSERS BY
COULD SEE. O.O
YOU CANT MAKE THIS SHIT UP.
ITS BRILLIANT
HE'S 42 YRS OLD!
FUCKING GET A LIFE YOU PERV.

I SEE MICK O'DONNELL HUNG HIMSELF RECENTLY IN
STRANGEWAYS. HE WAS ONLY 29 YR OLD.
HE MADE A GOOD ESCAPE OFF A VAN ONLY A COUPLE OF MONTHS AGO
BUT GOT CAUGHT DAYS LATER.
WHAT A SAD ENDING.
IT ALWAYS SADDENS ME TO HEAR IT OO
ESPECIALLY WHEN ITS GOOD PEOPLE
I CAN NEVER WORK IT OUT WHY.. ITS SENSELESS.
A WASTE OF A GOOD LIFE

IM GONNA GET MY SIT-UPS DONE NOW. THEN HAVE A STRIP
WASH. READY FOR BED
ILL HAVE ABIT OF IAN COLLINS ON TALK SPORT RADIO LATER
HE TOOK OVER FROM JAMES WHALE.
    THE WHALES NOW ON LONDON . L.B.C.

        " I LOVE MY RADIO   (
            BEATS ANY TELLY .

NEWS. PLAYS. MUSIC. DOCUMENTRIES. YOU CANT BEAT A
GOOD RADIO.
        IVE NOW GOT A SONY D.A.B.
            DOES ME LOVELLY. (ONLY COST ME A BULLSEYE)

        NOT NOT A BAD DAY.   ' (
    " APART FROM THE BOLLOCKS OVER MY BOOIT SENT IN ,

            RIGHT IM OFF .
            STAY COOL .
                " BE LIKE ME
                    THE ICE-MAN WHO DONT MELT !

                                        YOUR OLD CHINA

        PS

        IM FEELING LUCKY .
            WATCH THIS SPACE ..
        SOMETHING GOOD IS COMMING MY WAY.
            I CAN FEEL IT MY BONES .

In replying to this letter, please write on the envelope:

Number A8076AG   Name BRONSON

Wing C.S.C.

16-9-2010

F W_ _G
HM PRISON
5 LOVE LANE
WAKE_ _ELD
_ _ _ _AG

Hi. CHRIS

BAD NEWS FOR ME TODAY.
A PAL OF MINE NEIL BUCKLEY 'BUCKO TO ME' HAS BEEN DOING SOME INVESTIGATING FOR ME.
COZ SOMEBODY CLOSE IN MY FIRM HAS BEEN SELLING BITS OF MY ART ON e-BAY, FOR QUITE A LONG TIME UNDER THE NAME JAMES.
70 PIECES OF MY ART TO BE EXACT.
(OBVIOUSLY MOST WOULD BE COPIES).
     TODAY I NOW KNOW WHO IT IS, AND HES DONE IT BEHIND MY BACK. WITHOUT EVEN SORTING ME A TEA BAG OUT.
          THANKS . 'JIM DAWKINS .
NO WONDER HES NOT WROTE ME IN 18 MTHS.
     TO BUSY SELLING MY ART
ALOT OF IT IVE DONE FOR GIFTS TO HIS KIDS

WHAT A CHEEKY FUCKER.

There's NO EXCUSE.

IT WOULDN'T BE SO BAD IF HE HAD SORTED MY
MOTHER OUT A DRINK.

IT'S NEVER FORGOT.

I'LL LEAVE IT AT THAT!

HEY! HE AIN'T THE FIRST TO BE CAUGHT
OUT. HE WON'T BE THE LAST EITHER.

I'VE GOT A LITTLE BLACK BOOK FULL OF PARASITES
WHO HAVE SUCKED OFF OF ME.

SOME ARE IN FOR THE SHORT OF THERE LIFE.

ANYWAY 3 CHEERS TO BUDU.

HIP HIP HURAY, HIP HIP HURAY.
HIP HIP HURAY

WELL DONE MY OLD SUNSHINE.
{ EAT YOUR HEART OUT COLUMBO }

WHOSE NEXT ?

I GOT A PILE OF MAIL TODAY. MAL ISANGA
STEVIE SWATTON. DI BROWN. MY SON MIKE
CLARE RAPER. AND SIX NEW ONES.

ONTOP OF THAT LOT
I GOT MY CANTEEN.

FRUIT. NUTS. CHOC BARS. EGGS
SQUASH AND TOILETRIES

FUCK ME IT'S

37

ALMOST 2 QUID FOR A TUBE
OF AQUFRESH TOOTHPASTE
"DAYLIGHT ROBBERY"

I WOKE UP AT 6 AM TODAY WITH CRAMP IN MY LEFT
CALF. "AGONY" - IT MUST HAVE BEEN ALL THEM
SQUATS I DONE YESTERDAY.
"FUCKING MURDER" - IT'S LIKE A RAT INSIDE YOUR
LEG BITING TO ESCAPE

I HAD A NICE JOG ON THE YARD - AND AN HOUR
ON THE MULTI-GYM
    (NOT ENOUGH WEIGHT FOR ME)
I NEED A GOOD 400 POUNDS TO BENCH PRESS
WHATS ON THAT MULTI GYM I COULD LIFT THAT
WITH MY BELL-END "OO"
    "EASY"

I SEE THE POPE'S UP IN SCOTLAND RIDING ABOUT
IN HIS POPEMOBILE
    WHY NOT BATMAN IN HIS BATMOBILE?
WHO REALLY WANTS TO SEE THE POPE?

HE SHOULD BE CONSENTRATING ON HIS PAEDOPHILE
PRIESTS, "SACK THE LOT OF THEM"
    WHAT A DISGRACE THAT IS TO THE CATHOLIC CULTURE.
        "I CANT STOMACHE RELIGION."

38

There was a religious freak in Broadmoor back
in 1979 on my wing who kept trying to convert
me to God. He said I was the son of Satan..

Hell. He was in for raping his granny
and strangling her.
And he was calling me evil
'No wonder I broke his jaw!
(Sorry God)'

I'm having a late night tonight.
A good films on at 10 PM on Channel 5
"Outlaw"
Sean Bean and Bob Hoskins is in it.
And Danny Dyer.
It should be a blinder.
It fucking better be,
Coz it dont end till gone midnight
"I like my sleep."

Anyway.. Jim Dawkins eh?
You sad little man..
You've sold me out like a rat in a sewer..
I knew id catch you up.
It had to be somebody close.
I'm glad it's you and
not somebody closer

Alive + kicking

SUNDAY
19.9.2010

Bronson. A8076AG. CSC.
H.M.P. Wakefield.
W. Yorks.
WF2 9AG

Chris

Your card in .... Cheers
Sandra Gardner was up today. She looked her
lovely self. I dont know any woman whose always
so smartly dressed. She got me 3 banana milk shakes,
and six choc-bars. Lovely jubbly ☺
   It really was a nice visit. The 2 hours just
flew. She's flying to China on Friday for her
charity walk. Good luck to her.
   I got her a chain to wear for luck. But the fucker's
not arrived yet ☹ Looks like she wont get it till she's
back from the walk...
   I see the Beast of Broadmoor "Fisher" just confessed to two
murders back in 1998. And got another life sentence.
One of his victims was 75 year old Beryl O'Connor.
   "Brave fucker aint he? (There all the same them monsters).
   Ok well. Lets hope his next move from Broadmoor is the local
Crematorium. One way ride.
   I had Roast Beef today. Roast spuds and carrots.
   I covered it in tomato sauce.
   Washed it down with a pint of squash. (Robinsons) only the best!
I'm ready for tomorrow. Got me some workouts to do.
   X-Factor was on last night. And its on again tonight
(I'm just waiting for it to come on)
There was a scouse girl on last night, mixed race. Singing
a Sam Cooke number. She was brilliant.
   A real soul girl. Fantastic.
   I love soul. I'm a born soul man - Believe it.
I shaved my head at breakfast. Felt clean and fresh.

40

Then covered it in baby lotion till it shone like a snooker ball ☺

I see George Michaels been moved to a cushy jail already. Thats how it works for the celebs ... Double fast.
I've been waiting all my life for a cushy move ?!!

It's about time we was allowed conjugal visits like in some of the european jails, Holland - Germany, Finland, ect.

Why not? It's only human rights after all. What would I do for a good long slow fuck? 😡

It's not normal going all these years without sex. How can some countries allow it and others dont?
Are we not all in the european laws?
There must be a legal case here worth fighting?

Sandra could of stayed the night. Breakfast in bed ☺
Why not? What harm? Wishfull thinking.
Well she is a very elegant, sexy, woman.

Man. U. stuffed Liverpool 3 - 2 today.

Well ... I'm gonna have a walk up and down my cell for an hour waiting for X. Factor.
Clear my head abit. Prepare for a new week tomorrow.

The cold weather is creeping in. These old cells are like freezers. The coldest cell I've been in was Armley (Leeds) back in 1975. I was on B/1 the Dungeon, my windows were smashed out, the snow and wind was blowing in. My nose was dripping. I was fucking freezing. There was no heating.

Tough times. But I buzzed on it.

Hell I've been so cold in bed, that I've jumped out to do 500 press-ups to warm up.

Them days it was a privilage to get a hot bowl of porridge... we loved our porridge.
Now days ... its Rice fucking Krispies ?!!
Do me a favour ... wake me up when it's home time.

STAY WELL !!!

21. 9. 2010

BRONSON. A8076AG
C.S.C. UNIT.
H.M.P. WAKEFIELD
W. YORKS. WF2.9AG

" Hi CHRis "

Di BROWN AND HER DAUGHTER ELLE
WAS UP TODAY. We ALWAYS HAVE A GOOD LAUGH.
BUT.. SHe FORGOT MY 'BANANA MILK SHAKES.. xx
THAT TO ME is THE END OF THE WORLD.
        [I COULDN'T BELEVE IT]
SHe GOT CHOC-BARS AND CAKE AND COFFEE.
        BUT No. MILK SHAKES 😞

Di AND ELLE HAVE VISITED ME FOR YEARS
        THERE FAMILY TO ME.. ELLE WAS ONLY A LITTLE GIRL
WHEN SHe FIRST VISITED ME, NOW SHES A BEAUTIFUL WOMAN.
        "HOW TIME FLIES WHEN JOUR HAVING FUN 😊

THEY RUN A CAR.. "THE TEA CUP" IN HAYLING ISLAND
Di WAS SAYING THAT JIMMY TIBBS SON PETER CAME IN THE
OTHER DAY. AND WAS TELLING HER ABOUT ONE OF MY UNLICENSED
FIGHTS IN EAST LONDON WHEN THE CROWD STARTED SMASHING ME
WITH CHAIRS... "THE GOOD OLD DAYS" 😊
        PETERS DAD JIMMY HAS BEEN IN THE BOXING WORLD FOR
YEARS. A GOOD MAN. "ONE OF THE BEST".
A GOOD EAST LONDON FAMILY THE TIBBS
        "MY RESPECT TO THEM".

        I SEE YOUNG SCOTT BEVAN HUNG HIMSELF IN SWANSEA JAIL
YESTERDAY. He WAS ONLY 21. SERVING A PONY 8 MONTH SENTENCE.
HOW TRAGIC IS THAT?
        OUT OF 8 MONTH He WOULD ONLY SERVE 16 WEEKS!!
        IT ALWAYS SADDENS ME TO HEAR OF SUCH SAD ENDINGS.

42

I CAN NEVER WORK IT OUT WHY

IT TAKES ME BACK TO WANDSWORTH JAIL IN THE LATE 80'
WHEN TONY CUNNINGHAM TOPPED HIMSELF ON D. WING
HE WAS ON THE EXERCISE YARD WITH ME AND NOEL TRAVIS IN THE
MORNING. LAUGHING AND TELLING JOKES. HE WAS A TOP GEEZER
THEN LATER ON THAT SAME DAY THEY FIND HIM SWINGING IN HIS CELL.
IT BLEW ME AWAY THAT DAY..
YOU NEVER CAN FORGET SUCH SADNESS.
THE CRAZY THING IS ... WHO KNOWS WHY THEY DO IT ..

. HA. HA. WANNA LAUGH? ANN WIDDECOMBE IS ON
STRICTLY COME DANCING! WHAT A JOKE.
WHAT SANE PERSON WANTS TO WATCH HER DANCING?
THATS SPOILT THE SHOW THIS YEAR...
IT's FUCKING PATHETIC ...
I FEEL SORRY FOR THE PRO-DANCER WHO HAS TO PARTNER HER.
            COZ SHE CANT DANCE .. NOR EVER CAN .
WHEN SHE WALKS SHE WADDLES ..

I HAD LIVER AND ONIONS TODAY. NOT BAD EITHER
    NO MAIL TODAY.. YEH .. UNBELIVABLE .. I DONT BELIEVE IT .
THERE PROBABLY IS - BUT ITS HAD BEEN CENSORED. IT'S PILED UP ON
SOME DESK. I GET POST EVERY DAY..
        GET ON THIS .. YOUR LOVE IT
                PRISON STATISTICS

                POPULATION   JUNE 2010

        COUNTRY   PRISON POPULATION

        RUSSIA   ---   850,800
        TURKEY   —   119,112
        ENGLAND, WALES —   84,966
        GERMANY   ---   70,817
        NETHERLANDS —   15,614
        GREECE   —   12,300
        SCOTLAND   —   7,953
        SWITZERLAND —   6,084
        DENMARK   —   3,967
        CYPRUS   ---   671
        ICELAND   —   175
        GIBRALTAR   -   51   ?

        THAT RUSSIA TAKES SOME BEATING EH

43

OH well ... I've Now Gotta Do Elle's Boyfriend "Brad" A Piece of ART. Thats My Mission Before Z Climb into Bed. I think Ill Do one of Me, Saying-- ☺

TREAT MY Elle With Respect or else!

I've Also Got To Write To My Lawyer Harriett. Its High Time She Pulled Her Finger out ☺

This is MY LIFE Being Sucked AWAY ...

Fuck. All on The Telly Tonight...
So ill Have My Beloved RADO on.
The Heating Pipes Got Turned on Today
So we Got Nice Hot Pipes in My Cell ☺
These Cells Are Lovelly And WARM in The WiNTER.

Not Like Years Ago Here". There Was No Pipes in The Cells. "Freezing" it Was
Now its All Cosy.
Like A Chimp in A Cage!

Which Reminds me.... Di was Telling me About A Wrestler Who Z Know As Chris. (Hes Been Taking Liberties) (Turned into A Right Bully Boy) "IM Not Happy About It".
I Cant Stand People Who Abuse Trust, And Friendship.
"Familiarity Breeds Contempt"

OH well". THATs Me,
A Great Day.
Roll-on Tomorrow... Coz Ive A Few Choc Bars To Work off. "I Love it"   ?
Who Said There's No Heaven ?   ☺

Adios-Amigo

24.9.2010

BRONSON A8076AG
C.S.C UNIT
H.M.P. WAKEFIELD
W. YORKS
WF2.9AG

Hi CHRis

I've HAD THAT MANY LETTERS OVER THE LAST COUPLE OF DAYS IT'S BLOWN ME AWAY.
Some HAVE BEEN CRACKER'S TO. FANTASTIC.
ALL BASICALLY SUPPORTING MY FIGHT FOR FREEDOM.
THIS ONE FROM 'AMANDA KIRTON' FROM NORTHWICH ILL SHARE HER VERSE SHE CREATED FOR ME.

"AN EAGLE HELD IN A CAGE MAY BE CONFINED TO THE GROUND, BUT WHEN ITS HEART SOARS FREE AND ITS MIND IS UNCONTAINED, NO CHAINS CAN HOLD IT DOWN. WITHIN ITS MIND IT SURVAYS THE WORLD FROM HIS ROYAL THRONE. FROM ITS HEART A CRY BURST FORTH AND THE BIRD BREAKS FREE. NOTHING CAN STOP IT OR HOLD IT BACK, THE EAGLE WILL FLY FREE AGAIN AND SO WILL YOU."

HOW GREAT IS THAT? FROM A STRANGER. AMAZING.
IN YEARS TO COME I THINK ILL PUBLISH ALL MY MAIL.
IT WILL MAKE A UNIQUE BOOK. IT REALLY WOULD.
THE BRONSON BOOK OF LETTERS FROM SUPPORTERS ALL OVER THE WORLD.

THE PHOTOS HAVE STARTED TO ROLL IN OF THE BRIGHTON FIGHT NIGHT, SOME CLASSICS TOO. ALL ARE ON THE SITE.. SO HAVE A BUTCHERS.
I CALLED DAVE TAYLOR AND MAL VANGO LAST NIGHT.
We ALWAYS HAVE A LAUGH. TWO OF THE BEST.
MAL WAS TELLING ME DAVE COURTNEYS HAD A STOMACHE BAND FITTED : "I've FUCKING HEARD IT ALL NOW 'Q.O'

DO SOME SIT-UPS YOU FAT LAZY FUCKER.
A GOOD DIET. A REGULAR JOG. SOME SWIMMING.
YOU DON'T NEED A STOMACHE BAND. NOBODY DOES 'Q.O'

I See That Beast "Oliver Longcake" Copped A Life Sentence For Killing His Girlfriends Baby Daughter. "One Year Old Alisia" The Coward Bashed Her To Death.

All He Got Off The Judge is A Tariff of 11 Years
Longcake is Only 21 Now. He Could Be Free At 32.

What A Pathetic Sentence..... Why Not 30 Years Tariff?
It Makes Me Sick... It Really Does.
The System Can Sit Back And Watch Me Rot Away
But They Will Free A Baby Killer In No Time...
"Sick".

Marik Williams Has Just Created The Bronson Bedlam Set
I Told You This Guy is A Genius, He Makes Sculptured Heads
Straight Out Of Your Worst Nightmares...

Dave Taylor Was Telling Me About A "Big-Band" Out In
Australia Called "Bronson". (I Salute You Boys)
Everyday I Get Blown Away By Something New Going On.

In The Early Hours Of This Morning in Virginia. U.S.A
They Executed There 1st Woman In 98 Years..
Can You Believe This!
She Was A Grandmother. (So The Next Time You Hear
Of The U.S.A. Going On About Human Rights Atrocities In Other Countries)
"Remember The Granny They Put To Death Today".

I See Our Governor This Morning, I Asked Her.
"How Come All The Notorious Sex Cases Find Jesus Soon As They
Enter Prison"?
Could it be Anything To Do With Parole I Wonder?

I Had A Lovely Pump-Up On The Multi Gym Today
I Really Felt Strong.
(Not Enough Weight On There For Me Though)

So z Work it Slow... Like A Dynamic... To Get The Pump.
Work The Mind... Feed The Muscle
You Gotta See it... To Understand...

I Got Some New Lotion From The Canteen
"Enliven"
Its Got Vitamin A And E In it.
Good Stuff... After A Shower I Cover Myself
In it... It Makes Me Feel Fresh And Alive. (Almost Free) :)

46

So WHATS THE PLAN FOR TONIGHT? COZ TODAY IS OVER! ITS 5PM,
FRIDAY IS AN EARLY TEA. IVE GOT 15 HOURS TILL MY DOORS UNLOCK AGAIN.
  IVE GOT SOME MAIL TO REPLY. I WANT TO DO AN ART FOR SOMEBODY
IM GONNA WATCH CORONATION STREET, ITS ON TWICE FRIDAY.
  IVE GOT TO GIVE MY FLOOR A GOOD CLEAN AND SHINE.
      THERES ALWAYS SOMETHING TO DO IN THIS SOLITARY LIFE...
IF NOT - THEN FIND IT. ˘ŎŎˋ

      I SEE JODIE MARSH IS LEARNING TO BE A TATOOIST
ALL THE LADS WILL BE GOING TO HER STUDIO TO GET ONE DONE ON THERE
COCK ... 'JODIE DONE THIS' ☺
  SHES GOOD STUFF JODIE ... I KNOW ALOT OF HER CIRCLE OF FRIENDS
SHES HAD ALOT OF BAD PRESS SHE DONT DESRVE.

      DID YOU KNOW THE MOST SUCCESSFUL BANK ROBBER IN U.S.A
WAS 'CARL GUGASIAN'
    HE ROBBED 50 BANKS IN A 30 YEAR REIGN!
    HE WAS DUBBED THE FRIDAY NIGHT BANK ROBBER
      AND HE WORE A FREDDY KRUEGAR MASK.
SADLY ... FUCK ALL EVER LASTS...   HE GOT CAUGHT IN 2002 AND
SENTENCED TO 115 YEARS ˘ŎŎˋ

    WHY CANT THE BABY KILLERS GET THAT?
            WELL? (FOOD FOR THOUGHT).

    I HAD CHIPS PEAS AND PORK CHOP FOR TEA
        "NOT BAD" —   IVE HAD ALOT WORSE (x)
      ITS BEEN ALONG TIME SINCE Z HAD BETTER. ⌢
MUMS LETTER IN TODAY - SHES WELL... WHAT A CUNT SHE IS ☺

    I DREAM OF FOOD SOME NIGHTS... I SHOULDNT BUT Z DO.
OH' GOTTA FILL IN MY CANTEEN FORM FOR TOMORROW.
IT GOES IN AND GETS PROCESSED FOR THURSDAY.
 'MUST GET MY 48 EGGS. I NEED THEM egg whites.

      ANYWAY IM OFF FOR A MUG OF TEA AND CATCH UP
ON MY BITS AND BOBS
    A CONVICTS DUTIES ARE NEVER DONE.
        NOT ENOUGH TIME. ˘ŎŎˋ

"
IM OFTEN ASKED BY 1ST TIME WRITERS
    " CHARLIE - DO YOU EVER WANT TO GET OUT ?

" IT FUCKING WINDS ME UP THAT '
        WHAT A QUESTION TO ASK A GUY WHOSE
    BATTLED THROUGH 3½ DECADES OF SHIT.

BUT LET ME PUT IT STRAIGHT ONCE AND FOR ALL -
    " " IT DONT REALLY MATTER WHAT I WANT '
        IT'S WHAT THESE WANT ' "

LET ME PUT IT ANOTHER WAY ...
    IF SOMEBODY RIPPED YOUR ROOF OFF
        AND SMASHED YOUR HOME UP
            AND KIDNAPPED A FEW OF YOUR OWN -

    " WOULD YOU DO HIM ANY FAVOURS ?

            " DO I MAKE MYSELF CLEAR ?

    LET ME TELL YOU NOW ... WHAT WILL BE WILL BE '
        IF ITS FATE THAT I NEVER GET FREED
            THEN THATS HOW THE COOKIE CRUMBLES
                NOW FUCK OFF AND LEAVE ME ALONE
                    " CORONATION STREET ON SOON

When writing to Members of Parliament please give your previous home
address in order to avoid delay in your case being taken up by the M.P.

In replying to this letter, please write on the envelope:

Number A8076AG   Name Bronson

Wing C.S.C. UNIT

Sat 25. 9. 2010

F WING
HM PRISON
5 LOVE LANE
WAKEFIELD
WF2 9AG

CHRIS

A GREAT NIGHTS KIP. LIKE A BUG IN A RUG.
I WAS UP AT 6AM DOING PRESS UPS.
I DREAMPT ABOUT THE GRANNY THEY EXECUTED IN
U.S.A. I WAS WONDERING WHAT HER LAST WORDS
WERE? "MINE WOULD OF BEEN. ILL SEE YOU LOT
IN HELL LATER. NOW GET ON WITH IT.
OH: BY THE WAY HER NAME WAS TERESA LEWIS
SHE HAD BEEN ON DEATH ROW FOR 8 YEARS, FOR
DOUBLE MURDER.
                        THEY DONT FUCK ABOUT IN THE
GOOD OLD U.S.A.
     I NEVER HAD BREAKFAST. JUST A MUG OF
TEA. COZ WE HAVE A FRY UP AT 11-30 AM HERE.
TODAY I HAD 2 SAUSAGES. 2 EGGS. BEANS. TOMATOES AND
2 FRIED BREAD. WITH 8 BREAD ROLLS.
     IT WAS FUCKING AWESOME.

49

I WORKED IT OFF LATER ON THE YARD. I FELT FREE WITH
THE COLD WIND IN MY FACE. "ALMOST". '00'

AFTER MY SHOWER I GOT A PILE OF MAIL.
ONE WAS A LARGE A/4 FROM DEE MURRIS. WHICH AS
GONE INTO MY PROPERTY "UN-READ".
    THATS HOW I AM... WHEN I CUT-OFF. I MOVE ON.
    WHATS THE POINT IN READING THE PAST.?
      I JUST WISH HER WELL COZ SHES A GOOD SOUL.
    MAYBE ONE DAY WHEN IM FREE I'LL READ IT ALONG.
    WITH HUNDREDS MORE I DONT BOTHER READING.

      I LEARNT TODAY ALAN RUDKIN DIED ON TUESDAY.
    HE WAS ONLY 68... A CHAMPION BOXER IN THE
    1960's. HE WAS A GOOD-UN.
            , AND DON PARTRIDGE DIED ON THE SAME DAY
    AS ALAN. DON WAS THE ORIGINAL BUSKER
        HE WAS 68 TOO.
      HE HAD A COUPLE OF BIG HITS IN THE 1960'
            "ROSIE" AND BLUE EYES

        WE LOST 2 GOOD UN'S THERE.
            REST IN PEACE BOYS. "RESPECT".

          I GOT A FANTASTIC SKETCH SENT IN
          FROM DEAN SHEPHERD.
            HE'S ONLY CREATED ME WITH MY MUM
          AND BROTHER. "HOW RESPECTFUL IS THAT?
            A NICE SURPRISE
      (HE ALSO ENCLOSED A £20 POSTAL ORDER FOR ME)

So my next canteen will be on
Dean Shepherd...
Lovelly Jubbley."

I also got 6 Jail Mail..
From Cons wishing me well..
Yeh its been a Top-Day.
Abit of X-Factor put the Cherry
on the Cake. :)

There's a Tom Cruise Movie on Now.
'Fuck That'.
I've got 'Heart' Radio on
and Al Green's 'Let's Stay Together'
is just on... "What a Song.
What a Singer.
Unbeatable.

I'm a True Soul Man Me.
Tamla. Soul. Blues, I love it all.
Guys Like us we bleed it.
We are it.
Born to be Soulful.
It's in the Blood.
Pumping Around the Body.
You Better Believe it.

My Brother is up to see me this
Tuesday... Just us for a Nice Chat

Then he's off to Spain with the chaps
to celebrate his 50th Birthday.

I've done well for visits this month 😄
          I tell the Governors. "Send me to Mars
and I'll still get visits"
          I fucking would to ....
My firm don't let me down ... (ever) ...

Alot of cons are forgotten within 6 months
of being inside. "Thats a fact".

Oh .. I found out "today my new book"
          Bronson ③ up on the roof is selling
like hot cross buns ..
          I told you my books are the bollocks.

The publishers will be climbing over each other to
get my 'Freedom book'
          (if) and (when) I ever get out to do it.

I'll write that baby with a golden pen on
the beach with a few beers and a bit of pussy -
          - close by.
                         You know it buddy 😄

          He. He
          He - He
          - He -
          Die. Laughing.

          Laughter is the true medicine.   ?

BRONSON .A8076AG . C.S.C
H.M.P. WAKEFIELD

29.9.2010

CHRIS.

GREAT VISIT YESTERDAY WITH MY BROTHER.
I POLISHED OFF 2 BANANA MILK SHAKES AND 6 CHOC-BARS AND A CAKE.
HE ALSO GOT ME 4 BAGS OF CRISPS — FUCK KNOWS WHY COZ I
DONT EAT THEM. IT'S ALWAYS A TREAT TO SEE MARK.
BUT THE BAD NEWS IS.. BEFORE MY VISIT Z WAS INFORMED BY
THE PRISON POLICE LIASON OFFICER THAT THE MILTON KEYNES POLICE ARE UP
TO SEE ME ON THE 11TH OCTOBER OVER INCIDENTS THAT OCCURED AT
WOODHILL PRISON 'ᴏ̈' SO THAT PUT A DOWNER ON MY DAY.'
"SUCH IS LIFE".. WHAT WILL BE WILL BE."
THE INCIDENT IS IM ALLEGED TO HAVE SMASHED UP A GYM, RIPPED
A DOOR OFF. ATTACKED A GUARD DOG. AND CRASHED INTO THE RIOT MOB.
'FUCKING FULL HOUSE THERE' 'BINGO' ,
NO-MAIL TODAY. BUT Z GOT A PILE YESTERDAY.
IAN FROSTS FROM BRIGHTON WITH MORE PHOTOS FROM THE BOXING
SHOW'. MY LAWYER HARRIETT. JOHNNY GRIFFITHS AND RED MENZIES
AND AN OLD BUDDY FROM MAIDSTONE JAIL "CHRIS DRUMMOND"
THATS A RIGHT OLD JAIL MAIDSTONE.
GOES BACK TO THE 18TH CENTURY
THEY DONE ALOT OF EXECUTIONS THERE.
ONE OF THE FAMOUS ONES WOULD OF BEEN GEORGE JOSEPH SMITH
HE WAS THE BRIDES IN THE ~~BOTH~~ MURDERER. BACK IN 1915.
BATH

THE LAST OFFICIAL EXECUTION THERE WAS "SIDNEY FOX" BACK
IN 1930.
HOW DO I KNOW ALL THIS YOU ASK ?
"IM A WALKING LIVING BREATHING HUMAN PRISON ENCYCLUPIDIA."

OH BY THE WAY SIDNEY FOX WAS SENTENCED TO HANG FOR THE
MURDER OF HIS MOTHER.. 'ᴏ̈'
ALSO Reg KRAY WAS MARRIED

53

there.. WHAT A FARCE THAT ENDED UP. SHE EVEN MESSED UP HIS
FUNERAL.. A VERY SAD DAY FOR MANY OF REGGIE'S LOYAL MATES WHO
HAD STOOD BY HIM FOR YEARS..
MY OTHER MAIL WAS SUPPORTERS... ONE SENT ME 20 QUID.

TODAYS BEEN A MUGGY OLD DAY WEATHER WISE.
MY SON MIKE CALLED THE JAIL UP FOR A VISITING ORDER.
BUT HE'S NOT GETTING ONE.. (HE KNOWS WHY) (PERSONAL")

CHIPS BEANS tw PIE FOR TEA. FUCK KNOWS WHAT SORT OF PIE?
BUT ONCE Z COVERED IT IN RED SAUCE.. WHO CARES.

IM HAVING AN EARLY NIGHT TONIGHT
THERES FUCK ALL ON TELLY.
IT'S DARK AND COLD AND WET OUTSIDE.
SO IM IN THE RIGHT PLACE ☺

A NICE BIT OF PEACE.
IVE GOT MY EAR PLUGS, SO ITS BACK INTO MY WORLD OF
DARKNESS, SILENCE AND DEEP THOUGHT
"LOVELY"
YOU CANT BEAT IT.

WHEN YOU LIVE INSIDE A TOMB LIKE ME FOR DECADES,
YOU BECOME A BRICK IN THE WALL.
NOTHING PENETRATES.
ITS ABIT LIKE FLOATING AROUND IN SPACE.
YOUR JUST A FEATHER IN A TORNADO..
HANGING ON FOR SANITY.

"IN THE DARKNESS WE ARE ALL THE SAME.

Hi-Mum

PS. AS MY BUDDY IFTY ALWAYS SAYS.
"SALAAM BROTHER!

54

When writing to Members of Parliament please give your previous home
address in order to avoid delay in your case being taken up by the M.P.

In replying to this letter, please write on the envelope:

Number A8076AG   Name Bronson

Wing C.S.C.

INSANITY Gone MAD

HM PRISON
5 LOVE LANE
WAKEFIELD
WF2 9AG

Hi CHRIS

LAST DAY OF THE MONTH BUDDY... SOON BE CRIMBO
NOT THAT IT MATTER'S TO ME. COZ SANTA STAYS WELL AWAY
FROM THESE PLACES. THE FAT SLOB...

A LITTLE SPARROW WAS SINGING AWAY EARLY THIS MORNING
ONTOP OF MY CAGED WINDOW... "I THOUGHT". THIS IS CRAZY
MAN IN CAGE.. BIRD FREE.. SOMETHING DONT ADD UP.
THEN AGAIN SOME DO CALL ME THE BIRDMAN.
"TWEET. FUCKING. TWEET."

I HAD 500 PRESS UPS POLISHED OFF BEFORE BREAKFAST
AND A 100 KICKS ON BOTH LEGS.

A BOWL OF RICE KRISPIES   CAN YOU BELIEVE IT ?
RONNIE BARKER WOULD TURN IN HIS GRAVE.
WHATEVER HAPPENED TO GOOD OLD PORRIDGE? A MANS
BREAKFAST. WITH BACON AND EGGS..
FUCKING RICE KRISPIES. DO ME A FAVOUR!

VF004 Printed for the Prison Service at HMP Norwich

Nice Bit of Mushroom Soup For Dinner. I had 7 mushrooms in it - A right result. And 6 bread rolls went down well. A pile of mail too. Stu Godfrey sent me some photos of the Brighton Bash and one of his daughter Amber handing over a pile of Dosh To Little Dylan.

"That's what I love to see... a nice few Quid for needy Kids. Fantastic."

Dawn Peters sent me in $20 For my canteen. She's a lovely soul.

I got 8 prison letters, one from a con up in Durham asking me to design him a cell work-out to keep fit.

I get alot of them.

I've got cell work outs you would not believe. I use my chair, table, and bed for dynamic exercises. It's all in my Solitary Fitness Book.

Talking of Books my Publisher Blakes just posted me in "Bronson (3) up on the roof (security say I cant have it)

I bet Jeffrey Archer never got this crap. So I now cant have my own books sent in by the publishers? (Life in jail can be very childish)

I see Karen Easterbrook just copped her 4th life sentence for attempted murder on a prison guard at Bronzefield. That's where old fatty Rose West is.... Great name for a jail.

Karens 55 now... So she's gonna be a very old lady before she breathes freedom again.
"Believe it or not" she's really a good soul. She just has issues. (Its sad really)

Poor old Tony Curtis passed away last night. He was 85. (What a true Hollywood star he is)
He made some classics.
And what a life he lived.
My fav film he did was Viltings with Kirk Douglas. "Awesome"

Tea was stew.. (No dumplins) :: How can you have a stew without dumplins?
Its like a car without wheels. OO

I called Mum. She had just received a framed drawing from Lorraine.
Lorraine had done a fantastic portray of my late brother John. Along with a brilliant poem.
"She's a bloody star"
And it really did make my mums year.
(we never forget such things).

Cantern day as well today.
I got my regular goodies
And I treat myself to a new toothbrush
£2.80 OO Fuch me its not even gold.
I remember when that was 30 pence.

It's a lovely brush though. I do love a good
brush.. cos I do it 6 to 8 times a day.

Oh my lovely friend Leanne Mayers got her
parole last week.. so she will be partying! :)
Johnny Griffiths sent me in some signed boxing photos
thats 10 this month. even one off Joe Bugner
signed to me.
    All the boxers never forget me.
    it's one big family

    Its been a nice day
Gym. Shower. Yard. Mail. A call. Canteen.

    Coronation Streets on in 10 min :)
    Io give that Becky one :)

Oh well 1st. Oct. Tomorrow.
    Lets hope it brings some luck.

    As my old mate Ronnie Kray used to
always say. 'Bring it on'. Lets do it !

    └ Eggs have rights !

58

CHRIS

THATS WHAT ITS ALL ABOUT
LOADS OF LOLLY FOR THE KIDS.

THATS WHY I SLEEP GOOD
AND AWAKE A PROUD MAN!

2010

CHRIS
    ITS BANG ONTOP
2 OF MY POST TO YOU HAVE BEEN STOPPED ✓
2 OF YOURS WITH A BOOK HAS BEEN STOPPED ✓
(REASONS) THEY BELIEVE Z AM DOING A BOOK
WITH ALEX..   (NOSY TWATS) ☹
Z SHALL SORT YOU A V/O FOR NOVEMBER ✓
   ITS A BRILLIANT IDEA ☺

Z THINK YOUL LIKE IT.
  (IF) NOT.. THEN THATS SHOWBIZZ ☹

SAW OLD BILL YESTERDAY WITH HARRIETT OVER WOODHILL
   8IT DAMAGE. ASSULT ON SCREW AND DOG
½ WAY THROUGH INTERVIEW Z REACHED THROUGH BARS GRABBED
RECORDER AND SMASHED IT.. TOLD THEM TO FUCK OFF AND
HOW LUCKY YOUR NOT IN MY ROOM COZ ZO WRAP YOU
BOTH UP LIKE THEM TURKEYS
  IM BEING STITCHED UP OVER WOODHILL..
   (ILL TELL YOU WHEN Z SEE YOU) ☹
 SUCH IS LIFE... ONE MUSNT GRUMBLE...

12/10/2010   POON EXPRESS

17.11.2010

BRONSON A8076AG. C.S.C.
H.M.P. WAKEFIELD
W. YORKS WF2 9AG

Jeff! I Bet Your THINKING ... Where's old CHARLIE
Been HIDING .. Clock The DATE '00'

THINGS HAVE Been GOING ON ... ALOT of SILLY BOLLOCKS ..
BUT I MUST ADMIT, SOMEBODY OUTSIDE CAUSED ALOT of UNNECESSARY
PROBLEMS FOR ME TO CONTINUE THIS PROJECT.
THAT PERSON KNOWS WHO HE IS. AND WHAT He DONE, SO ILL LEAVE IT
AT THAT. ONLY I KNOW IT WAS A BIG MISTAKE He REGRETS.
I DID WRITE TWO PAGES TO CHRIS COWLIN, BOTH Were STOPPED FROM
LEAVING THE JAIL IN OCTOBER 8TH.
AND ONE of His LETTERS WAS STOPPED TO ME. (SUCH IS LIFE)
He AINT THE FIRST, He WONT Be THE LAST TO Be BANNED FROM CONTACTING
ME. I KEEP TELLING PEOPLE ALWAYS Re-READ YOUR LETTERS YOU POST ME
COZ THERE ALL READ BY SECURITY ...
ANYTHING IN IT THEY SEE AS A THREAT TO THEM OR AN EMBARASSMENT
TO THE SYSTEM THEY WILL STOP IT - IT WILL BE PUT INTO MY PROPERTY.
ILL NEVER SEE IT TILL IM RELEASED ..
I HAVE SACK LOADS of MAIL TO READ WHEN I GET OUT.
THATS NOT COUNTING THE PARCELS IVE NEVER SEEN WITH BOOKS.
MAGS. CLOTHES, SHOES. DIARIES. PENS. CD' TAPES .. EVEN GIRLS
KNICKERS. (YES BAGS of THEM) 'CRAZY WOMEN'.
WHO THE FUCK DO THEY THINK I AM ?
THERE GETTING ME MIXED UP WITH SOME POP STAR.
DONT THEY RELEAZE WHO AND WHAT I AM ?
ANYWAY, THINK WHAT YOU WRITE AND POST ME.
ALWAYS THINK ... DONT LET THE ENEMY KNOW WHAT YOU PLAN
DONT TELL THEM NOTHING. THEY NEED NOT NO -
IF YOU HAVE A MESSAGE FOR ME, TELL IT TO ME ON A VISIT - OR
TELL ONE of MY TRUSTED VISITORS TO TELL ME.
ITS REALLY SO SIMPLE ...
WHAT THIS MOB DONT KNOW DONT MATTER
SO DONT FEED THEM WITH INFORMATION THAT ONLY CAUSES ME
PROBLEMS.
OH! AND WILL THE IRISH BIRD BETTY STOP POSTING ME IN BIBLES.
SHE'S SENT IN EIGHT THIS YEAR. AND NINE LAST YEAR.
TOLD THE SECURITY TO SLING THEM ALL IN THE BIN.
GODS A FAGGOT. I PREFERE SATAN .. YOU KNOW WHERE YOU
STAND WITH THE DEVIL .. PLUS ITS MUCH MORE FUN ☺

61

So WHAT IM GONNA Do NOW is PuT THE RECORD STRAIGHT ON THIS LATEST Bollocks ⟶

Daily Mirror, 15 November 2010:

BUTTER NUTTER

SMEARED AND NAKED BRONSON'S JAIL RIOT
Exclusive by Jeremy Armstrong

Crackpot Charles Bronson covered himself in butter while naked and took on 12 prison warders in his latest jail rage.

The 57-year-old flipped after growing more and more furious over his latest failed bid to be freed.

He took on six warders, then another six in a specialist restraint team who rushed to help before finally being dragged back to solitary.

At least four officers were injured in the rampage on the notorious F-wing at Wakefield jail, West Yorks.

An insider said: "He was naked and covered himself in butter so staff trying to restrain him could not take him down. He assaulted four before they sent in six members of the control and restraint team to get him.

"They finally managed to control him and he was taken back into solitary confinement.

"Charlie has not been in the news for a while and his failed appeal last year hit him hard. He was moved to Long Lartin and thought he was going to get out.

"Then they had to take him back to the highest security at Wakefield.

"He knows this is it for the rest of his days, and he is desperate."

Lifer Bronson, first jailed for armed robbery in 1969, is likely to be in solitary indefinitely. He has spent the vast majority of his 36 years behind bars alone.

Bronson was last locked up in 1974 for another armed raid. He has taken a string of hostages in 10 sieges, attacked at least 20 officers and caused £500,000 damage in rooftop protests.

He got life for kidnapping prison teacher Phil Danielson at Hull jail in 1999.

His appeal against that sentence failed last year. A film, Bronson, has been released based on his life.

His art work, including dark depictions of jail life, has won awards, and can earn £2,500 a canvas.

The Prison Service said of Friday's rampage: "A prisoner was involved in a minor incident in the gym area."

You JUST CANT MAKE MY LIFE up.
ITS BECOME A FuCKING RUNNING SAGA.
iT WOULD MAKE A GREAT OPERA.
OR A 12 PART T.V PLAY.

So LET ME NOW PUT THE TRUTH OVER.

INSTEAD OF READING iT FROM THE PAPERS FED TO THEM BY A GREEDY SCREW.

He PROBABLY GOT A COUPLE OF GRAND FOR THIS SHIT.
THE CUNT NEVER EVEN GIVE ME A BOX OF MARS BARS

ON SAT 13TH NOVEMBER 2010 STARTED OUT AS ANY OTHER DAY.
THE ONLY DIFFERENCE iT WASN'T SAT, OR THE 13TH ⊙⊙

"I BET YOUR CONFUSED NOW?
MY FAULT ... iT WAS FRIDAY 12TH .... MY MIND is GoiNG
SO I WOKE uP ON FRIDAY, FRESH, ALIVE AND PREPARED FOR THE DAY.
I HAD A Good CRAP. ONE OF THOSE CRAPS THAT MAKES A MAN FEEL PROUD
TO BE ALIVE. (LETS FACE REALITY HERE) HOW MANY PEOPLE ON THE PLANET HAVE
TO SHIT INTO A COLOSTOMY BAG?
HOW MANY SUFFER WITH CONSTIPATION ... OR HAVE PILES?
PLEASE BELIEVE ME .... US CRAPPERS ARE SO LUCKY. BLESSED. BE THANKFUL.

It was Rice Krispies. OO That don't help for a good start.
I made my applications, exercise. Shower. And gym.
And I had a chat with Governor Raven, through the gate of my cage.
She's a lovely human. With a beautiful smile.
   She really does try her best. But she's only a mouth piece for
These creepy crawlies up in H/Q
   I had a nice mug or tea. And 4 custard creams. And sat in
Silence for ½ hour. "Thinking" 'OO'   Bad Thoughts

   I started to wind myself up... Why am I kept in a cage.
Why am I forever isolated. Why are security fucking about with
my mail. Phone calls. And Visitors.
   I got my list of Visitors they have stopped (for no reason)
Here is the list.... Tammy Miller. Amanda Richardson Ryan Dubois
Tony Fear. Stevie Swatton. Spencer and Daniel Wilder. Mark Sharman
Gary White Dave Taylor. Andy Dutrice. Ian Frost
Zahrah Iftkhar John.H Stracey Guffy Iftkhar
Matt Legg Dawn Peters
        Thats all the ones I've applied to be put onto my visit list
(all have been given no reason)
     Because there is no reason.

Then there's then lot who have been taken off my list and
   Banned from visiting me.
Leighton and Lindsey Frayne. . Mark Fish . Alan Rayment
Tom Hardy . Danny Hansford.
        (Again no reasons)
     Because there is no reason.   its all Bollocks.

So put yourselfs in my shoes.
     Your serving a life sentence... Never knowing when or if
Your ever be freed.
              And these spineless fuckers are stopping you seeing
old Friends.
         How would you feel?
     Ill tell you how I feel.... Angry. Frustrated. Mad.
I feel betrayed, and De-humanized
     its like Im being cut off from the real world
     not being. I am. And I've had my lot.
     This is the Real story _____ "OO"

I Love Lurpak Butter... The Best Butter in the World.
Its my little treat from the Canteen.
I like to spoil myself occassionally.
So I stuffed it down my pants ready for some action."

They unlocked me for my gym session. Searched me, and metal
detected me. And escorted me to the gym cage.
Its a 20 feet by 10 feet area. In a zoo cage.
I'm locked in there on my own for one hour.
But today... its all about to change

I stripped off and covered myself in my Lurpak.
I really am a slippery fucker.
I tore up my T shirt to make some fist wraps. And a head
band. And shouted out.

Lets Fucking have some
Ready to Rumble.
Jippeeeeeeeeeo..

4 hours later I'm still waiting to Rumble.
I've smashed all the lights out... I prefere to rumble in the
shadows of hell...
Then they appear like an army of space men.
The special force... The Tornadoes.
They look like the S.A.S. Walk like John Wayne...
They've all got the attitude look.
Dont Fuck with us
They surrounded the cage...
One brave one said... We're gonna break your arms + legs
another said. Branson your going to die in prison —
— Today could be the day.

Then im told I will be gassed...

Fuck me... Get on with it you bunch of Pussies.
You lot would give a fucking aspirin a headache.
Stop yapping and lets get this show on the road.

Then out of nowhere one sprayed me with a jet of liquid
through the bars (Brave Bastard)
It got me full in the eyes
I went blind... I was in agony. I could hear shouting

64

I heard the door slam open... So I rushed to the door and began to lash out at them in a blind fury.

Soon I was sprayed again.. Most of it hit the back of my throat. I could not breathe, I was in panic.

My eyes were burning up.

I was now being punched and kicked. Lots of shouting going on.

I felt myself slipping into darkness.

Then I was carried off and slung into the Concrete Coffin which is a cell with a hole in the floor for a toilet and a slab of rock for a bed.

The door has a feeding hatch in it like a cat flap.

No, its not Alcatraz......... its Wakefield.

I'm left blind... in agony. Burning up.

Fuck me...... What a day...

Bumps, lumps, bruises, and totally dehumanized.

oh! They left me some water, and a blanket.

It took several hours for my eyes to work.

It took 4 days to get back to health.

I remained in the coffin for 3 days.

I did NOT see a doctor.

That on its own is a disgrace.

I have since found out I was sprayed with Parva which immobilizes the nervous system.

My symptoms were

Blindness, eyes, throat, chest, burning up.

Vomiting. Sweating. Agony. Shakes. Loss of balance. Disorientation. Palpitations of the heart. Dizzy.

Its now 17th Nov. and im still not myself.

Let this be a lesson to all you youngsters who are about to take on a life of crime!

You will be Tortured!

And smashed into another world

A world with no pussy and no sweetness.

Give it a wide birth.. and stay free.

ILL NOW GO BACK TO OCTOBER ... TO SOME OF THE DATES I MISHD.

MONDAY 11TH

THE MILTON KEYNES OLD BILL COME TO INTERVIEW ME OVER MY RIOT IN WOODHILL

HARRIETT MATHER MY LAWYER WAS PRESENT.

THEY SAT IN ONE ROOM, AND ME IN ANOTHER BEHIND BARS..
THEY PUT THE TAPE MACHINE ON THE SHELF - BETWEEN US.
AND BEGAN THERE QUESTIONS.

AFTER 10 MIN.. I HAD ENOUGH.
      SO I GRABBED THE MACHINE AND SMASHED IT
   " INTERVIEW OVER " __   FUCK OFF ..

HARRIETT AND ME SPENT THE NEXT HOUR ALONE DISCUSSING IT ALL
APPARENTLY WOODHILL HAVE IT ALL ON FILM -
    SO WHY BOTHER ASKING ME ... ⊙⊙

SAT 16TH OCT

      JOHNNY GRIFFITHS AND SANDRA GARDNER VISITED
      WHAT A LAUGH. ☺
I HAD 3 BANANA MILK SHAKES AND LOTS OF CHOC BARS
SANDRA LOOKED HER LOVELY SELF.
SHE HAD JUST GOT BACK FROM HER CHARITY WALK IN CHINA.
      LORRAINE SENT ME IN A BULLSEYE
            THANKS LORRAINE .... ILL GET SOME CANTEEN ON YOU X
WHAT A GREAT ARTIST SHE IS.
      ONE OF MY FAVOURITES.

21ST THURSDAY

            BIG STEVIE SWATTON HAS BEEN STOPPED FROM VISITING ME.
            (WATCH THIS SPACE).
      YOU GUTLESS, SPINELESS CUNTS.
      YOU LOT COULDNT CLEAN STEVES BOOTS.
      HE'S ONE OF BRITANS STRONGEST MEN. HE OWNS HIS OWN GYM
      HE'S A GOOD HONEST MAN --- AND YOU HAVE VICTIMIZED HIM.

66

AGAIN THEY GIVE NO REASON WHY?
. COZ THERE IS NO REASON YOU CAN GIVE
STEVE WONT ACCEPT IT THATS FOR SURE.

26TH TUESDAY
        ITS MY NIECES 13TH BIRTHDAY RACHAEL
            HAPPY BIRTHDAY. ☺
    BIG JACK BINNS WAS UP TO SEE ME TODAY.
    WE GO BACK 40 YEARS
NOW THIS IS A GEEZER YOU DONT FUCK WITH -
    HE'S 76 NOW - AND CAN STILL HAVE A PUNCH UP.
JACKS ONE OF A HANDFULL OF GUYS WHO HAS RIPPED A CELL
    DOOR OFF ITS HINGES
THERES ONLY A FEW OF US -
        ME.. ROY SHAW . JACK. FRED MILLS. AND GEORGE WILKINSON
    OH. AND FRANKIE MITCHELL.. (SORRY FRANK) HOW COULD I FORGET.
ITS A VERY SPECIAL RARE CLUB TO BE IN..
            THE CELL DOOR WRECKERS ☺
    MINE WAS IN ARMLEY JAIL. 1975 IN THE SEG BLOCK
    (WHAT A KICKING I GOT FOR THAT) ☺☺ ' GOOD TIMES...

            I PHONED LORRAINE TODAY SHES GREAT
    WE HAVE ALOT IN COMMON -- PLUS SHE MAKES ME LAUGH

        A GREAT DAY
            AND IT WAS LIVER AND ONION FOR TEA

27TH
        THEYVE STOPPED A VISITING ORDER BEING SENT OUT TO
    CHRIS COWLIN.
            HE IS NOW OFF MY VISIT LIST.
                WHOSE NEXT?
        IT COULD BE YOU?
    SOON ILL HAVE NO FUCKER LEFT..
        THATS WHAT THEY WANT..
            THE CUNTS...

67

31st

Big Protest outside this Jail Today.
"Free Bronson"
My Supporters never Let Me Down
Its why they cant kill me ... Ive to many eyes on them.
Thanks everybody.
But one Guy let me Down Big Time. Marit Jones
He only Lives 200 Yards from this Jail
He Promised me he will have Loads on the Protest
"Talks Cheap Mate"
You Let Yourself Down ... and Made a Cunt out of me
Coz I Praised You ... I Told All my Friends Youd be there
and You Let me Down
You had Loads of Warning All the Contacts
Maybe one Day You will be inside a Coffin.
Trapped.
Then Youd think of what you never Done.

What you have Done is Lost a Good Friend and the
Respect I Drummed up for you.

Fuck me ... I even Got You a Fucking invite to my Film
Premiere in London Last Year
and you cant Give my Support Group a bit of Support.
Fuck You.

Ifty Also Visited Today. well Done my Brother
You Done the Protest Proud

Salaam Brother

1. 11. 2010 Monday

Just Sorted my angel Goddaughter Some Dosh for her Birthday
Happy Birthday Sahra x
And can You Believe it these Gestapo Bastards wont let me see her mum.
You cant make this Shit up if you Tried.
Called mum ... She has a Bad Cough
it Gave me a Headache Hearing it.

68

I Also Called Dave Taylor. And Got Some Sad News
      My old Mate CLIFFY Field Died on Sunday
Cliff was a True Survivor.
      He Fought The Best And Won.
He Beat Roy Shaw. And Lenny McLean.
He was Also A Royal Navy Boxing Champion
      " Ti me" He was The Original Tough Nut That All Dream
of Being. Ive Sorted My Reef of Respect
          So Long CLIFF
                    Never Forgotten By So Many
      And Respect To Reoo Menzies And Dave Taylor For
Showing My Respect at The Funeral on The 12th
      (Which So Happens To Be My Riot Day) 'OO'
                                                    ͜

I Also Got A Pile of Mail.. One was From A Paddy
   Called "Patsy O Connor" Asking me if I ever Pulled
out anybody's Teeth 'OO'
                                ͜
              Hello".... He's Free. And im Locked up.
Somebody Please Get me out of Here Before I Go Mad.

      it was Pie and Mash Tonight For Tea'
"Well".. Thats What They Call it'... '
its A Fucking Insult To The Cockneys'

2/11/2010 Tuesday
          Eddie Clinton was up Today For A Chat.
      Great To See The old Rascal.
      We Go Back Some Years.
    Ed's old School.. very Loyal.
Its One Guy You Really Dont Want To Upset.
      'You Have Been Warned'

7.11.2010 Sunday
          Since Tuesday. Heres A List of All The Mail
   Ive Had Sent In. Mum. Brother. Aunty Eileen. Stu Godfrey.
Tammy Miller. Amanda Richardson. Al Rayment. Lorraine. Jffy.

69

JOHN GRIFFITHS. STEVE SWATTON— TONY FEAR. MARK WILLIAMS.
MAL VANES. REDD MENZIES. STU CHESHIRE. LEYTON FRAYNE.
    PLUS 14 PRISON LETTERS
NOW SEE WHY I SAY .. ENCLOSE A S.A.e..
    I COULD WRITE REPLY TO SO MANY... IMPOSSIBLE

    I CALLED STEVE SWATTON.. HE IS FUMING OVER BEING STOPPED FROM
VISITING ME. AND BEING GIVEN NO REASON.
        HE IS SEEING HIS LOCAL M/P.
                (WATCH THIS SPACE)

        STEVE WONT ACCEPT IT ''
    THEY'VE JUST MADE A SERIOUS ENEMY'.
                ''
                CUNTS   ''
        NOW LETS SEE WHAT REASON THEY GIVE TO THE M.P.'

    COZ THE M/P WILL DEMAND ONE FROM THE PRISON MINISTER
            (YOUR FUCKED WHO EVER STOPPED IT)   ''
        NOW JUSTICE IT YOU POWER FREAKED TWAT.'
        _____

8/11/2010 MONDAY
        SAW MY INDEPENDANT PSYCHIATRIST TODAY TO PREPARE MY
REPORT FOR MY NEXT PAROLE BOARD IN MARCH 2011
        DR MARC LYALL.. A NICE CHAP FROM LONDON -
SO GOOD TO HEAR A SOUTHERN ACCENT.
        COZ I FEEL LIKE AN ADOPTED YORKSHIRE MAN UP HERE FOR SO LONG.
    HE IS NOT HAPPY WITH THE VISIT ROOM
            CAMERA--- BARS BETWEEN US
            HIS WORDS .. " BARBARIC'.
    CALLED LORRAINE... AND SANDRA GARDINER
            GREAT DAY
        ALSO HIT MY 3½000 PRESS.UPS
            ' LOVE IT '   ☺
            _____

70

11/11/2010 THURSDAY

Spencer and Daniel Wilder Both Got Refused To Go onto my Visit List.

Daniel is a Teenager into His Boxing.
Spencer his The Father

The Helped His Son as if He was my own
(with Diet - Training Tips) ect
its Totally Shocked me.. I Feel Sick
and Daniel is Heart Broken over it

(The System as Kicked This Lad in The Head For No Reason)

All I've ever Tried To Do is Help This Boy Along on His Fight Career
With His Dads Blessing

Daniel even Calls me His 2nd Dad
He Also Wears my Name on His Robe

Your Mindless Cunts
Spineless Fudt Faces

Whoever Made This Latest Decision I Hope You Get Bowel Cancer
and You Die in Agony.

You Have Insulted Mr Wilder. And Devastated Young Daniel
All Because You Can Do it. If You Wish To

Again With No Reason Why.

You Cant even Put it in Writing or Sign it. So we can
See Who You Are ... Your A Coward.

You Need Your Jaw Breaking To Wake You Up

I Can Accept Such A Decision if There Criminals .. or Smart Heads
or Piss Heads.

Mr Wilder Has No Record of Crime
Nor Does Daniel

There Goes Decent Honest Folk

Your The Fucking Criminal By Humiliating Them
They Do everything Right.

Fill Your Security Forms in

You Then Send The Forms To The Police
Who Then Interview Them . They Say No Problem. You Get

71

The police reports and forms back
Then you say NO
Your going to be exposed you evil cunt
(even your fellow screws say its bollocks)
Its Bronson month. Lets upset Bronson.
Lets see how far we can push him again
Lets fuck him up for his parole.

We all cant be wrong in thinking its a stitch up.
' is now all stopped by you (whoever you are)

I called Mal Vango today and told him how I feel.
Sick. Tired. Fed up. Cut off. Angry.
And very very confused...

Mal said. "CHILL OUT CHARLIE - its a fit up.'

(Again) Nov 12th Friday
Remember this word. "PARVA SPRAY
And pray you never ever get it in your face.

Adios - Amigus

↑s   Get CLIFF Fields Booit.
        " A Cut Above The Rest '
        (www . New Breed Boots . Co . u.it)
              Price £12.99
(all fight fans are in for a treat)

18.11.2010

I THINK ITS TIME I INTRODUCED YOU TO THE RESIDENTS ON
OUR HIGH SECURE CONTROL UNIT (ALL SIX OF US)
BUT LET ME FIRST EXPLAIN ABOUT F. WING.
ITS CUT IN HALF... ONE SIDE IS US - AND THE OTHER SIDE IS THE SEG
BLOCK FOR PUNISHMENTS
WE OCCASSIONALLY SEE THEM ON THE YARD...
OUR SIDE IS CALLED THE C.S.C. UNIT. FOR LONG TERM SOLITARY
THERE SIDE IS SEGREGATION WING FOR SHORT SPELLS.
AT THIS MOMENT ON THE OTHER SIDE IS APPROX A DOZEN INMATES
SOME YOU MAY WELL OF READ ABOUT
"COPELAND" THE NAIL BOMBER.
HE LET SOME BOMBS GO OFF IN LONDON IN A GAY BAR
HE'S INTO THE NATIONAL FRONT SKIN HEAD MOB... HE HATES BLACKS
BUT IN JAIL HE IS A MOUSE -
SCARED TO SAY A WORD
HE IS ACTUALLY IN THE SEG FOR HIS OWN PROTECTION
A FRIGHTENED RABBIT
I WOULD RESPECT HIM IF HE STOOD AND FOUGHT FOR HIS BELIEFS
(NOT HIDE AWAY)

THEN THERES GRIFFITHS... WHO CALLS HIMSELF THE CROSSBOW CANNIBAL
HE'S WAITING TO GO UP ON TRIAL FOR 3 MURDERS OF PROSTITUTES
(I BEST SAY ALLEGED) COZ WE ARE ALL INNOCENT TILL PROVEN GUILTY
YOUR SOON SEE IN THE MEDIA WHAT HE DONE.

I SAW HIM THE OTHER WEEK BEING ESCORTED TO THE VISIT ROOM.
I SHOUTED... OY CROSSBOW - WHAT DID THE HEART AND KIDNEYS TASTE LIKE.
HE SMIRKED AND SAID... "TOUGH"
WAS IT IN A STEW OR CURRY I SHOUTED
STEW HE SAID WITH A SMILE... OO
GET ME OUT OF HERE I'M A CELEBRITY.

THEN THERES "PETER BROWN" AWAITING TRIAL ON A DOUBLE MURDER.
(A SERIOUS FIT UP)
I KNOW PETE. HE'S ALOT OF THINGS BUT NOT A KILLER.
IT STINKS OF A POLICE FIT-UP.
INFACT HIS TRIAL BEGINS TOMORROW AT NOTTINGHAM COURT.

ANYBODY WHISH ANYBODY AS A SPELL OVER ON THE SEG BLOCK HERE.
I FIRST HIT THERE BACK IN 1974.
I WAS BRUTALIZED. BEATEN BLACK AND BLUE STUCK IN A STRAIT
JACKET FOR DAYS. IT WAS GREAT FUN OO THE GOOD OLD DAYS ☺
IN RECENT YEARS A FEW NAMES YOU WILL HAVE READ ABOUT WHO HAVE
SPENT TIME ON THERE,
HUNTLEY. MICHAEL STONE. BAMBER. NIELSON. MY OLD MATE FERDI LIEVELO
WARREN SLANNEY. SO MANY.. COLIN IRELAND. GLYN WRIGHT

    SOME OF THESE GUYS ARE SERIAL KILLERS.
    BAMBER KILLED 5 OF HIS FAMILY
    NIELSON KILLED 15.
    WE ARE TALKING SERIOUS MAD BASTARDS !

OVER THE LAST 40 YEARS THIS GAFF AS HAD THEM ALL.
    NOW HAVE Z EXPLAINED WHY ITS CALLED MONSTER MANSION ?
"BELIAVE ME".. ALOT OF CONVICTS HERE EVEN LOOK WHAT THEY ARE
            PSYCHO MAD KILLERS - WITH BULGING EYES AND
RAZOR SHARP TEETH.
    ITS ALSO PAEDOS PARADISE.
        THERE ALL HERE... BLACK. COOKE - WHITING. BABY KILLERS
SERIAL RAPISTS. GRANNY BUGGERERS
        YOUR WORST NIGHTMARES..

THANK FUCK IM ALONE IN MY CAGE.
    OR I COULD WELL BECOME A MASS KILLER HERE LET AMONGST
THESE REPTILES.
" COULD YOU LIVE WITH SUCH SHIT ? COULD YOU ?

THERES PLENTY OF SORE ARSES IN THIS JAIL.
    THEY EVEN WALK FUNNY
        AND THATS ONLY THE STAFF ☺ HA. HA. HA. HA.

NOW LETS GET ONTO MY LITTLE UNIT.
    "WELCOME TO HELL"   ☺   IM NOT KIDDING.

74

IM IN CELL Nº 6 ON THE TWO'S LANDING
ITS A CELL WITH 2 DOORS..
THE OUTSIDE DOOR IS SOLID STEEL.. THE INSIDE DOOR IS A GATE WITH WIRE
ON IT,
ITS 18 FEET LONG. AND 8 FEET WIDE. AND 12 FEET HIGH.
ITS GOT A SINK AND TOILET MADE OF STEEL.
ITS GOT A CAGED WINDOW.
THE FURNITURE IS A TABLE & CHAIR AND A CUPBOARD
I HAVE A T.V SET, RADIO, AND ALL MY ART PENS.
I HAVE BARE WALLS. NO PHOTOS OR POSTERS (MY CHOICE)
A CELL IS A CELL TO ME.. NOT A HOME.
    ITS CLEAN, MY BED IS A STANDARD ISSUE BED.
    I HAVE 3 BLANKETS AND A PILLOW.
   THIS IS WHERE I LIVE FOR APPROX 23 HOURS EVERY DAY
   SOME DAYS 22 HOURS
      ON A VISIT DAY 21 HOURS.
   BUT THIS CAGE IS MY LIFE ... MY WORLD.
   DAY TO DAY. WEEK TO WEEK, AND YEAR TO YEAR.

CELL 5 NEXT DOOR IS THE INFAMOUS FREDDIE LOWE
   IVE KNOWN FRED FOR 30+ YEARS
    A BIG MAN, A DANGEROUS MAN BUT A HEART OF GOLD.
 FRED HAS KILLED TWICE IN PRISON
         A CON IN GARTREE JAIL AND ANOTHER CON IN LONG LARTIN
 HE JUST ENJOYS KILLING.
    HE IS A GOOD NEIGHBOUR! HE READS ALOT! AND SLEEPS ALOT!
   I RARELY SEE HIM.
       IN A YEAR I MAY SEE HIM 4 OR 5 TIMES (ON A GOOD YEAR)
 FRED TO ME IS FRED. A NICE GUY
     TO YOU HE IS FREDDY KRUGER..
          DONT FUCK WITH FREDDIE..
            YOUR ONLY DO IT THE ONCE.
 THE CON HE KILLED IN GARTREE, HE STABBED 38 TIMES

75

He Looked Like A Tea Bag
IM Glad To Say The Con Was A Bad Nonce
So He Wont Be Playing With Anymore Children
Fred Should of Been Awarded The O.B.E.
But Sadly He Received His 3Rd Life Sentence
Fred Will Die in PRison.
Maybe even in Cell 5
But Knowing Him As I Do ___ He Dies With A Smile.

Cell 4. It's our Very own "Hannibal The Cannibal.
(Bob Mad Dog Maudsley)
What else, Can Be Said on Bob That Hasn't Been Said
A Million Times Before?

He Got Sent To Broadmoor Asylum For The CRiminally Insane
Back in 1974 For Killing A Faggot in Kings CRoss.
Whilst in The Asylum He Killed Alan Francis. And Ate
Part of The Brain-:(Raw):
For That He Got A Life Sentence And Sent To Prison
(Now Thats Insane)
He Kills outside And Gets Sent To Broadmoor.
He Kills inside And Gets Sent To Prison

He Arrives Here in 1978 And Kills Again.
"Twice"
Bobs Now Been in A Cage For over 30 Years.
Sadly We Fell out Some Years Back
He Now Dreams of eating my Brain.
And I Dream of Breaking His Jaw.
He Spends His Day Playing His Music
He Loves Classical.
And He Plays Chess on A Computorized Set
He Rarely Speaks To Anybody.

He walks like a zombie with dead eyes.
He smells like death too.
Bub died long ago.
        Nothing or nobody bothers our cannibal..
Satan sucked away at his soul years ago.
You only have to hear him laughing in his sleep
        It's creepy.
Even the spiders and cockroaches stay away from No 4

N° 3   The one and only Gary Nelson

        Gary copped a life sentence over a cop shooting in London.
A shooting he never done.
        A total stitch up.
But it's left him with a life sentence.
        I've known Gary since he was nicknamed "Tyson"
He even looks like Tyson.
He even knows Mike Tyson

        Gary is a man of respect
I've known him for 20+ years

        He's a tough cookie.
Sadly we fell out awhile back.
        Nothing serious. Just a dispute.
I can never run him down
        Nor do him a bad turn.
(It's our problem) Personel

    I will speak up for him though

He has been set-up by the C.S.C. bosses.

    He should never be on this unit

These just afraid of the guy.
    He has alot of supporters in and out of jail
(They don't like that)
    He will expose them.   Good luck to him!

Cell '2'

The Giant of the C.S.C.
6 Feet 4 and 22 Stone.
I call him The White Man of The Green Mile.
Big Robbo Robinson

A True Prison Legend
He could eat a Horse in one Helping.
Robbo is on his 2nd Life Sentence.
He knows this is now his World.
He just Survives it.
Plods on
Never Moans
If He's got a Problem they either Sort it
or He Sorts them.

it's That Simple with Robbo.
Don't Play Games with me!

He's Knocked out More Prison Guards than any Con Alive.
Sometimes 3 at a Time

(all for a Good Reason though)

Robbo is Respected Around the System.
Plus He Stops Alot of Trouble.
He Wont Stand By and Watch a Liberty Be Taken.
He's Stood up for Alot of Cons.
I Admire The Man.

I've Known Him For Years And I've Never Heard a
Bad Word Spoke of Him.

He Lives For His Sport - especially Football.
It's Great To Hear Him Cheering Some nights When
The Football's on - or the Boxing
Just Don't Upset The Man (you Have Been Warned)!

78

Cell 1

Legendary Reg Wilson

Reg has spent the last 14 years in Solitary.
He's a Lifer, and a very silent man
     But when he speaks it's worth listening to.
He does alot of study. He knows about worlds... planets... space.
He knows more than most ever will.
     He does alot of meditation, yoga, and Tai-Chi.
He has the rage under control... 'A Master'
He once stabbed a prison governor in the eye.
     But the slag deserved it --- most of them do.
I've known Reg for a good 15 years
     No doubt it could be, well another 15 years 😊
          (if the Governors have there way)

Reg is also one of the best artists in UK Jails.
     I mean a genius
If your lucky enough to own a Wilson Masterpiece
     Then your blessed.
He don't eat much. He always leaves me is eggs.
I eat 14 boiled eggs a week.
     and
24 raw   thats 38
I only wish it was chickens instead

_____

Thats us. in an egg shell.
     Love us or hate us we are surviving..
          We always will ....

     Men like us are born for a challenge..
          We don't like it any other way
You fuck with us.. and you'll get seriously hurt
     I could saw your leg off and bash your skull in
with it. Then feed Maudsley with it
     You really don't want to mess with something
You don't understand
A Broadmoor official once described me as the most
     unpredictable man in Britain. (Now thats a label)

After 36 years of this insanity... with a total of eleven hostages. 9 roof protests. (10 riots on my own) scores and scores of assults on guards. Millions of pounds in destruction.
Let me tell you now .... every day was a challenge. And I passed.. with flying colours.

Now at 58 years of age I really do need a break. What else is left? What more can they do to me? I've had it all a 100 times over. They must be sick of me .. as I am of them

Mum's just had her 80th birthday. Its time to go home. She needs me out there.

My art alone would make me a good living so why not let me free?

Lets face up to the truth ... prison created me. And society forgot me. Now nobody wants me..

Well... my mother still loves me. And so do all the ones who know the real Charlie Bronson. I'm not such a bad guy.

Join the fight to . free me. And at the same time help me expose this evil corrupt system.

Believe me its a buzz when you see one of these gutless fuckers squirm under pressure. The truth hurts these firm.

Hey! its not to late for me to stand for parliament.. Bronson MP. I'll fight for the real people... You know it.

HM Prison   **Telephone   01924 246000**
Wakefield   **Fax Number   01924 246280**
West Yorkshire
WF2 9AG   **18 November 2010**

Dear Chris Cowlin

I regret to inform you that your application to be placed on the Approved Visits List of visitors for

     BT1314   CHARLES   BRONSON

HAS NOT BEEN APPROVED BY THE HOME OFFICE.

Your photographs are enclosed.

Yours sincerely,

Intelligence Unit
for the Governor

BRONSON A8076AG C.S.C
HMP WAKEFIELD

Redd Menzies was up to see me today 20/11/2010.
Top Geezer in my book.
He does alot for me behind the scenes.
And if it wasn't for him there would be no Cliffy Field book.
Redd done 90% of the research to that.
Plus it was Redd who got Cliff out of the gutter, and put clothes on him when Cliff was at his worse.
Redd really come up to tell me about the funeral, and I'm pleased to say it was a proper good send off.
This is what Redd wrote, and read out at the service at Dunstables Priory Church on 12th November.

CLIFF

"What can I say about this man.
I'll try to describe him the best I can.
In the Navy he travelled far
In his local pub, propped up the bar.
Eight rounds set in a boxing bout.
He just took one to get the knockout.
Sometimes saint, sometimes sinner
Seldom a loser, but often a winner.
Going forward, his only aim
Whether Ali, Dunne, or Lennie Mc'Lean.
Modest, Dapper and reasonably shy.
Sometimes rich, then sometimes poor.
Sometimes working on the door.
Easy come and easy go,
If it bothered him, then it didn't show.
A childlike grin, that couldn't offend
Cliff the Iron Man was his name.
All throughout his boxing fame
He kept attacking and wouldn't yield
God Bless you Champ
My friend Cliff Field.
By Redd Menzies

82

WHATS LEFT TO SAY. BUT.. A TRUE LEGEND!
MAX-RESPECT.

I'M GETTING BORED OF THE CROSSBOW CANNIBAL STEVE GRIFFITHS Suicide ATTEMPTS.
Fuck me.. CANT SOMEBODY SHOW HIM HOW TO DO IT.
ITS GETTING LIKE THE HUNTLEY SAGA.

THIS TIME HE'S SWALLOWED 4 PENCIL BATTERIES AND SOME PILLS.
UP TO NOW HE'S CUT HIS WRISTS AND THROAT.
PUT A PLASTIC BAG OVER HIS HEAD
SWALLOWED A PLASTIC BAG.
A NOOSE AROUND HIS NECK.

TALK ABOUT ATTENTION SEEKING.
HURRY UP AND DIE YOU CUNT...

" SOMETIMES YOU JUST CANT WIN!
I THOUGHT ID BE A GENTLEMAN AND HOLD THE DOOR
OPEN FOR A YOUNG LADY.
ALL I GOT WAS ABUSE...
SHUT THAT FUCKING DOOR SHE SCREAMED, I'M TRYING
TO HAVE A SHIT. ♫ ☺

" I RANG FOR A TAKEAWAY LAST NIGHT FROM CHINA-
- KING RESTARAUNT .
"HERRO, IM WAN KING" THE CHEF.
I SAID.. YOU FILTHY BASTARD ☺   ♫

" FOR SALE _ COMPLETE SET OF ENCYCLOPEDIAS.
45 VOLUMES, EX-CONDITION, £100.0.N.O
NO LONGER NEEDED, GOT MARRIED AND THE WIFE
KNOWS FUCKING EVERYTHING. ♫

HEY! WHO WOULD BE A TURKEY CHRISTMAS TIME?
'IF I WAS'... ID GO ON A HUNGER STRIKE OCTOBER TIME.
NO FUCKER WOULD WANT A SKINNY BIRD..

A DAY IN THE LIFE!

· CHARLES · ARTHUR · BRONSON ·

Guy's only Dream
of Doing what I Do..
I Live The Dream....
I Fear Nothing –
– only Myself....

You Really Don't
Want To Enter into
My World..

Stick To Reading
My Book's..

Only A Fucking Lunatic Does What
I Do...
It's A Mission of Madness at it's Very Best.

SANDRA GARDNERS UP TOMORROW. WE ALWAYS HAVE A LAUGH.
ADIOS AMIGO

SUNDAY 21ST NOV 2010

BAD NIGHT. COULDN'T SLEEP, TOSSING AND TURNING
I STOOD AT THE WINDOW FOR AGES LOOKING OUT
    (NOT THAT I'VE GOT A MAGNIFICENT VIEW)
MORE FOR THE COLD BREEZE ON MY FACE...
        DEATH'. WHAT IS IT ALL ABOUT?
            WHOSE EVER GONNA KNOW?

THIS IS ONE BIG CRAZY JOURNEY THROUGH LIFE.
I DON'T THINK I CAN DO IT WITHOUT THE ODD BUTTER FIGHT.
I NEED A BIT OF MADNESS IN MY LIFE
IT'S MY RELEASE OF INSANITY "OO"

    A MAN CAN'T SURVIVE ALL THESE YEARS IN SOLITARY WITHOUT
SOME FUN"

WE'VE JUST HAD ANOTHER MONSTER ARRIVE AT THE MANSION
        GARY ALCOCK
    HE BRUTALLY KILLED A 15 MONTH BABY.
            LITTLE VIOLET MULLEN HAD 35 SEPERATE INJURIES'
WHAT A FUCKING PIECE OF SHIT...
            28 YRS OLD AND HE SMASHES TO DEATH A LITTLE
ANGEL...
    HE JUST GOT LIFE. WITH A 21 YR TARIFF.
    HE WILL ONLY BE 48 WHEN HE GETS FREED.
        "BRITISH JUSTICE FOR YOU" "OO"

SO ALCOCK'S NOW UP ON THE WING. A NICE WARM CELL.
GYM. POOL. TABLE TENNIS. COOKING MEALS. MIXING WITH OTHER
MONSTERS. OPEN VISITS. T.V. C.D. D.V.D. LIBRARY.
    WHILST BRONSON REMAINS IN A CONCRETE COFFIN
    SOMEBODY WAKE ME UP WHEN IT'S TIME TO GO HOME.
THERE'S ONLY ONE PUNISHMENT FOR CHILD KILLERS
        "HANG THE FUCKERS". "CASE CLOSED".

SANDRA LOOKED HER LOVELY SELF... ALWAYS A WELL TURNED OUT LADY.
AND SHE NEVER FORGETS MY BANANA MILK SHAKES.
   I HAD ROAST BEEF FOR TEA. SPUDS. COLLIE. GRAVY.
       IT WAS BLOODY LOVELY.
     A GREAT DAY...
   I ENJOY SUNDAYS...
     I EAT AS MUCH AS I CAN GET A HOLD OF.
THERE'S BEEN NO GYM SINCE THE "RUMBLE"
   COZ ALL THE LIGHTS ARE STILL SMASHED
THE LADS ARE NOT TO HAPPY ABOUT IT EITHER.
     'ME'... I REALLY DON'T GIVE A FUCK.
     COZ I STILL DO MY WORK-OUT IN MY CELL AND ON THE
YARD.. "WHO NEEDS A SILLY GYM"?
   X-FACTOR RESULTS TONIGHT ☺
       (DON'T WE LOVE IT)?
     CHEERS SANDRA FOR A SMASHING VISIT

THURSDAY 25/11/2010
     I'VE JUST SUBMITTED 15 COMPLAINT FORMS..
   GIVE THE CUNTS SOMETHING TO DO ☺
   I BET YOU CAN GUESS WHAT FOR?
       YEH.... PERSECUTING MY VISITORS
         :(WATCH THIS SPACE): ☺

SAT 27/11/2010
       RAY KRAY PHONED IN TO CANCELL THE VISIT.
         'SNOW. DRIFTS'
     HE LIVES UP IN CUMBRIA... THEY ALWAYS GET IT
BAD UP THERE.. POOR SODS..
       'SOLUTION'.. MOVE'!
   NO BIG DEAL... I'LL HAVE A GOOD DAY.
       I ALWAYS DO.

Years ago I used to get so wound up over cancelled visits. I was very insecure. Unbalanced and dangerous. I just lost control of reality!

I would even blame the screws and governors I wouldn't believe it was cancelled it was a fit-up..

There having a fucking laugh!

But if my visitor never phoned to cancel it, I would get myself so worked up my head would explode.

That would be me wrapped up and slung into the box for a couple of days.

Now days I'm so much better.
Probally grown up.. Matured.
But I really was a nasty bastard!
Insanity gone beserk

But what does it matter in prison?
Let's face it... This is a crazy way of life.
Everything about prison is un-real.
False and un-natural.
It's another world.
I fucking hate it..
I dont want to be locked up.
Do you?

I'll tell you whose a lucky guy.
Angel Alvarez
He's a New York Mobster.
He got shot 21 times and _
_ survived.
That's what I call a legend.
I salute Mr Alvarez
21 fucking bullet holes in one hit
Eat your heart out Superman.

87

I RECENTLY READ "NEZAR HINDAWI" IS AT THE APPEAL COURTS FOR A LEGAL BID TO FREE HIM.

He GOT 45 YRS IN 1986 FOR PLOTTING TO BLOW UP A PLANE BY USING HIS PREGNANT GIRLFRIEND.

CAN YOU BELIEVE THAT!

"CUNT"

MY PAL "VALERIO VEICCI" CHINNED HIM IN PARKHURST.

IT'S BLOODY FREEZING TODAY.
ICE ON THE YARD.
BONES COLD.
EYE'S STING.
FINGERS RIGID.
TOES FREEZING.

"Hell" — I LOVE IT..
STILL DONE MY PRESS UPS
ALIVE AND KICKING.

ALL THEM MOTHER FUCKERS OUTSIDE WHO HAVE SUCKED OFF MY NAME FOR ALL THESE YEARS:
SOLD MY ART BEHIND MY BACK.
RIPPED ME OFF.
ABUSED MY TRUST AND FRIENDSHIP.

I ONLY KEEP STRONG FOR YOU CUNTS.
I DO IT WITH A BIG SMILE

COZ I'M COMMING FOR MY DOSH.
I'M BANGING ON YOUR DOORS.
THE TAX MAN IS ON HIS WAY.
YOU SLAGS THOUGHT I WAS BURIED... LONG GONE.

EVEN IF I'M ON A ZIMMER FRAME, THERE IS NO ESCAPE FROM ME... I REALLY AM YOUR WORST NIGHTMARE.
AND I WANT INTREST LOTS OF IT.
YOU FUCKING PARASITES...
HAVE A NICE LIFE...

It's MONDAY 29/11/2010
MY LAWYER CALLED TO CANCEL OUR VISIT
THIS BLOODY SNOW..
  IT'S CAUSING ALOT OF PROBLEMS.
    MY SON MIKE is UP TOMORROW.
      THAT'S IF HE DONT GET SNOWED OFF!

FUCKING WEATHER!

No GOOD FOR A
    BANK JOB.

  SLIPPING ALL OVER
    THE PLACE.
  DROPPING THE
      LOOT.

  CAR WONT START.

Fucking WEATHER.

OH WELL..
  IM HAVING AN
  EARLY NIGHT.

ADIOS AMIGO.

MY SON MIKE SHOULD OF BEEN UP TODAY!
THE SNOW PUT A STOP TO THAT.
THAT'S MY BANANA MILK SHAKE FUCKED.

But I DID WATCH REG WILSON MAKE A SNOWMAN
ON OUR YARD FROM MY WINDOW.

THAT'S MEMORY LANE AS A BOY GROWING UP IN LUTON.
We USED TO SLIDE DOWN FARLEY HILL FIELDS.
AND THAT'S ONE BIG FUCK OFF HILL.

GREAT TIMES.

We ALWAYS HAD SNOW THEM YEARS. LOTS OF IT
NOW WE GET SOME SNOW AND THE COUNTRY COMES TO A
HALT..

THE OLD STEAM TRAINS KEPT GOING.
LOOK AT THEM NOW? A POXY LEAF ON THE TRACK
STOPS THEM TODAY

THE WHOLE COUNTRY IS RUN BY PUSSIES!
'IT'S TRUE'

FUCK IT. WHO NEEDS A MILK SHAKE ANYWAY.

I COPPED 18 LETTERS TODAY. 9 WERE FROM CONVICTS.
WHAT DOES THAT TELL YOU?

SEEN YOUR MOVIE. READ YOUR BOOKS. LOVE YOUR ART.
DOING YOUR SOLITARY FITNESS ROUTINE. DO YOU REMEMBER MY
DAD IN PARKHURST BACK IN THE 1970'S
MY GRANDAD WAS WITH YOU IN RISLEY IN 1969.
'IT BLOWS ME AWAY'
IT'S LIKE ONE BIG FAMILY
BROTHERS IN ARMS
THANKS LADS...
But SOME ARE LOONIES.. DANGEROUS NUTTERS
OFF THERE HEADS ON SMACK
YOUR BE AMAZED AT HOW MANY BEGGING LETTERS I GET.

NOW I KNOW WHY JOHN LENNON GOT DEPRESSED.
   NO WONDER ALOT OF STARS TURN TO DRINK. DRUGS AND
DISAPEAR.   THERE SICK OF THE LEECHES.
      "BEGGING ME"   A MAN IN A COFFIN!
      YOU FUCKING SPINELESS PARASITES...
            ROB YOUR OWN BANK.

            I HAD A BEEF STEW FOR TEA.
            ={NOT MUCH BEEF IN IT}=
               "IS THERE EVER?"
            I HAD 6 BREAD ROLLS WITH IT!
         WASHED DOWN WITH A MUG OF SWEET TEA.

      FUCK ALL ON TELLY.
            I CANT GET INTO THAT JUNGLE BOLLOCKS
      WHATS LINFORD CHRISTIE DOING IN THERE?

         I WATCHED MIRANDA AT 10 PM ON B.B.C.2.
            NOW SHE'S A FUNNY BIRD.
      10.30 PM I WATCHED THE SNOW.
            SO PEACEFUL.
               SILENT
         I STOOD THERE NAKED AT MY WINDOW JUST
      DRIFTING AWAY, I FELT FREE.
            IM GOING MAD 'OO'
                     ◡

      FUCK THE SNOW.
      FUCK THE MILK SHAKES.

      SON... SEE YOU LATER
         , MAKE YOURSELF A SNOWMAN.
      ILL BE DOING PRESS UPS IN IT TOMORROW
                  ADIOS. AMIGO

PS!   IVE DECIDED TO ADD A LETTER
AND TWO POEMS FROM A CONVICT I GOT TODAY.
WHAT I BELIEVE TO BE VERY SPECIAL FROM A GIFTED YOUNG MAN!

91

Daniel Gibbons A7963AC
Hmp Manchester
Southall street
Manchester
Strangeways
M60 9AH

Alright Charlie,

How you doing? I'm Gibbo, im 23 and im from Manchester, as you can probably tell from the address I'm sat in Strangeways, im on a 10½ year IPP sentence for attempted murder. My kids uncle was a no good bully so had to use a knife when the shit hit the fan and I put it on his toes for a straightener. For two and a half years he took liberties and when I finally rose to him he took the piss and come out worse off, fucking Coward!

I'm Just writing to tell you how much your Solitary fitness book has changed my life. Me personally, I like the cow punch chapter, its helped me a lot, I always use to doubt myself and what I was capable of, I had low self esteem and was severly depressed, but now, im more confident in myself, im always smiling and the got a new spring in my step, all thanks to your book, thankyou Charlie.

I know that you love art and poetry so I put a painting that I did and a couple of poems in with this letter, I wrote one of the poems "A letter from Within," to my babies mum when I first come to prison, its from the heart so I hope you like it, the other one "Sexual Desires" is just one that I put together for a laugh, I find it relaxing and a great way to ~~stre~~ express deep feeling. I recently did an anti-bullying poster for one of the course's I did with a painting and a poem about bullies and the teacher loved it, she said its an explosive piece of work and has sent it off for an award or something that recognises prisoners art work, I forget what it's called. I read one

92

of your poems in the good, the mad, the bad and the Ugly that I really enjoyed. "All dried up", the message I got from that was, that we're all walking robots controlled by the system and we need to wake up and see the world for what it really is, I really liked that one. Also one by Ted Currie "Lest we forget", my kid brother is in the army, he's only 17 so I liked that one too.

Whilst I was reading your Solitary fitness book I had a thought, imagine Bronco doing a bail facts army getting us all in shape and making us change our ways, and getting paid off HMP for it (haha) how ironic would that be? I had to laugh.

Anyway Charlie, im gunna leave it here mate, I hope they let you out soon and give you the opportunity to prove you have changed, what I think it is with these people is, they know that you are no longer a threat and they know that they should have let you out years ago but their too scared to admit they are wrong, they're all shit houses if you ask me.

Thanks again Charlie for helping me change my life and giving me my confidence back, I hope to hear from you soon

all the best mate

Gibbo

P.S - I hope that the painting isn't ruined from me folding it, I fucking hate folding my pictures/art work but it's the only way I could get it to you.

Best wishes for your birthday Charlie.

93

Sexual Desires

I'm a pussy lickin', fanny flickin', foul mouth prick,
I'll be munchin' on your pussy whilst your suckin' on my dick,
I love a sixty-niner with a sexy arse chick,
I'll suck out all your juices as your fanny starts to drip.

Now your havin' orgasms you know you can't fake,
Your toes curl up and your body starts to shake,
I taste your pussy essence with every breath that I take,
and your heart starts beatin' at a triple x-rate.

Then I'll bend you over and I'll fuck you half to death,
Your pussy's soakin' wet and you can't catch your breath,
I fuck you hard and fast whilst i'm cheekin' on your breasts,
we're bumpin' and we're grindin' and your screamin' "Ohh yes!"

I'm rearin' six-inches off your tight fanny walls,
You reach underneath and grab on to my balls,
Your pussy starts drippin' and looks like Niagra falls,
I climb underneath you and suck out every drop,
Your howlin' out my name, screamin' "Daniel please don't stop!"
You tell me that i'm filthy and you wanna suck my cock.

So I put my cock up against your lips,
and you caress my balls with your finger tips,
with one arm wrapped around my hips,
then you give the head just one little kiss
You look up and ask "are you ready for this?"

Then you blow away without a care in the world,
you've got my cock throbbin', your a very naughty girl,
It feels good that, what you do with your tongue,

94

I could let you do that baby, all night long
You look up at me with a sexy look,
I wanna lick your pussy but you just wanna fuck.

So you climb on my cock and ride it like a rodeo,
Your ridin' me like you're never rode before
I'm holdin' on your hips and I can't let go,
You keep scratchin' at my chest and it makes me want you more,
we fuck on the bed and fall on to the floor,
we fuck up the walls and up against the door.
we have frantic sex it's a spiritual cure.
Then I throw you down on the bed
Your lyin' on your back and your legs are spread.
I begin to kiss you on your thighs
I work my way up 'til I'm lookin' in your eyes.
Then you wrap your legs right around my back
You say "fuck me fast I wanna hear your balls slap against my crack"

So with every thrust my balls slap against your bum,
your face screws up and you beg me not to cum.
and I ram my cock really hard in your slit,
Your watchin' it go in whilst your friggin' on your clit
I'll nibble on your nipple and hold the other tit
Now that's multi-taskin', I'm sure, isn't it?

Before we started fuckin' your pussy was really tight,
but then it went soft, warm, loose and wet as we fucked all night,
and just as the sun comes up,
I feel my balls begin to erupt
you pull me close so it all goes up
One last thrust is all it took
and we was well and truely fucked.

95

Hija Babe,

I hope your okay, I'm writing this letter for you just to say, I miss you so much, your smell, your taste and your sweet gentle touch. When I first met you I knew it was love, I felt blessed like the Angels sent me a gift from above, now I'm sat in a cell with nothing to do, my mind's messed up I'm only thinking of you, and the way that you use to be, the way you use to love and care for me, and I know you wont be there when they set me free, but I'll always cherish every memory, like the way you use to dance for me so sexially, see me and you, we were meant to be. It makes me sad, for everytime that I created you had, you blessed me and made me a dad but I threw it all away everything that I had for a twelve by four shitty little pad. But I need you to know that I never cheated, you was my all and could never be defeated, my one and only girl, my whole world, the love of my life, I should have whisked you away and made you my wife, but I cant turn back time and change history, I can only reminis on what use to be but I swear I'll love you for eternity.

I cant hide what I'm feeling inside, I'm only human, I thought you'd always be mine, because I'm lost without you, I cant be without you, I'm helpless, and I just dont know what to do. I just wish that I could see your face, kiss you once just to taste your taste, I cant believe I let my life go to waste, with you I finally thought I'd found my place, but obviously someone up there has a different plan, what it is I dont know and I dont understand, I just wanted to be your man and grow old with you, hand in hand.

I sit on my bed looking through the bars, thinking about you as I stare at the stars, I'm a broken man with

Internal Scars. Everytime I close my eyes, I see your cute smile and your gorgeous green eyes, and everytime I go to sleep, I dream a dream and your always there or so it seems but I get woke up by jingling keys, and im here in this concrete Hell, I was in heaven with you but then I fell, what's waiting for me only time will tell but I never wanna come back to a jail cell.

My Intentions to your brother was never to kill, now without you im left feeling ill and for a broken heart they can't prescribe a pill, you know you made me feel warm when there was a chill, I was on top of the world, I was king of the hill. Babe you know you was the best and I want nothing less, to me you looked so sexy whenever you undressed, when you use to shake your bum I was incredibly impressed, but now without you my love I've got nothing left, no hopes, no dreams, no direction to go, where we would have ended up, I guess we'll never know.

Now the time has come to say good bye, and I write these words with a tear in my eye, because there was only you who could love me enough to stand by me when times were tough, I guess it got too much. So with these words I send all my love, with millions of kisses and millions of hugs, goodbye my love, you'll be truely missed, I sealed this envelope with one last kiss, lots of love

Your Man,
Dan
X

WHAT CAN YOU SAY ABOUT THAT?

I KNOW WHAT I SAY : " FUCKING BRILLIANT.

THIS GUY DANIEL GIBBONS is A GIFTED YOUNG MAN.

A WRITER. A POET. A PHILOSOPHER. AN ARTIST

AND A REAL NICE FELLA.

NOT AFRAID TO SHOW is TRUE SELF.

I RESPECT THE GUY. ILL WRITE BACK TO TELL HIM TO

STAY COOL, AND KEEP ON CREATING.

I THINK HE HAS A FUTURE IN THE PUBLISHING WORLD.

I CAN FORSEE A BOOK OR SIX AHEAD FOR DANIEL.

ALL HE'S GOTTA DO is KEEP A HOLD OF SANITY.

DONT FALL INTO THE HOLE OF HOPELESSNESS.

AND STAY CLEAR OF THE DRUG DEALERS.

COZ PRISON is FULL OF SMACK NUTS.

ALOT OF YOUNG CONS ARE TRAPPED, HOOKED AND ABUSED.

ON THERE KNEES SUCKING COCK FOR A FIX.

Believe me... IT'S A FUCKING WAR ZONE.

So let's HAVE 3 CHEERS FOR DANIEL GIBBONS

HiP·HiP HORAY ... HiP HiP HORAY . HiP HiP HORAY

Well DONE SON.

AND ALL YOU GIRLS OUTSIDE. DROP HIM A LINE

GIVE HIM SOME HOPE.

YEP! . I THINK THATS A SPECIAL LETTER THAT

DESERVES TO BE SEEN.

IT'S UNUSUAL. SPECIAL. IT STANDS OUT FROM MOST

AFTER I READ IT I THOUGHT. FANTASTIC.

WE CAN ALL LEARN SOMETHING FROM IT.

THAT COULD BE ANYBODY IN THAT CELL.

EVEN YOU, OR YOUR DAD. OR BROTHER.

He KNOWS He FUCKED UP.

DONT WE ALL HAVE A BAD DAY AND DO

SOMETHING WRONG.

His BAD DAY COST HIM 10 YEARS.

IT'S ALOT TO LOSE.
STAY STRONG BUDDY
MAX-RESPECT.
AND YOU MADE IT INTO A BRONSON BOOK
{ONLY THE BEST EVER DO THAT} t.t

2.12.2010   (THURSDAY)

GOT UP AT 6 AM. IT'S FUCKING FREEZING
STRIP WASH. FEEL ALIVE, COLD BREEZE FLYING IN.
TODAY I MEET LORRAINE.
                    (IF SHE MAKES IT) oo
The SNOWS BAD ALL OVER BRITAIN
SHE'S TRAVELLING ON THE TRAIN FROM LONDON...
IF SHE MAKES IT SHE DESERVES A MEDAL.

BREAKFAST... RICE KRISPIES (PISS TAKE) I FUCKING HATE IT
MEN DONT EAT BABY FOOD
We NEED SAUSAGES, EGGS AND BACON...
MUSHROOMS. BEANS AND TOMATOES
THAT'S WHAT WE NEED!
Rice FUCKING KRISPIES!
(DO ME A FAVOUR)

THANK FUCK I'VE A MALT LOAF FROM MY CANTEEN.
"FILL THE HOLE".

I WATCHED JEREMY KYLE AND TRISHA.
IT ALWAYS MAKES ME FEEL LUCKY AND BLESSED.
SOME of THOSE CREEPS WOULD MAKE A LEPER FEEL LUCKY.

DINNER WAS MUSHROOM SOUP AND 6 BREAD ROLLS AND A
BEEF AND PICKLE SANDWICH.
I HAD A BIT OF LOOSE WOMEN THEN... I LOVE THAT.

99

THERE ALL A GOOD LAUGH..
VISIT IS GETTING NEAR..
I PACE THE CELL... UP AND DOWN.
WILL SHE, WONT SHE, WILL SHE.
UP AND DOWN IN A DREAM STATE.

I HATE NOT KNOWING.
THIS SNOW IS NOW GETTING ON MY NERVES
1.45 PM MY OUTSIDE DOOR OPENS.
ITS "MR CHAPMAN" A GOOD OLD SCREW. ONE OF THE OLD FELLAS.
HE'S BEEN IN THE JOB YEARS. HE KNOWS HOW TO TREAT PEOPLE.
IT COMES WITH EXPERIENCE.
    YOU <u>DONT</u> LEARN TO BE A PRISON GUARD OUT OF BOOKS
YOU LEARN THE JOB BY OPENING DOORS.
            ABIT LIKE A BOUNCER...   YOUR VISITOR'S ARRIVED ☺

Fuck me .. She's MADE it ☺
          " I'M BUZZING "
BUT VISITING BRONSON ISN'T THAT SIMPLE.
   NOW, SHE'S GOTTA GO THROUGH, THE SECURITY CHECKS.
CAMERAS, DOORS, X RAYS, SEARCH, THE BOLLOCKS.
   THEN SHE'S ESCORTED TO THE CANTEEN TO GET MY FOODIES ☺
UNLIKE OTHER VISITORS SHE IS THEN ESCORTED OVER TO THIS SPECIAL
ISOLATED MAX SECURE UNIT

   2. 15 PM I AM LET OUT OF MY CAGE AND ESCORTED BY
7 GUARDS TO THE 'ZOO' ROOM
        ' OUR VISIT BEGINS ☺

SHE IS BLOODY LOVELLY
      TALL, SLIM, PRETTY, SHORT BLACK HAIR, BEAUTIFUL EYES.
AMAZING TEETH, GOOD FACIAL BONE STRUCTURE, CLEAR SKIN
      AND HER OUTFIT WAS BRILLIANT
              BLACK AND GREY.
      A SILK BLACK SHIRT, GREY 3/4 LENGTH SKIRT, BLACK SHOES.
AND A BLACK JACKET, NICE MATERIAL.
           ' SMART ', STYLISH, VERY ELEGANT.
   AND WHAT A TREAT FOR ME TO HEAR A COCKNEY VOICE ..
      ☺ (LETS FACE IT, MY WORLD IS YORKSHIRE) ☺
SHE GOT ME 2 BANANA MILK SHAKES AND A TRAY OF CHOC BARS.
   SHE ATE A 'BOUNTY BAR'.
   I MADE HER A CUP OF TEA.
      AND WE CHATTED TILL 4PM THROUGH THE BARS.

   GOTTA SAY NOW. IT'S MY BEST VISIT THIS YEAR !
      I REALLY ENJOYED IT

      " ONE VERY INTRESTING LADY "
           : THANKYOU LORRAINE.
                    FANTASTIC.

101

AND SHE MADE IT. GIVE THAT WOMAN A MEDAL.
A BIT OF SNOW NEVER STOPPED HER. ☺

"LOVE IT" - I DO LOVE A WINNER!

YEP. A LOVELY DAY.

WHY CANT EVERY DAY BE SO NICE.

The ONLY THING THAT SPOILT IT WAS MY PHONE
CALL TO DAVE TAYLOR WHOSE SEEN The SCRIPT OF The
BRONSON DOCUMENTARY BEING DONE FOR T.V IN FEB 2011.

THERES THINGS IN IT THAT PORTRAY ME AS A RIGHT CUNT.
EVEN DOUBTING MY SEXUALITY.

"ME A POOFTER OO"

"DO ME A FAVOUR"!

THERES MORE CHANCE OF ME SHAGGING A KANGAROO THAN
A GEEZER.

The VERY THOUGHT OF PUMPING A MANS ARSE MAKES ME FEEL
SICK. I COULDNT DO IT.

EVEN A BLOW JOB. OO   DROP IT OUT

SO IVE TOLD DAVE TO SEE MY BROTHER TO HAVE A WORD WITH
The DIRECTOR   (EITHER DO IT RIGHT The FACTS) OR PULL The PLUG

CAT I DONT NEED ANYMORE BAD PRESS.

IM IN JAIL. IN A COFFIN FOR FIGHTING THIS PENAL SYSTEM
NOT FOR PUTTING ARSE HOLES. OO

DAVE ALSO SAID THERES A SCENE WHERE I SLING A WOMAN
AROUND A ROOM BY HER HAIR?

FUCK ME. IM CHARLIE BRONSON ... NOT CHARLES
FUCKING MANSON.

PUT IT RIGHT JIM SLAGS.

IVE ACTUALLY WROTE TO The DIRECTOR ...

TELLING HIM ... BE VERY CAREFUL HOW YOU PORTRAY ME
COZ ONE DAY IT COULD WELL COME BACK AND BE YOUR WORST EVER.

NIGHTMARE."

WHAT DO PEOPLE DO IT? STICK TO THE TRUTH...

SURE IM NOT AN ANGEL, WHO WANTS TO BE?
I FUCKING DONT.

ANYWAY... MY BROTHER WILL SORT IT.
" WATCH THIS SPACE "

IM ABIT CONFUSED OVER IT THOUGH. COZ Z WAS TOLD ITS A
DOCUMENTRY ON MY LIFE, INTERVIEWING MY FAMILY + FRIENDS.
PLUS MY ART SHOWS, AND CHARITY FETES ECT...

" NOT SOMEBODY PLAYING ME "

A GOOD DOCUMENTRY IS INTERVIEWS. X SCREWS. X CONS.
GET THE TRUTH HEARD FOR ONCE.

THATS WHAT PEOPLE WANT...
WHAT REALLY GOES ON BEHIND OUR WALLS.

GIRL SAYS TO PADDY. "WOULD YOU LIKE A BLOW JOB?
PADDY REPLIES - ' I DONT KNOW, WILL IT AFFECT
MY JOB SEEKERS ALLOWANCE ".

:)

A SMALL GEEZER IS SAT AT A BAR WHEN ALL OF
A SUDDEN A THUG SMACKS HIM IN THE FACE AND SAYS
" THATS KUNG FU FROM JAPAN "

ABIT LATER HE SMACKS HIM AGAIN AND SAYS
" THATS KARATE FROM KOREA "

THE LITTLE GEEZER LEAVES THE BAR.
AND RETURNS 10 MIN LATER AND SMACKS THE THUG
KNOCKING HIM OUT COLD.
HE SAYS TO THE BARMAN
TELL THAT CUNT WHEN HE WAKES UP
THAT WAS A SHOVEL FROM B+Q.

:)

103

ALSO GOT CANTEEN TODAY.
AND HAD MY FAV... LIVER AND ONIONS FOR TEA.
VISIT! CANTEEN, CALL, SHOWER. GOOD GRUB.
    A BIT OF CORRIE STREET
(TYRONE AND MOLLY ARE HAVING A TOUGH TIME ☺)
I LOVE BECKY IN THE ROVERS BOOZER
    I'D GIVE HER ONE FOR REAL.

ANYWAY... BE HAPPY.
        BE THANKFULL TO BE ALIVE.
        IT'S A WONDERFUL WORLD
    WE ARE ALL SO LUCKY TO BE HERE.
        = (IT DON'T FUCKING LAST) =

    TIME RUNS OUT FAST..

            ENJOY

PS
    THIERRY BAUDRY WASN'T SO LUCKY ☹
HE WAS SHARING A PRISON CELL WITH CANNIBAL NICK COCAIGN
WHO KILLED HIM, THEN CUT HIM OPEN AND ATE HIS HEART.

    NOW THAT'S WHAT YOU CALL INSANITY.
        INSANITY GONE MAD ☺

    COCAIGN TOLD THE JUDGE.
        HE WAS CURIOUS IN HOW BAUDRY TASTED!

'FUCK ME'... I'M A CELEBRITY GET ME OUT OF HERE FAST.'

BRONSON A8076AF. C.S.C.
WAKEFIELD CAGE.

WHOSE BIRTHDAY TODAY?
58 YRS OLD. 😊

I COME AWAY AT 21.. ALL BUT 3 MTHS I'VE BEEN INSIDE
MAX SECURE.. A COFFIN.
    BUT I'M PROUD! I'M ONE OF LIFE'S TRUE SURVIVORS.
DONT GET ME WRONG IM NOT PROUD OF MY CRIMES
    IM ACTUALLY A PRATT FOR GETTING CAUGHT.
GOOD CRIMINALS DONT EAT PORRIGE.
    I'VE EAT A SWIMMING POOL OF IT. IM TIRED
BORED TO DEATH.
        YEP! IM A SURVIVOR!
        WILL I DIE IN JAIL?
        IS IT ALL OVER?
        IS IT ALL A DREAM?
        A LIVING DEATH..

                " FUCK KNOWS".
        I JUST SURVIVE IT.

    SO I'VE DECIDED TODAY TO TELL A FEW STORIES.
A FLASH BACK IN TIMES OF MADNESS.
    PICTURE ME ON A STAGE- YOUR MY AUDIENCE!
YOUR PAID £30 A TICKET TO HEAR ABOUT MY JOURNEY
THROUGH HELL.

        SIT BACK AND ENJOY, AND PRAY MY LIFE NEVER
BECOMES YOUR OWN..   . WELCOME TO INSANITY!
TODAY YOUR ABOUT TO STEP INTO A WORLD OF NIGHTMARES!

105

MOST GUYS GET SENT DOWN. THEY BUCKLE UNDER. THEY ACCEPT IT. AND DO THERE TIME IN PEACE.
  IN NO TIME THERE OUT ON PAROLE.
  SOME STAY OUT -- MOST RETURN .. THAT'S HOW IT WORKS.
Me' I COME IN AND GOT MYSELF TRAPPED AND LABELLED A PRISON ACTIVIST.
    THATS ALL IT IS.
SOME MEN CAN ACCEPT IT . OTHERS CANT.
    FORTUNTLY FOR THE SYSTEM. I AM A VERY SMALL MINORITY.
IF ALL WERE LIKE ME .. PRISONS WOULD BE ON TOTAL LOCK DOWN.
A PRISON CAN ONLY RUN SMOOTHLY WITH MEN OF PEACE.

SO I STARTED OUT AS I CHOSE ... A REBEL. AND IT'S COST ME 31 YEAR TO DATE.
   IT'S ACTUALLY BEEN FUN.
     I'VE ENJOYED IT
I WOULDNT RECOMMEND IT.
        IT CAN BE A VERY EMPTY EXPERIENCE AND TOTALLY DARK AND GLOOMY AND AT TIMES PAINFUL.
   IF YOU ATTACK THE SYSTEM ... EXPECT TO BE ATTACKED BACK.
"YOU THROW A PUNCH, AND BELIEVE ME NOW YOUR TAKE 20 BACK.
   " SO DONT THROW IT, IF YOU CANT TAKE IT

   Me .. I FUCKING LOVED IT. I THRIVED ON IT ALL.
IT MADE ME FEEL SPECIAL"
    I WAS A SOMEBODY .... EVERYBODY KNEW .... "DONT FUCK WITH BRONSON"
   EVEN SCREWS AND GOVERNORS HAD A KIND OF RESPECT FOR ME.
   I WAS TREAT DIFFERENT.
   I WAS DIFFERENT.
   I FUCKING LOVED THE RUMBLES
   I LOST EVERYONE OF THEM. HOW COULD I WIN ?
     I LOST EVERYTHING. EVEN MY SANITY.

IT WAS BACK IN HULL JAIL 1974 I REALLY TASTED MY
FIRST VICTORY OVER THIS VINDICTIVE SYSTEM.. AND BULLY BOY GUARDS.

I SMASHED A SCREW WITH A STICK IN A WORK SHOP.
AND ASSULTED TWO MORE BEFORE I WAS RESTRAINED

IT FELT MAGICAL. I HAD COME ALIVE.

Even AFTER ALL THEY DONE TO ME.. THE BEATING, THE STRONG BOX
THE DEGRADATION, THE HUMILIATION.

I COME ALIVE
THE RULES WERE MADE THAT DAY.

FUCK WITH ME AND YOU FUCK WITH HELL.

"IT WAS SO SIMPLE"
THE BATTLE BEGUN.

ON MY PRISON FILE.. IT HAS ONLY THERE STORY.
SO WHY DID I ATTACK THE GUARDS THAT DAY.

"SIMPLE". ONE HAD BEEN TAKING SERIOUS LIBERTIES.
HE WAS A "BULLY SCREW" A BIG MAN. A RUGBY PLAYER.
A CHAMPION BOXER IN THE ARMY

BUT IN JAIL HE BULLIED THE WEAKER CONS.

I WAS A YOUNG MAN. "FEARLESS"
WHY SHOULD I TAKE HIS SHIT

AND THATS HOW IT ALL STARTS.

EVEN A TRANSFERE TO ANOTHER PRISON, YOUR FILE FOLLOWS
ON... YOU DONT ESCAPE IT ... MORE BULLY SCREWS.
"GET BACK TIME"

HEY! EVEN THE DECENT SCREWS HATE THE BULLY ONES!
IVE HAD GOOD SCREWS GIVE ME A MARS BAR FOR CHINNING
ONE OF THERE OWN ☺

ITS A BIT LIKE THE FORCES.
"SURVIVALISTS"
THATS ALL WE BECOME.

WANDSWORTH 1975 Punishment Block

I can close my eyes and see it now.
  My door opens. I rush out and just start punching.
It's like a cowboy movie, an old John Wayne battle.
Im fighting with 6.
  The bells gone... Dozens more come running.
Im kicked, sticked, and punched all the way to the
  strong box and put in a body belt and ankle straps
Im also injected with a psychotropic tranquiliser
  they leave me in a terrible mess.
  Choking on blood.
  My balls are like swollen balloons
  Even my toes are bleeding
  I cant see out of my eyes.
              And
        Im feeling magic...
  A fight to be proud of.
  When it's all over, days, weeks later. They will all
  know not to fuck with Bronson.

      Thats how it was... How I was. How they was.
  (Now see why I got treat so different)

        To get an extra shower or food or a blanket
  (You have to suffer)

  And boy did I suffer...
Screws have spit in my food. Pissed in my tea.
Wet my mattress. Stole my photos.
      Denied me the basic of human rights
  So when Ive become violent I feel justified
      Ive attacked for my own sanity.

They know it... We all know it... It's life at its best.
Attack or be attacked.
Be a mouse or a lion.
We all must chose our way to sanity.

And with every act of violence comes humour..."
" Believe me you will laugh about it later "
Prison is a very funny way of life.

Full Sutton 1989

I was strolling around the exercise yard with
one of the I.R.A Balcome Street Mob " Harry Duggan "
He had spent years on the Secure Units
I got on well with the Irish cons
(Dont get me wrong) I despise there crimes
But in jail they are top men with good morals.
" Any prison riot, Your always count on the Irish lads.

So there we was on a sunny day on our exercise.
Chatting about the worlds problems.
Sudenly a crowd of civilians appeard, having a look around
" watching us " like a fucking zoo.
I ran over and grabbed a geezer hostage."
All the others ran off.
It turned out the cut I grabbed was a trainee
Probation officer, it was his 1st and last day in the job.

Now thats what I call humour.
Prison madness at its very best
You dont get out of bed and plan such events
It's fate... Meant to be, " You act on impulse "
(split second action) " magical "

109

I DO WHAT MOST ONLY DREAM OF.
I PICKED HIM UP LIKE A SACK OF SPUDS :
  SQUEEZED HIS BOLLOCKS AND WHISPERED.
    "WHO THE FUCK ARE YOU LOOKING AT CUNT"
WHEN I LET HIM GO HE LOOKED LIKE ONE OF THESE THUNDERBIRD
PUPPETS BOBBING ALONG
          HE HAD LOST ALL CONTROL OF HIS ARMS + LEGS "
  THATS HOW FAST AN INCIDENT CAN HAPPEN.
    THATS WHAT HAPPENS WHEN BRONSON COMES ALIVE !
          " EXCITEMENT
      I CHEER THE WORLD UP...
      I MAKE A BORING DAY SPECIAL.
      IM NOT A NASTY FUCKER
        (IF) I WAS I WOULD OF SNAPPED HIS NECK.
    IT WAS A LAUGH...
          A MOMENT OF MADNESS...
              WE LOVE IT ""
          IT LIVES ON.
              FOREVER". t·t   ,
        A WONDERFUL MEMORY.

BROADMOOR 1978

  I WAS SITTING IN THE DAY ROOM OF SOMERSET WARD 1
MINDING MY OWN BUSINESS, WATCHING TOP OF THE POPS.
  WHEN SOME LOON APPROACHED ME..
      " CAN I HAVE A PRIVATE WORD ":
          " WHAT" IM WATCHING TELLY'
              PLEASE HE SAID !
              PLEASE. PLEASE.
  " WHY ME". DO I HAVE A MAGNET TO ATTRACT THESE LOONIES?

110

So I says.. Okay.. Go Down The Recess And i'll Be Down in
    5 Mins."
15Min Later I Shot Down To See What He Wanted!
        Right! Whats Your Problem Pal'?
        He Looks me Straight in The eyes And Asks Me To Hit Him"
WHAT? Are You For Real'." You Want me To Hit You'
        " Yes He Said"
        WHY, WHAT FOR I SAY.'?
        Coz I Like it He Says
        Well Fuck off I SAY.
            Please Hit Me.
            Fuck off I SAY
            Please.
            Fuck off.
            Oh Please.
What Would You Do?
        Anyway I Hit The Cunt
            "Crack"
        I Hit Him 3 more Times Before He Hit The Floor
            (He was out Cold)
    So I Dragged Him To The Toilet Cubicle And Splashed
    His Face With Water.
        As His eyes Started To Flicker And He Woke up
    He Said Something ill Never Forget.
        " THAT Was Lovelly"

    There's Alot More To This Story...
            Come To My Show Later And Hear The Rest
                Your Fucking Love it.
    You Wont Believe it _ But it's "Brilliant"

111

WANDSWORTH. D. WING 1986

The closest I ever come to escaping was here..
I had 6 bricks out of the back of my wall
I had a rope and grappling hook.
I had some clothes and dosh.
        And a shinny little cunt of a cleaner grassed.''
I got put in patches (escape list)
I lost 180 days remission and 3 mths punishment'
    He later got a luv stitches in his boat..
'Fate'.. it wasn't meant to be.' ☺

Imagine me on the run?
    It would be the S.A.S come for me!
        ''Body-bag ending''

WALTON JAIL 1985 (Bath House)

One of the best punch ups ever.

I had just had my shower, and all I had on was
    a towel as I lined up at the serving hatch for clean
clothes.
'Now' the scousers are a funny lot, I love em.
There a good breed.. But this cocky cunt got lemon
with me, so I chinned him through the hatch.
    Next thing his mate grabs my arm and im pulled
through this fucking hatch in the wall
        My towel falls off and im confronted by
half a dozen scousers all throwing punches and shouting
you cockney cunt.
    I opened up with a cluster of hooks and crosses
''mostly body shots''
        It was a mad fuckoff brawl.

112

LOADS OF SCREWS PILED IN AND THEY STARTED ON ME -
IT WAS OPEN DAY FOR SMASHING BRONSON.
ANYONE AND EVERY FUCKER WAS TAKING A SHOT !!

MY RIGHT THUMB WAS ½ BITTEN OFF, MY BODY WAS CRUSHED.
MY FACE WAS A PULP

IT WAS MAGICAL.

I HAD TO HAVE A TETNUS. X RAYS. STITCHES
AND GUESS WHAT?

YOUR NEVER GUESS?

I WAS NICKED FOR BEING IN AN UNAUTHORIZED PLACE
UN-ESCORTED !!.

NOBODY WAS NICKED OVER THE FIGHT.

MY DEFENCE WAS ... "GOVERNOR" I DONT KNOW WHAT
WENT DOWN... I JUST WOKE UP IN HOSPITAL ?

"YOU CANT MAKE THIS SHIT UP"
IT'S HISTORIC

I STILL LOVE THE SCOUSERS THOUGH.

WOODHILL 1993 (Seg Block)

ONE OF THOSE BORING DAYS THAT NEEDED SOME ACTION
YOU KNOW THE SORT...

I'VE JUST FINISHED MY WORK OUT ON THE YARD
AND IM BEING ESCORTED BACK TO MY CELL.

WHOSE ON THE LANDING "THE LIBRARIAN GUARD"
"ANDY LOVE". I WALK OVER TO GET A BOOK AND I

113

GRAB HIM IN A NECK HOLD..
        MOVE CUNT AND I'LL SNAP YOUR VERTIBRAY".
. WITHIN 10 SECONDS WE WERE BOTH IN MY CELL WITH THE DOOR
SLAMMED SHUT. BARRICADED AND SAFE..

    "DEMANDS".
HELICOPTOR.' UZI. 10,000 ROUNDS. AN AXE.
    CHEESE ROLLS WITH PICKLE

' COME ON '... THIS IS MADNESS AT IT'S VERY BEST!
    DONT WE FUCKING LOVE IT ?
THAT DAY COST ME AN EXTRA 7 YEARS..'
    BUT WHAT A MEMORY ..☺

NOW DO YOU SEE WHY IM ALWAYS LAUGHING'.
I ONLY HAVE TO CLOSE MY EYES AND GO BACK IN TIME.'
    IT'S WONDERFUL.

HULL. SPECIAL. UNIT 1991
THE DAY I HIT MAD JACKO ON THE HEAD WITH A WOK
AND LAY HIM IN THE FREEZER ☺

LINCOLN SPECIAL UNIT 1992.
    THE DAY I KNOCKED OUT GOVERNOR PRATT
        LOVELLY MEMORIES

PARKHURST SPECIAL UNIT 1986
    THE DAY I RUN 10 TIMES AROUND THE YARD WITH
    GEORGE HEATH ON MY BACK IN THE BLAZING SUN
        FOR A BET

PARKHURST F/2 1978.
    THE DAY I CUT A SCREWS EAR LOBE OFF
        (EAR TODAY GONE TOMORROW)

HIGHDOWN 1994

The DAY I BROKE The GOVERNORS CHEEK BONE.
(BUT) He WAS SO LUCKY COZ I ACTUALLY TRIED TO STAB
HIM IN THE EYE WITH A TOOTHBRUSH ☺

BULLINGDON 1994

The DAY I KIDNAPPED MY SOLICITOR 'ROBERT TAYLOR'
OH HOW WE LAUGHED
I HAD SO MUCH FUN

ALBANY 1985

The DAY I TOOK The Seg Block OVER
IN MY OWN RIOT.

WINCHESTER 1986

The DAY I TOOK OVER The Seg Block OFFICE
AND CALLED A NATIONAL NEWSPAPER AND SANG
"WHAT A WONDERFUL WORLD"

ALBANY 1989

The DAY KELLY ANNE VISITED Me AND SAT ON MY COCK
IN The VISIT ROOM. SUCH MEMORIES
"PURE MAGICAL"
BOUNCING UP AND DOWN LIKE A FUCKING LUNATIC!
WHEN I SHOT MY LOAD ITS A MIRACLE IT NEVER BLEW
The TOP OF HER HEAD OFF
THAT HAD TO BE The CRAZIEST FUCK I EVER HAD.

DURHAM 1988

The DAY I CHINNED A SCREW ON The YARD
IT ALMOST CAUSED A RIOT

LEICESTER 1987

UP ON The ROOF
The SKY's The LIMIT. SUCH FUN

115

RAMPTON 1978

The DAY I STRANGLED John WHITE A PAEDOPHILE.
SADLY The NURSES BROUGHT The MONSTER BACK To LIFE

PARKHURST 1976

The DAY I SPAT IN IAN BRADY'S FACE THROUGH
B/Wing GATE
I WATCHED The SPIT DRIP DOWN His FACE.
"WHAT A SHOT"
We USED To SHIT IN A SOCK AND GET A CLEANER
To PUT IT IN His BED.

Beautiful Memories

PARKHURST 1976. MY 1st XMAS WITH The KRAY TWINS

PARKHURST 1992. HOW I SURVIVED A MULTIPLE STABBING
(I Keep TELLING You ALL I'M The TRUE SURVIVOR)

The RIOTS. The Violence. The Sieges.
Its Been A WONDERFUL Journey.
ONE DAY I WILL Be ON STAGE TELLING ALL
STORIES.
There's So MANY Tell.
The Legends I've MET. "The ICONS."

Let me Tell You NOW
ITS ALL Been AN experience.
it's PRiceless.
TODAY ON MY BIRTHDAY... PETER BROWN GOT SENTENCED To
A DOUBLE LIFE FOR TWO MURDERS.
His JOURNEY Begins
GOOD LUCK PETER...
FOR ME... The DREAM GOES ON. WITH A Big SMILE ☺

116

Memorandum

To: Mr Bronson - A8076AG
CSC

From: Complaints Clerk
Re: Complaint

....

Thank you for your Comp 1 which has been emptied out of the complaints box.

In order for the complaint to be accepted and logged please can you state what your complaint is without using offensive language.

Thank you

Complaints Clerk

There's Fifteen Complaints Here All Submitted on The 24th November 2010.

Not one of them Have Been Answered!

I only Done it To Prove it's All A Farce.

And To expose This System As A Joke!

Now You can UNDERSTAND WHY AT Times I explode With Pure Anger and Despair.

These People can Do Whatever They Wish, Whenever They Wish.

But in A COURT OF LAW They Would Be Forced To Answer These Questions.

Prison Law is A Law UNTO ITSELF.

(I Rest My Case)

6/12/2014

FORM COMP 1
PRISONER'S FORMAL COMPLAINT

Establishment

Serial N°

Read these notes first

1. This form is for you to make a formal written complaint under the complaints procedure. Complaints should wherever possible be sorted out informally by speaking to your wing officer or making an application. Use this form only if you have not been able to resolve your complaint this way.
2. A written complaint should be made within 3 months of the incident or of the relevant facts coming to your notice.
3. Keep the complaint brief and to the point.
4. When you have completed the form, sign it and post in the box provided. The form will be returned to you with a response.
5. If you are unhappy with the response, you can appeal on a separate form (COMP 1A).
6. Some subjects are dealt with only by the Area Manager or Prison Service headquarters. If your complaint is about one of these subjects, the reply will take longer.
7. There is a separate pink form (COMP 2) for confidential access complaints.

Your details (use BLOCK CAPITALS)

Surname	BRONSON	First name(s)	CHARLES ARTHUR
Prison number	A8076AG	Location	C.S.C.

Have you spoken to anyone about your complaint ?   Yes ☐   No ☐
If so, who did you speak to ?

GOVERNORS

Your complaint

WHO is THE NAME - RANK - AND NUMBER - OF THE SECURITY OFFICER WHO MADE ALL THE DECISIONS ON MY APPROVED VISITORS -

AS MY SOLICITOR NEEDS IT A.S.A.P.

" ENOUGH is NOW ENOUGH "

Does your complaint have a racial aspect ?   Yes ☐   No ☐
Is your complaint about bullying ?   Yes ☐   No ☐

What would you like to see done about your complaint ?

I AIM TO TAKE THE PATHETIC BEHAVIOUR AND DECISIONS TO COURT AND PROVE YOUR JUST TAKING THE PISS. AND CAUSING SERIOUS UNNECESSARY STRESS TO GOOD HONEST PEOPLE, AND A 16 YEAR OLD BOY WHOSE SUFFERED TERRIBLE SHOCK OVER YOUR SILLY DECISIONS.

Signed _____   Date 24/11/2010

VF 011   Printed at HMP Kingston 4334 03/2003

118

Response to the complaint *(including any action taken)*

```
┌─────────────────────────────────────────────────────────────┐
│                                                               │
│                                                               │
│                                                               │
│                                                               │
│                                                               │
│                                                               │
│                                                               │
│                                                               │
│                                                               │
│                                                               │
│                                                               │
│                                                               │
│                                                               │
│                                                               │
│                                                               │
│                                                               │
└─────────────────────────────────────────────────────────────┘
```

Name in block capitals _____ Position _____

Signed _____ Date _____

This section for official use only			
Sentence	Category	Status	
Release date	Ethnicity	Location	
Date received by complaints clerk	Date received by responding member of staff	Passed to RRLO on (date)	Date of interim reply
Reserved subject ? (tick box) ☐	Referred to	On (date)	Date received by Area Manager or HQ
Outcome of complaint Upheld ☐ Rejected ☐		Reserved Subject Upheld ☐ Rejected ☐	
Action taken (where complaint upheld)			

OPS

F2059

FORM COMP 1
PRISONER'S FORMAL COMPLAINT

Establishment WDCm
Serial Nº WD 397 10F

Read these notes first

1. This form is for you to make a formal written complaint under the complaints procedure. Complaints should wherever possible be sorted out informally by speaking to your wing officer or making an application. Use this form only if you have not been able to resolve your complaint this way.
2. A written complaint should be made within 3 months of the incident or of the relevant facts coming to your notice.
3. Keep the complaint brief and to the point.
4. When you have completed the form, sign it and post in the box provided. The form will be returned to you with a response.
5. If you are unhappy with the response, you can appeal on a separate form (COMP 1A).
6. Some subjects are dealt with only by the Area Manager or Prison Service headquarters. If your complaint is about one of these subjects, the reply will take longer.
7. There is a separate pink form (COMP 2) for confidential access complaints.

Your details (use BLOCK CAPITALS)

Surname	BRONSON	First name(s)	CHARLES ARTHUR
Prison number	A8076AG	Location	C.S.C. UNIT

Have you spoken to anyone about your complaint?   Yes ☐ No ☐
If so, who did you speak to?

GOVERNOR

Your complaint

I BELIEVE THERE IS A MASSIVE CONSPIRACY GOING ON BY SECURITY AND H/Q.

TO CUT ME OFF FROM THE OUTSIDE WORLD, AND TO DRIVE ME MAD.

YOUR STRESSING ME OUT AND MAKING ME FEEL VERY CONFUSED..

DONT KEEP DOING IT.
THERE WILL BE A MASSIVE EXPLOSION IN MY HEAD.

Does your complaint have a racial aspect?   Yes ☐ No ☐
Is your complaint about bullying?   Yes ☐ No ☐

What would you like to see done about your complaint?

WHAT is THIS GAME YOUR PLAYING?
EVEN THE UNIT SCREWS AGREE WITH ME THAT ITS WRONG IN WHATS BEING DONE
YOUR DECISIONS ARE BECOMING PATHETIC.

Signed _____   Date 24/11/2010

VF 011 Printed at HMP Kingston 4334 03/2003

120

Response to the complaint *(including any action taken)*

Mr Bronson,

Having looked in to this matter I can assure you that there is no conspiracy against you, on the contrary we have always attempted to process your visits/ telephone numbers in a timely fashion. I would ask you to take in to consideration the volume of applications submitted and the stringent processes used to ensure the good order or discipline of the establishment and the safety of both staff and prisoners. In closing may I state that we will continue to process your applications in a fair and transparent manner to ensure your rights as a serving prisoner are upheld.

SO WHY NOT ANSWER MY QUESTIONS ?
WHY ARE THEY BANNED ?

Name in block capitals _____   Position __S·O·__

Signed _____   Date __29·11·10__

This section for official use only			
Sentence	Category	Status	
Release date	Ethnicity	Location	
Date received by complaints clerk	Date received by responding member of staff	Passed to RRLO on (date)	Date of interim reply
Reserved subject ? (tick box) ☐	Referred to	On (date)	Date received by Area Manager or HQ
Outcome of complaint Upheld ☐ Rejected ☐		Reserved Subject Upheld ☐ Rejected ☐	
Action taken (where complaint upheld)			

FORM COMP 1
PRISONER'S FORMAL COMPLAINT

OPS   F2059

Establishment WDCM
Serial Nº WD 396 10F

Read these notes first

1. This form is for you to make a formal written complaint under the complaints procedure. Complaints should wherever possible be sorted out informally by speaking to your wing officer or making an application. Use this form only if you have not been able to resolve your complaint this way.
2. A written complaint should be made within 3 months of the incident or of the relevant facts coming to your notice.
3. Keep the complaint brief and to the point.
4. When you have completed the form, sign it and post it in the box provided. The form will be returned to you with a response.
5. If you are unhappy with the response, you can appeal on a separate form (COMP 1A).
6. Some subjects are dealt with only by the Area Manager or Prison Service headquarters. If your complaint is about one of these subjects, the reply will take longer.
7. There is a separate pink form (COMP 2) for confidential access complaints.

Your details (use BLOCK CAPITALS)

| Surname BRONSON | First name(s) CHARLES ARTHUR |
| Prison number A8076Ag | Location C.S.C. 2UN17 |

Have you spoken to anyone about your complaint ?   Yes ☑ No ☐
If so, who did you speak to ?
Several Governors

Your complaint

TWo Weeks AGo Security Refused TONY FEAR To Go onto MY APProved Visit List.

NoW You CHANGE Your MIND AND PUT HIM ON

So WHY did You WRITE HIM AND SAY No

AND WHAT WERE Your ReAsons ?

Does your complaint have a racial aspect ?   Yes ☐ No ☐
Is your complaint about bullying ?   Yes ☐ No ☐

What would you like to see done about your complaint ?

STop STRESSING Me OUT.
AND STop CAUSING PRoBlems To MY FRieNDS OUTSIDE.
WHo DoNt Deserve To Be VicTimized BY You Lot.

(JusT TeLL THe TRUTH FoR once)

Signed [signature]   Date 24/ 11/ 2010

VF 011 Printed at HMP Kingston 4334 03/2003

Response to the complaint *(including any action taken)*

So WHY WAS HE BANNED ? ?
"PUT IT IN WRITING SO WE CAN
ALL SEE YOUR REASONS. ?
OR MAYBE YOU __CANT__ . COZ YOU HAVE NONE ,

Mr Bronson,

Having re-visited the risk assessments for Mr Tony Fear I am satisfied he now meets the criteria for approved visits. Mr Fear will be notified in writing shortly.

Name in block capitals ▓▓▓▓▓▓▓▓▓   Position S.O.

Signed ▓▓▓▓▓▓▓▓▓   Date 29.11.10

F2059

FORM COMP 1
PRISONER'S FORMAL COMPLAINT

Establishment

Serial Nº

Read these notes first

1. This form is for you to make a formal written complaint under the complaints procedure. Complaints should wherever possible be sorted out informally by speaking to your wing officer or making an application. Use this form only if you have not been able to resolve your complaint this way.
2. A written complaint should be made within 3 months of the incident or of the relevant facts coming to your notice.
3. Keep the complaint brief and to the point.
4. When you have completed the form, sign it and post it in the box provided. The form will be returned to you with a response.
5. If you are unhappy with the response, you can appeal on a separate form (COMP 1A).
6. Some subjects are dealt with only by the Area Manager or Prison Service headquarters. If your complaint is about one of these subjects, the reply will take longer.
7. There is a separate pink form (COMP 2) for confidential access complaints.

Your details (use BLOCK CAPITALS)

Surname	BRONSON	First name(s)	CHARLES ARTHUR
Prison number	A8076AG	Location	C.S.C. UNIT

Have you spoken to anyone about your complaint ? Yes ☑ No ☐
If so, who did you speak to ?

SEVERAL GOVERNORS

Your complaint

ZARAH IFTIHAR is THE MOTHER OF MY GOD DAUGHTER.
SECURITY REFUSED TO PUT HER ONTO MY APPROVED VISIT LIST.
(WITH NO REASON GIVEN.)
MYSTERIOUSLY SHE IS NOW ON MY LIST.
So WHY WAS SHE VICTIMIZED AND UPRT BY YOU ?
WHAT REASON COULD YOU OF HAD
TO REFUSED HER
THEN WEEKS LATER CHANGE YOUR MIND AGAIN ?

Does your complaint have a racial aspect ? Yes ☐ No ☐
Is your complaint about bullying ? Yes ☐ No ☐
What would you like to see done about your complaint ?

STOP CAUSING TROUBLE TO MY FRIENDS OUTSIDE.
OR WAS THIS A RACIST DECISION ?
You HAVE CAUSED THIS YOUNG MOTHER ALOT OF STRESS
OVER YOUR PATHETIC DECISION

Signed _____ . Date 24/11/2110

VF 011 Printed at HMP Kingston 4334 03/2003

Response to the complaint *(including any action taken)*

SO WHY WAS SHE EVER BANNED?
COULD IT BE YOUR A RACIST?

Mr Bronson,

Having re-visited the risk assessments for Mrs Zarah Iftikhar I am satisfied she now meets the criteria for approved visits. Mrs Iftikhar will be notified in writing shortly.

PLUS SHE'S A MISS - NOT A MRS.

Name in block capitals _____ Position __S. O.__

Signed _____ Date __29.11.10__

This section for official use only			
Sentence	Category	Status	
Release date	Ethnicity	Location	
Date received by complaints clerk	Date received by responding member of staff	Passed to RRLO on (date)	Date of interim reply
Reserved subject ? (tick box) ☐	Referred to	On (date)	Date received by Area Manager or HQ
Outcome of complaint Upheld ☐ Rejected ☐		Reserved Subject Upheld ☐ Rejected ☐	
Action taken (where complaint upheld)			

F2059

FORM COMP 1
PRISONER'S FORMAL COMPLAINT

Establishment

Serial Nº

Read these notes first

1. This form is for you to make a formal written complaint under the complaints procedure. Complaints should wherever possible be sorted out informally by speaking to your wing officer or making an application. Use this form only if you have not been able to resolve your complaint this way.
2. A written complaint should be made within 3 months of the incident or of the relevant facts coming to your notice.
3. Keep the complaint brief and to the point.
4. When you have completed the form, sign it and post in the box provided. The form will be returned to you with a response.
5. If you are unhappy with the response, you can appeal on a separate form (COMP 1A).
6. Some subjects are dealt with only by the Area Manager or Prison Service headquarters. If your complaint is about one of these subjects, the reply will take longer.
7. There is a separate pink form (COMP 2) for confidential access complaints.

Your details (use BLOCK CAPITALS)

Surname BRONSON	First name(s) CHARLES ARTHUR
Prison number A8076Ag	Location C.S.C UNIT

Have you spoken to anyone about your complaint ?   Yes ☑   No ☐

If so, who did you speak to ?

SEVERAL GOVERNORS

Your complaint

TWO WEEKS AGO SECURITY REFUSED SPENCER WILDER AND HIS SON
DANIEL TO GO ONTO MY APPROVED VISIT LIST
    NOW YOU CHANGE YOUR MIND AND PUT THEM ON
SO WHY DID YOU WRITE THEM AND SAY NO ?
    AND CAUSE THEM ALOT OF STRESS AND DEPRESSION ?

WHAT ARE YOU PLAYING AT ?

Does your complaint have a racial aspect ?   Yes ☐   No ☐

Is your complaint about bullying ?   Yes ☐   No ☐

What would you like to see done about your complaint ?

STOP CAUSING ME PROBLEMS -
    AND STOP UPSETTING MY FRIENDS OUTSIDE

(TELL THE TRUTH WHY YOUR DOING IT) ?

Signed _____   Date 24/11/21/0

VF 011 Printed at HMP Kingston 4334 03/2003

126

Response to the complaint *(including any action taken)*

SO WHY DID YOU BAN THEM WEEKS Ago?
AND NOW SAY ITS OKAY.

CANT YOU WORK IT OUT IT MAKES YOU A MUG?
ONE WEEK THERE BANNED. THEN THERE NOT.
= (YOU SHOULD BE SACKED FOR INCOMPITENCE)

Mr Bronson,

Having re-visited the risk assessments for Mr Spencer Wilder and his son Daniel Wilder I am satisfied they now meets the criteria for approved visits. Mr Wilder will be notified in writing shortly.

YOUR PROBABLY BAN THEM AGAIN NEXT WEEK.

Name in block capitals ▓▓▓▓▓▓▓ Position S.O.

Signed ▓▓▓▓▓▓▓ Date 29.11.10

This section for official use only			
Sentence	Category	Status	
Release date	Ethnicity	Location	
Date received by complaints clerk	Date received by responding member of staff	Passed to RRLO on (date)	Date of interim reply
Reserved subject ? (tick box) ☐	Referred to	On (date)	Date received by Area Manager or HQ
Outcome of complaint Upheld ☐ Rejected ☐		Reserved Subject Upheld ☐ Rejected ☐	
Action taken (where complaint upheld)			

F2059

FORM COMP 1
PRISONER'S FORMAL COMPLAINT

Establishment WDCm
Serial Nº WD 398 10f

Read these notes first

1. This form is for you to make a formal written complaint under the complaints procedure. Complaints should wherever possible be sorted out informally by speaking to your wing officer or making an application. Use this form only if you have not been able to resolve your complaint this way.
2. A written complaint should be made within 3 months of the incident or of the relevant facts coming to your notice.
3. Keep the complaint brief and to the point.
4. When you have completed the form, sign it and post it in the box provided. The form will be returned to you with a response.
5. If you are unhappy with the response, you can appeal on a separate form (COMP 1A).
6. Some subjects are dealt with only by the Area Manager or Prison Service headquarters. If your complaint is about one of these subjects, the reply will take longer.
7. There is a separate pink form (COMP 2) for confidential access complaints.

Your details (use BLOCK CAPITALS)

Surname	BRONSON	First name(s)	CHARLES ARTHUR
Prison number	A8176AF	Location	

Have you spoken to anyone about your complaint ? Yes ☑ No ☐

If so, who did you speak to ?

GOVERNOR RAVEN

Your complaint

I WAS TOLD 4½ MONTHS AGO ... ALL THESE GUYS WERE TO BE REVIEWED IN OCTOBER FOR BEING PUT BACK ON MY APPROVED VISITORS LIST.

ITS NOW A MONTH IM AWAITING YOUR DECISION AND THE REASONS WHY THEY ARE BANNED.

TOM HARDY. ALAN RAYMENT. MARIT FISH. DANNY HANSFORD. LEIGHTON AND LINDSEY FRAYNE.

We STILL DONT KNOW WHY THEY WERE ever BANNED OVER 18 MONTHS AGO.

Does your complaint have a racial aspect ? Yes ☐ No ☐

Is your complaint about bullying ? Yes ☐ No ☐

What would you like to see done about your complaint ?

WHY CANT YOU JUST GIVE SOME HONEST ANSWERS INSTEAD OF LYING ALL THE TIME

THESE GUYS NEED THE REASONS?

"THE TRUTH" (THATS ALL WE WANT)

Signed _____   Date 24/11/2010

VF 011 Printed at HMP Kingston 4334 03/2003

Response to the complaint *(including any action taken)*

Mr Bronson,

Having re-visited the risk assessments for Mr Tom Hardy, Mr Alan Rayement, Mr Mark Fish, Mr Danny Hansford, Mr Leighton Frayne and Mrs Lindsay Frayne I am satisfied they do not meet the criteria for approved visits. I understand how distressing this may be however my responsibility is to ensure the good order or discipline of the establishment.

SO WHAT HAVE THEY DONE WRONG ?
OR HAVN'T YOU GOT A REASON ?
HOW CAN THIS BE RIGHT ?

Name in block capitals _____ Position __S·O·__

Signed _____ Date __29·11·10__

F2059

FORM COMP 1
PRISONER'S FORMAL COMPLAINT

Establishment WDCM

Serial № WD 398 10F

Read these notes first

1. This form is for you to make a formal written complaint under the complaints procedure. Complaints should wherever possible be sorted out informally by speaking to your wing officer or making an application. Use this form only if you have not been able to resolve your complaint this way.
2. A written complaint should be made within 3 months of the incident or of the relevant facts coming to your notice.
3. Keep the complaint brief and to the point.
4. When you have completed the form, sign it and post it in the box provided. The form will be returned to you with a response.
5. If you are unhappy with the response, you can appeal on a separate form (COMP 1A).
6. Some subjects are dealt with only by the Area Manager or Prison Service headquarters. If your complaint is about one of these subjects, the reply will take longer.
7. There is a separate pink form (COMP 2) for confidential access complaints.

Your details (use BLOCK CAPITALS)

Surname BRONSON	First name(s) CHARLES ARTHUR
Prison number A8076AJ	Location C.S.C. UNIT

Have you spoken to anyone about your complaint?   Yes ☑   No ☐
If so, who did you speak to?

GOVERNORS. (NONE HAVE ANSWERS)

Your complaint

SECURITY HAVE REFUSED STEVE SWATTON TO GO ONTO MY APPROVED VISIT LIST.
    WHY?
    WHAT HAS THE MAN DONE WRONG?
    THE POLICE PASSED HIM.
    He HAS NO CRIMINAL RECORD.
    AND
    He is A TRUE FAMILY FRIEND.

Does your complaint have a racial aspect?   Yes ☐   No ☐
Is your complaint about bullying?   Yes ☐   No ☐
What would you like to see done about your complaint?

WHY is THIS MAN BEING VICTIMIZED?
    AND WHOSE DOING IT?
    (WE NOW NEED THE TRUTH)
        SO WE CAN EXPOSE WHAT YOUR DOING?

Signed _____   Date 24/11/2010

VF 011 Printed at HMP Kingston 4334 03/2003

Response to the complaint *(including any action taken)*

Mr Bronson,

Having re-visited the risk assessments for Mr Steve Swatton I am satisfied he did not meet the criteria for approved visits. Again I understand how distressing this may be however my responsibility is to ensure the good order or discipline of the establishment.

So WHAT's THE REASON ?

Name in block capitals _____ Position __S·O·__

Signed _____ Date __29·11·10__

This section for official use only			
Sentence	Category	Status	
Release date	Ethnicity	Location	

Date received by complaints clerk	Date received by responding member of staff	Passed to RRLO on (date)	Date of interim reply
Reserved subject ? (tick box) ☐	Referred to	On (date)	Date received by Area Manager or HQ

Outcome of complaint	Reserved Subject
Upheld ☐ Rejected ☐	Upheld ☐ Rejected ☐
Action taken (where complaint upheld)	

F2059

HM PRISON SERVICE

FORM COMP 1
PRISONER'S FORMAL COMPLAINT

Establishment

Serial Nº WD 398 10F

Read these notes first

1. This form is for you to make a formal written complaint under the complaints procedure. Complaints should wherever possible be sorted out informally by speaking to your wing officer or making an application. Use this form only if you have not been able to resolve your complaint this way.
2. A written complaint should be made within 3 months of the incident or of the relevant facts coming to your notice.
3. Keep the complaint brief and to the point.
4. When you have completed the form, sign it and post in the box provided. The form will be returned to you with a response.
5. If you are unhappy with the response, you can appeal on a separate form (COMP 1A).
6. Some subjects are dealt with only by the Area Manager or Prison Service headquarters. If your complaint is about one of these subjects, the reply will take longer.
7. There is a separate pink form (COMP 2) for confidential access complaints.

Your details (use BLOCK CAPITALS)

Surname	BRONSON	First name(s)	CHARLES ARTHUR
Prison number	A8076AY	Location	C.S.C UNIT

Have you spoken to anyone about your complaint ?   Yes ☑   No ☐

If so, who did you speak to ?

GOVERNORS

Your complaint

SECURITY HAVE REFUSED "TAMARA MILLER" TO GO ONTO MY APPROVED VISIT LIST.

THIS is A MOTHER WITH TWO CHILDREN.

SHE HAS NO CRIMINAL RECORD

SHE WORKS HARD.

AND is A GOOD HONEST DECENT WOMAN.

WHY AND _WHO_ is PERSECUTING THIS LADY

(HAVE YOU GOT AN ISSUE WITH WOMEN ?

Does your complaint have a racial aspect ?   Yes ☐   No ☐

Is your complaint about bullying ?   Yes ☐   No ☐

What would you like to see done about your complaint ?

I NEED THE TRUTH — IN WRITING.

SO I CAN THEN TAKE LegAl ACTION.

YOUR _NOT_ ABUSING MY FRIENDS NO MORE.

(ENOUGH is ENOUGH)

Signed _____   Date 24/11/2010

VF 011   Printed at HMP Kingston 4334 03/2003

Response to the complaint *(including any action taken)*

Mr Bronson,

Having re-visited the risk assessments for Ms Tamara Miller I understand she failed to comply with the 'Approved Visits' process therefore her application was turned down.

THe PoLiCe PASSeo HeR.

Name in block capitals _____   Position _____ S, O'

Signed _____   Date __29.11.10__

This section for official use only			
Sentence	Category	Status	
Release date	Ethnicity	Location	
Date received by complaints clerk	Date received by responding member of staff	Passed to RRLO on (date)	Date of interim reply
Reserved subject ? (tick box) ☐	Referred to	On (date)	Date received by Area Manager or HQ
Outcome of complaint Upheld ☐ Rejected ☐		Reserved Subject Upheld ☐ Rejected ☐	
Action taken (where complaint upheld)			

F2059

HM PRISON SERVICE

FORM COMP 1
PRISONER'S FORMAL COMPLAINT

Establishment
Serial Nº WD 398 10F

Read these notes first

1. This form is for you to make a formal written complaint under the complaints procedure. Complaints should wherever possible be sorted out informally by speaking to your wing officer or making an application. Use this form only if you have not been able to resolve your complaint this way.
2. A written complaint should be made within 3 months of the incident or of the relevant facts coming to your notice.
3. Keep the complaint brief and to the point.
4. When you have completed the form, sign it and post it in the box provided. The form will be returned to you with a response.
5. If you are unhappy with the response, you can appeal on a separate form (COMP 1A).
6. Some subjects are dealt with only by the Area Manager or Prison Service headquarters. If your complaint is about one of these subjects, the reply will take longer.
7. There is a separate pink form (COMP 2) for confidential access complaints.

Your details (use BLOCK CAPITALS)

Surname	BRONSON	First name(s)	CHARLES ARTHUR
Prison number	A8076Ag	Location	C.S.C UNIT

Have you spoken to anyone about your complaint? Yes ☑ No ☐
If so, who did you speak to?

GOVERNORS

Your complaint

WHY Is LEIGHTON and LINDSY FRAYNE STOPPED FROM VISITING me?
WHAT HAVE THEY DONE TO BREECH Security RULES.
"We DO-NOT NI"
We NEED TO BE TOLD.
IT'S GONE ON long ENOUGH.

Does your complaint have a racial aspect? Yes ☐ No ☐
Is your complaint about bullying? Yes ☐ No ☐

What would you like to see done about your complaint?

The REAL TRUTH.
PROOF IN WHAT YOU THINK THEY DONE?
(So we CAN CHALLENGE it)

Signed C Bronson   Date 24/11/2010

VF 011 Printed at HMP Kingston 4334 03/2003

134

Response to the complaint *(including any action taken)*

ITS MR LINDSEY FRAYNE YOU JOKER
YOU CANT EVEN GET THE SEX RIGHT -
So WHY ARE THEY BANNED ?

Mr Bronson,

Having re-visited the risk assessments for Mr Leighton Frayne and Mrs Lindsay Frayne I am satisfied they do not meet the criteria for approved visits. I understand how distressing this may be however my responsibility is to ensure the good order or discipline of the establishment.

IS IT COZ YOUR A POWER FREAK ?

Name in block capitals ████████ Position S·O·

Signed ████████ Date 29·11·10

This section for official use only			
Sentence	Category	Status	
Release date	Ethnicity	Location	
Date received by complaints clerk	Date received by responding member of staff	Passed to RRLO on (date)	Date of interim reply
Reserved subject ? (tick box) ☐	Referred to	On (date)	Date received by Area Manager or HQ
Outcome of complaint Upheld ☐ Rejected ☐		Reserved Subject Upheld ☐ Rejected ☐	
Action taken (where complaint upheld)			

F2059

FORM COMP 1
PRISONER'S FORMAL COMPLAINT

Establishment
Serial Nº (JJ) 398 10F

Read these notes first
1. This form is for you to make a formal written complaint under the complaints procedure. Complaints should wherever possible be sorted out informally by speaking to your wing officer or making an application. Use this form only if you have not been able to resolve your complaint this way.
2. A written complaint should be made within 3 months of the incident or of the relevant facts coming to your notice.
3. Keep the complaint brief and to the point.
4. When you have completed the form, sign it and post in the box provided. The form will be returned to you with a response.
5. If you are unhappy with the response, you can appeal on a separate form (COMP 1A).
6. Some subjects are dealt with only by the Area Manager or Prison Service headquarters. If your complaint is about one of these subjects, the reply will take longer.
7. There is a separate pink form (COMP 2) for confidential access complaints.

Your details (use BLOCK CAPITALS)

Surname	BRONSON	First name(s)	CHARLES ARTHUR
Prison number	A8076Ag	Location	C.S.C. UNIT

Have you spoken to anyone about your complaint ?   Yes ☑   No ☐

If so, who did you speak to ?

GOVERNOR

Your complaint

WHY is 'ALAN RAYMENT' STOPPED FROM Visiting me?
WHAT Did He ever Do WRong?
         We NEED To NO THe TRUTH.
   You HAVE A DUTY To Tell us WHY?

Does your complaint have a racial aspect ?   Yes ☐   No ☐

Is your complaint about bullying ?   Yes ☐   No ☐

What would you like to see done about your complaint ?

THe TRUTH!
       THATS ALL I WANT.

Signed _____   Date 24/11/2010

VF 011   Printed at HMP Kingston 4334 03/2003

Response to the complaint *(including any action taken)*

Mr Bronson,

Having re-visited the risk assessments for Mr Alan Rayement I am satisfied he did not meet the criteria for approved visits. Again I understand how distressing this may be however my responsibility is to ensure the good order or discipline of the establishment.

WHATS ALAN DONE WRONG ?

Name in block capitals _____ Position S.O.

Signed _____ Date 29.11.10

This section for official use only			
Sentence	Category	Status	
Release date	Ethnicity	Location	
Date received by complaints clerk	Date received by responding member of staff	Passed to RRLO on (date)	Date of interim reply
Reserved subject ? (tick box) ☐	Referred to	On (date)	Date received by Area Manager or HQ
Outcome of complaint Upheld ☐ Rejected ☐		Reserved Subject Upheld ☐ Rejected ☐	
Action taken (where complaint upheld)			

F2059

FORM COMP 1
PRISONER'S FORMAL COMPLAINT

Establishment

Serial Nº WD 398 10F

Read these notes first

1. This form is for you to make a formal written complaint under the complaints procedure. Complaints should wherever possible be sorted out informally by speaking to your wing officer or making an application. Use this form only if you have not been able to resolve your complaint this way.
2. A written complaint should be made within 3 months of the incident or of the relevant facts coming to your notice.
3. Keep the complaint brief and to the point.
4. When you have completed the form, sign it and post in the box provided. The form will be returned to you with a response.
5. If you are unhappy with the response, you can appeal on a separate form (COMP 1A).
6. Some subjects are dealt with only by the Area Manager or Prison Service headquarters. If your complaint is about one of these subjects, the reply will take longer.
7. There is a separate pink form (COMP 2) for confidential access complaints.

Your details (use BLOCK CAPITALS)

Surname	BRONSON	First name(s)	CHARLES ARTHUR
Prison number	A8076AG	Location	C.S.C. UNIT

Have you spoken to anyone about your complaint ?   Yes ☑   No ☐
If so, who did you speak to ?

SEVERAL GOVERNORS

Your complaint

TWO WEEKS AGO SECURITY REFUSED TO PUT MY FRIEND RYAN DUBOIS ONTO MY APPROVED VISIT LIST.

NOW YOU SAY HE CAN GO ON IT.

YOU HAVE WROTE AND TOLD HIM <u>NO</u>
AND NOW YOU SAY YES

IT'S BECOME A FARCE
AND ITS MUGGING good HONEST PEOPLE OFF.

Does your complaint have a racial aspect ?   Yes ☐   No ☐
Is your complaint about bullying ?   Yes ☐   No ☐

What would you like to see done about your complaint ?

STOP PLAYING GAMES WITH MY FRIENDS OUTSIDE.
AND START TREATING me LIKE A HUMAN.
(DONT YOU WANT ME TO HAVE VISITORS)?

Signed _____   Date 24/11/2010

VF 011 Printed at HMP Kingston 4334 03/2003

Response to the complaint *(including any action taken)*

Weeks Ago You Banned Him.
(For No Reason)
Now You Say He Fits The Criteria
(This PRoves Your A Joke)

Mr Bronson,

Having re-visited the risk assessments for Mr Ryan Dubols I am satisfied he now meets the criteria for approved visits. Mr Dubols will be notified in writing shortly.

Name in block capitals _____ Position __S·O·__

Signed _____ Date __29·11·10__

F2059

FORM COMP 1
PRISONER'S FORMAL COMPLAINT

Establishment
Serial Nº WD 398 10F

Read these notes first

1. This form is for you to make a formal written complaint under the complaints procedure. Complaints should wherever possible be sorted out informally by speaking to your wing officer or making an application. Use this form only if you have not been able to resolve your complaint this way.
2. A written complaint should be made within 3 months of the incident or of the relevant facts coming to your notice.
3. Keep the complaint brief and to the point.
4. When you have completed the form, sign it and post in the box provided. The form will be returned to you with a response.
5. If you are unhappy with the response, you can appeal on a separate form (COMP 1A).
6. Some subjects are dealt with only by the Area Manager or Prison Service headquarters. If your complaint is about one of these subjects, the reply will take longer.
7. There is a separate pink form (COMP 2) for confidential access complaints.

Your details (use BLOCK CAPITALS)

Surname	BRONSON	First name(s)	CHARLES ARTHUR
Prison number	A8176AY	Location	C.S.C UNIT

Have you spoken to anyone about your complaint ?   Yes ☑   No ☐
If so, who did you speak to ?

GOVERNOR

Your complaint

TODAY 24/11/2010. I AM GIVEN A VISIT LIST WITH ALL THE APPROVED VISITORS NAMES ON.

STUART AND KARYN GODFREY is NOT ON THERE.

THEY ARE FAMILY MEMBERS WHO HAVE VISITED ME FOR YEARS

So WHY ARE THEY MYSTERIOUSLY NOW OFF THE LIST?

INFACT THEY VISITED ME RECENTLY HERE.

So WHATS GOING ON?

Does your complaint have a racial aspect ?   Yes ☐   No ☐
Is your complaint about bullying ?   Yes ☐   No ☐
What would you like to see done about your complaint ?

WHY ARE YOU STRESSING ME OUT?
WHO WILL YOU BAN NEXT MY MOTHER?
WHEN is ALL THIS CRAP GOING TI STOP?

Signed _(signature)_   Date 24/11/2010

VF 011 Printed at HMP Kingston 4334 03/2003

140

Response to the complaint *(including any action taken)*

Look! THEY CANT EVEN GET KAREN'S NAME RIGHT.
OR EXPLAIN WHY THEY WERE TAKEN OFF MY LIST.
THERE COMPLETE IDIOTS .. (THEY MUST BE)

Mr Bronson,

Having re-visited the risk assessments for Mr Stuart and Kieran Godfrey I am satisfied they now meet the criteria for approved visits. Both Stuart & Kieran Godfrey will be notified in writing shortly.

Name in block capitals _____ Position ___S.O_____

Signed _____ Date___29·11·10_____

This section for official use only				
Sentence	Category	Status		
Release date	Ethnicity	Location		
Date received by complaints clerk	Date received by responding member of staff	Passed to RRLO on (date)	Date of interim reply	
Reserved subject ? (tick box) ☐	Referred to	On (date)	Date received by Area Manager or HQ	
Outcome of complaint Upheld ☐ Rejected ☐		Reserved Subject Upheld ☐ Rejected ☐		
Action taken (where complaint upheld)				

8.12.2010

BRONSON A8076AE
C.S.C.
H.M.P. WAKO

IT WAS BLOODY FREEZING LAST NIGHT. I GOT OUT OF BED TWICE
TO HAVE A WALK UP AND DOWN. I FELT ABIT STRANGE. CONFUSED.
I MUST BE GETTING OLD.
I WATCHED THE SNOW FALL IN THE DARK.
    RIGHT OUTSIDE MY WINDOW IS, A SECURITY LIGHT THAT BEAMS
ONTO THE EXERCISE YARD, SO IT'S A NICE CALMING SIGHT.
    'FUCK ME'. IT'S FREEZING.
THIS IS THE WEATHER WHERE A MAN NEEDS A SWEET AND
TENDER HOT PUSSY TO KEEP HIM WARM.
    THE VERY THOUGHT MAKES ME DRIBBLE.
    "WELL IM ONLY HUMAN" ∘ₒ∘ IT'S TRUE I AM.

 JACK BINNS AND RYAN DUBOIS ARE UP TO VISIT TODAY.
THAT WAS UNTIL THE SNIFFER DOG JUMPED ALL OVER THEM.
THATS WHAT JAILS ALL ABOUT TODAY .... "BOLLOCKS"

    1/ THE DOG SNIFFS THEM.
    2/ WHAT IF THEY WERE SAT NEXT TO A PERSON WHO SMOKES__
                                                    __ DOPE ?
    3/ ANY SCIENTIFIC DOCTOR WOULD CONFIRM THE SMELL COULD
        EASILY SPREAD ONTO OTHER CLOTHES.

BUT THATS PRISON LAW... IF A MUTT OF A DOG SNIFFS YOU.
    YOUR AUTOMATICALLY GUILTY. ∘ₒ∘

    SO THE SCREWS ON THIS UNIT ARE TOLD TO LOCK THE PLASTIC
    SHUTTER ON THE VISIT BARS, SO I HAVE A TOTAL CLOSED VISIT
            I SAY "BOLLOCKS"
        SO THE VISIT IS STOPPED.
        SUCH IS LIFE ....
        AND 30 YEARS TODAY JOHN LENNON WAS SHOT DEAD.
        SO MY LIFE'S NOT SO BAD...
        ONLY IM ACTUALLY BEING STITCHED UP AGAIN.
        'NOW IVE GOT PROOF FOR YOU ALL TO SEE. ∘ₒ∘

142

Daily Mirror, 6 December 2010:

BRONSON'S MONSTER MANSION 'ESCAPE BID'

BIRTHDAY ALERT ON VIOLENT CON

Exclusive by Jeremy Armstrong

A TOP security jail has been placed on high alert over a birthday escape plot by Charles Bronson – dubbed Britain's most dangerous convict.

He is 58 today. But after 36 years behind bars, 31 of them in solitary, a recent search by officers at Wakefield prison found that the window in his cell was unsecured.

A special staff meeting at the West Yorkshire facility – nicknamed Monster Mansion because it holds so many killers – heard the opening could lead him to an exercise yard.

And though superfit Bronson, who does 2,500 press-ups a day, would need to scale a wall to get his first taste of freedom since 1974, an insider said: "We know the significance of the window being disconnected.

"He remains very dangerous despite his age and could easily take out the watch in the yard before getting over the wall."

Warders were also placed on alert over a possible kidnap attempt three weeks ago when he took on 12 of them in the gym after covering himself with butter.

In 10 jail sieges, he has taken a string of hostages, attacking 32 officers and causing £500,000 damage in rooftop protests.

First jailed for armed robbery in 1969, he has had only 69 days of freedom since.

He has been moved 121 times due to his appalling record, including spells in Broadmoor and Rampton. And the insider said: "There are concerns about Charlie's state of mind. He is again finding it difficult to get his head around being locked up for life.

"He's been co-operative during searches but his behaviour has changed since the gym incident. He's a bomb waiting to go off."

Born Michael Peterson, Bronson changed his name to honour the late Death Wish film star when he was a bare-knuckle fighter.

Last jailed in 1974, he kidnapped prison teacher Phil Danielson inside Hull jail in 1999 and was told he must serve life. An appeal failed last year.

He has been the subject of a movie and his artwork can earn him £2,500 a canvas. Now he refuses to see prison psychiatrists.

THIS ARTICLE CAN ONLY OF COME FROM A PRISON GUARD. ITS ONE BIG MADE UP STORY! AND IT WAS DONE ON MY BIRTHDAY. AN EXCLUSIVE SUCH AS THIS WILL HAVE BEEN SOLD FOR 2 OR 3 GRAND.... THE SCREW GETS A HOLIDAY, AND I GET MORE PROBLEMS. THIS IS HOW IT ALL WORKS IN PRISON. 'LIBERTY AFTER LIBERTY.

This was done for one reason: To fuck up my parole. To make me look a dangerman. They even use a photo thats ten years old when I looked menacing.

Anybody who reads this shit must think: "Fuck me you cant let that animal out."

And this keeps going on. Its actually unlawful. Its a lie. Its really a national disgrace and the prison governors should be ashamed of it!

So what are they doing about it? O͜O

Who sold this story to the media?

Why?

How?

Let me make it 100% clear

1/ if this story was true I would automatically be charged with attempt escape.

2/ I would now be in patches (escape list)

3/ Im still in the same cell.

4/ I would of been moved to another prison.

Not one governor has been to see me over it O͜O
Because they know its an embarassment.
One of these officers has had an early Xmas on me.
"My name".
He/she sold my name.

My name is exclusive material.
And its a fucking piss take.

Now can you understand why I refuse to trust the system?

I cant afford to trust anybody.

Could you in my position?

They want me to work with psychologists!
In a room with C.C.T.V
"Are these people for real? O͜O
‿

it will all end up in the news of the world "

" Fuck THAT .
I'M NOT WARNING THEM.. end of ! " Fuck OFF " .

AGAIN I PROVE WHAT GOES ON .
When They TRY To COVER it up .
Here it is Again in BLACK AND WHITE FOR ALL To See .
" I DONT BLAME THE PAPERS .
They HAVE A JOB To DO..
it's These Fucking PARASITE LYING BASTARDS WHO NEED exposing .
(even ALOT of SCREWS ARE FUMING over it)
" PROBABLY JEALOUS THEY LOST OUT ON A FEW GRAND !

" YOUR LOVE THIS " ..... ☺
          PRISON OFFICER " EMMA BEARD " HAS JUST BEEN
     JAILED FOR 12 MTHS FOR GIVING A PRISONER A BLOW JOB
     IN HIS CELL AT FELTHAM PRISON .

WHATS THE SYSTEM GOT To SAY ABOUT THAT ? .⊙̈.

     I KNOW WHAT I'M GOTTA SAY .

               " LUCKY BASTARD " ?

     WHY CANT I MEET A NICE FEMALE SCREW To Give me
A BLOW JOB ?

     Did You KNOW it's 37 Years SINCE SLADE's No 1
     MERRY CHRISTMAS ?
       CAN You Believe THAT ? ' 1973 ' .
     I Remember it LIKE LAST Week .
               " FANTASTIC "
     I DONT THINK ANY XMAS SONGs ever BEAT it .
               " A PURE CLASSIC "

145

I've Been Watching Coronation Street This Week.
    The 50th Anniversary.
The Longest Soap in The World!
"Now" ill Let You into A Little Secret...
    "Tony Warren" The Script Writer in The 1960's
He Once Visited Me At Broadmoor Asylum With My
Uncle Jack Cronin" Back in 1979.
    It Was A Fantastic Visit. And He Told Me To My Face,
He Believed I Would one Day Make Something of My Life.

146

I DONT KNOW WHT He SAID iT BUT IVe NEVER FORGOT iT.

If THese FUCKERS WOULD STOP PERSECUTING ME, AND ALLOWED ME TO
PROGRESS AND GET MYSELF OUT. I PROBABLY WOULD DO well OUTSIDE.
BUT ITS A BOTTOMLESS HOLE WITH THIS LOT.
         THe FUCKERS WANT ME TO LEAVE PRISON IN A BODY BAG.

     IVe HAD A NicE FEW QUiD SENT IN TODAY FOR MY BIRTHDAY
£20 off STU CHeSHIRE
£20 off MY AUNTY EilEEN. (SHEs A STAR MY EilEEN)
£20 off STeve SWATTON.
£50 off DAWN PeTERS
£50 off MUM
£100 off MARY SHARMAN

                THANKS EVERYBODY
             ILL GeT SOME CANTEEN SORTED ". ☺

AS You CAN See I SPENT
20 QUID THis WeeK.
2 FuckiNG QUiD FOR A PLASTIC JAR
   OF HONEY.
CAN You BELIEVE iT?   ☹
iT WAS ONLY Sop WHEN I WAS OUT..
SOMEONEs TAKiNG THe PiSS..
   AND iT AiNT THe BEES.

Yeh. A STRANGE DAY ☹
WAS iT WORTH GETTiNG OUT OF BED FOR?

    You BET YOUR ARSE ON iT.
Hey! TAlKiNG OF ARSEs. Iu TELL You
WHose GOT A LoveLY ONE.
    ALEX JONES ON THe ONE SHOW x

147

Oh well.. it's the APPRENTICE TONIGHT
   Whose SUGAR GONNA FIRE?

THAT FINISHES AT 10 PM— THEN I'm OFF To BED.

            ADIOS AMIGO

ps! £2 FOR A JAR OF HONEY!
            YOU CUNTS.
      DAY LIGHT ROBBERY OO

      P.P.S
GOOD NEWS TO END..
         TALKING OF CUNTS.

   PAUL HUTCHINSON HAS BEEN FOUND DEAD
IN HIS CELL AT NOTTINGHAM JAIL
         YIPPEEEEEE..
He WAS ONLY A 52 YEAR OLD NONCE
         YIPEEEEE..
He RAPED AND KILLED 16 YEAR OLD COLETTE ARAM 26 YRS AGO..

   So LETS ALL CELEBRATE THE DEATH OF A MONSTER..

LETS HOPE IAN "CUNTLEY" IS NEXT.

      OOOPS SORRY
            HUNTLEY.

THE SOONER THAT CUNT'S DEAD THE BETTER.
   AND ALL SAY ALL OF US!

                  I'LL BE BACK!

148

SAT 11/12/2010

BRONSON A8076AG CSC (Cage)
MONSTER MANSION

Fuck.Me I HAD A CRAZY DREAM LAST NIGHT.
I WOKE UP AND SOMEBODY WAS SITTING AT THE BOTTOM OF MY
BED LOOKING AT ME.
I JUMPED UP AND GRABBED HIS HEAD AND STARTED TO SMASH
IT AGAINST THE WALL. I COULDN'T STOP. THE WHOLE CELL WAS
DRIPPING BLOOD. I WAS NAKED AND COVERED IN IT.
    THEN MY DOOR OPENED UP. AND A MOB OF SCREWS IN RIOT FEAR
RUSHED ME. IT WAS MENTAL.
    WHO WAS THAT GUY I SMASHED UP?
        IF DREAMS COME TRUE... YOU HAVE BEEN WARNED!
MAYBE A POTENTIAL CELL MATE? OR A HOSTAGE?
    WHAT A NIGHTMARE...
    ANYWAY HOW DOES A MAN WHO'S SPENT NEAR ON 4 DECADES
ALONE. END UP IN A DOUBLE UP CELL WITH A STRANGER?
    WHO WOULD WANT TO SHARE A ROOM WITH ME?
I DOUBT IT WOULD EVER HAPPEN...... WOULD IT? COULD IT?
The VERY THOUGHT OF SOMEBODY FARTING IN MY SPACE.
    SMELLY SOCKS. TOUCHING MY THINGS. BREATHING CLOSE TO ME.
WHAT IF I WOKE UP AND CAUGHT HIM BASHING HIS BISHOP 👀
        NAH! I COULDN'T HANDLE THAT!

OH WELL... ANOTHER SATURDAY.
            LOVE IT!
        X FACTOR LATER. ☺

HEY IVE HAD A GREAT WEEK!...
I CALLED UP DAVE TAYLOR, MY BRONSONWEAR CLOBBER IS GOING WELL.
LOG ON TO THE SITE, THERE'S SOME GOOD SPORTS WEAR ON THERE.
DAVE DOES ME PROUD. TOP GEEZER.

HEY! DID YOU READ ABOUT ANDY DYMOND WHO GOT SENTENCED
TO 4 MONTHS FOR HAVING ANIMAL PORN 👀
ONE WAS OF A GEEZER SHAGGING A SQUID 👀 A BIT FISHY TO ME! ☺

149

'Come on'. WHAT SANE GUY WANTS TO FUCK A SQUID?
WHAT'S THE TURN ON?

A SQUIDS LIKE AN OCTOPUS, WITH 8 ARMS.

I SUPPOSE IT COULD GIVE 8 WANKS ALL AT THE SAME TIME AND
A BLOW JOB 😊

"CRAZY PEOPLE"

SNOWS GONE, A NICE BREEZE COMING THROUGH MY WINDOW.
IT'S NOT COLD EITHER.

I HAD CORN FLAKES FOR BREAKFAST, I CUT A BANANA UP
AND PUT A SPOON OF HONEY IN.

4 JAM BUTTIES, AND A MUG OF ROSY LEA.
WITH 6 CUSTARD CREAMS

'LOVELY'

WELL IF I DONT SPOIL MYSELF WHO ELSE WILL? ☺

ATLEAST IM NOT A FAT LAZY BASTARD, LIKE ALOT OF SCREWS.
BELIEVE ME NOW. SO MANY GET TO 40 AND LET THEMSELFS GO.
BIG BEER BELLIES, FAT ARSES. 3 CHINS. AND THATS ONLY THE WOMEN ☺

THERES ONE WOMAN SCREW HERE. M'S WALTER. I WONT SAY HER AGE
BUT SHE WONT SEE 40 AGAIN

WELL SHE LOOKS 20... SHE KEEPS HERSELF SO SLIM AND FIT.
A GREAT INSPIRATION TO ALL. "CONS AND SCREWS"
I HAVE NOTHING BUT RESPECT FOR HER.

THERE WAS ONE SCREWESS HERE A FEW YEARS BACK SHE MUST
HAVE WEIGHED 18 STONE, SHE USED TO FART AS SHE WALKED. ☺

A LOVELY PERSONALITY THOUGH. BUT THAT FARTING SORT OF
TURNS ME OFF. DONT IT YOU?

I SUPPOSE IT TAKES ALL SORTS TO MAKE THE WORLD GO ROUND..

I DID 1½,000 PRESS UPS BEFORE BREAKFAST.
ALL IN 50'
A NICE PUMP UP...
I ENJOY IT, THATS WHAT COUNTS.

HEY! YOU GUYS WHO ARE JUST STARTING OUT INTO THE
FITNESS WORLD... HERES A TIP (ESPECIALY FOR PRISONERS)
WHEN YOU GO TO THE LIBRARY GET 6 BIG BOOKS. (THE BIGEST). 😊

150

Do Your Press ups on Them. 3 each side.
This Way Your Build Your Chest up.
Go Right Down on it. Slowly. Use it as a Dynamic.
Believe me Your Soon Build up.

THATS MY TIP OF The DAY Lads. (TAKE it OR Leave it)
You Know Im The DADDY OF Press ups ... So it's Best You Listen To
Sense!

I HAD Steak + Kidney Pie For Dinner .. ☺
        (Not Much Steak in it)

    I Covered it in DADDY Sauce. ☺ Lovely Jubbly.
The Mashed Spuds HAD Lumps in it.

        CANT Their Prison Chefs even Do Mashed Potato Without
Fucking it up ?

    No Wonder These Prison Chefs, And Not Hilton Chefs ?!
½ A Star Chefs. ☺

    Oh Z Forgot.
            I Got A Letter Off A Woman in Ireland
    Yesterday. CAROL WARD. She Asked me AM I MARRIED.?
OR In A RelATionsHip ?

    Well, CAROL... The TRUTH is ... Z DONT Do RelATionsHips.
I CANT. My World Is So Un-Real To Yours

        But Having said THAT . . . . .
    I Do Have Somebody Very SPECIAL In My Life
            LORRAiNe

    SHes A Massive INspiration To Me. ☺
        We BoTH Have So Much In Common.

    Z Would SAY IF There ever is To Be A Mrs BRonson
Then SHe is The ideal Woman For Me.
    Long Legs. Big eyes. Nice Mouth. Beautiful Teeth.
A Good Brain. An ARTist. Fearless.
    THATS MY SORT OF Woman CARoL..
        "Sex on Legs" ☺
    Like A STRAWBERRY Lollipop Melting in The Sun.

151

I HAD MY JOG ON YARD. A NICE HOUR OF FRESH AIR.
COME IN FOR A SHOWER. I FELT GOOD. "HAPPY"
I MIGHT EVEN BASH THE BISHOP TONIGHT... "WHY NOT"? IM ONLY HUMAN.
A GOOD OLD FASHION WANK BLOWS THE BLUES AWAY!...
       PLUS IT'S A GOOD STRESS RELEASE.
COVER THE DICK IN BABY LOTION AND GO FOR IT.
         " A SPEED WANK."
    I COULD ACTUALLY BE THE FASTEST WANKER IN BRITAIN AND
NOT REALISE IT.
      AND DONT FORGET. IT'S NOT JUST THE TECHNIQUE, ITS HOW
FAR YOU CAN SHOOT YOUR LOAD.
IVE ACTUALLY HIT THE DOOR FROM THE BACK WALL.
     IVE EVEN HIT THE CEILING.
        "HARD TO BELIEVE" BUT IT'S TRUE...
   SO YOU YOUNG CONS. HAVE ALONG WAY TO GO TO CATCH UP
WITH AN OLD WANKER LIKE ME. ☺
       SERIOUSLY. THE TRUTH IS I REALLY DO IT TO KEEP IT ALL
IN WORKING ORDER.
       LETS FACE FACTS... (IF) YOU DONT DO IT. YOUR BALLS
WILL EXPLODE.
'IF I WAS PRIMEMINISTER I WOULD ALLOW PRISONERS TO HAVE
SEX WITH THERE WIFES AND GIRLFRIENDS.
       (A TREAT FOR GOOD BEHAVIOUR ONCE A MONTH).
    SO START VOTING FOR THE BRONSON WANK PARTY.
HEY! I WONDER IF LORRAINE WILL VOTE FOR ME ?
             (I HOPE SO)
   THE QUESTION IS ..... COULD SHE HANDLE A NIGHT WITH ME ?
                      WOULD SHE WANT TOO ?
       COZ I MAKE NO. BONES ABOUT IT.
         I LOVE A SLICE OF PUSSY
      WHAT JAILBIRD DONT ?
EVEN THE WOMEN PRISONERS LOVE ABIT OF PUSSY.
 EVEN FAT MONSTERS LIKE ROSE WEST GET A GOOD LICKING.

152

WHY AS NOBODY EVER CREATED A BAG OF SWEETS IN FANNY JUICE TASTE?
"ONE DAY IT WILL HAPPEN"

IT'S A MAD OLD WORLD.

I GOT 11 LETTERS TODAY. NOT BAD FOR A SATURDAY
3 WERE PRISON MAIL.

ONE OFF A BIRD CALLED "SUZY" IN HOLLOWAY SERVING 9 YEARS
FOR DRUGS. SHE'S JUST READ MY BOOK "LOONTOLOGY"
AND SAYS SHE PISSED HERSELF LAUGHING. NICE ONE SUZY.
SHE WANTS A PEN FRIEND.
TO HELP HER THROUGH HER SENTENCE.

"WELL SUZY". BEST YOU DONT WRITE TO ME. COZ IT
WILL DAMAGE YOUR PAROLE.

HONEST LOVE — WRITING TO ME CAN ONLY DAMAGE YOUR
CHANCES OF EARLY RELEASE.

I HAD SALAD FOR TEA. AND BANANA + CUSTARD.
THEY DO A NICE CREAMY CUSTARD HERE.
SO ALL IN ALL A MAGICAL DAY.

IM NOW CHILLED OUT. AWAITING X FACTOR.
ILL END HERE.... BUT ILL BE BACK.

"PROMISE"

2 IRISH MEN LOOKING THROUGH A MAIL ORDER CATALOGUE.
PADDY SAYS "LOOK AT THESE GORGEOUS WOMEN.
THE PRICES ARE REASONABLE TOO!!"

MICK AGREES. "IM ORDERING ONE OF THOSE RIGHT NOW.!"

3 WEEKS LATER PADDY SAYS TO MICK. "HAS YOUR WOMAN TURNED
UP YET?

NO SAID MICK. "BUT IT SHOULDN'T BE LONG NOW.
COZ HER CLOTHES ARRIVED YESTERDAY!".

<u>SUNDAY 12TH DECEMBER 2010</u>

Got up at 6am. I had to. Coz I was bursting for a piss. One of those pisses that goes on forever. What a relief ☺ Then I had a good dump. Then a strip wash.

By 6.30am I'm into my stretching and press ups. I love Sundays. A nice chilled out day. I've no visit. So the day is all mine ☺

At 8am my doors unlock. I step outside and say
        Don't you lot ever go home

There's 4 outside my door, and 6.30 feet away by the hot plate I collect my Rice Krispies and bread rolls and return to my cell (with my razor). I've got Heart Radio Station on.

So I'm bopping away to the music. Whilst I shave my head. Then I make a jug of tea.

THIS is Living ☺

These fucking prison razors are shit
        4 cuts today.

I'll do my face tomorrow.

Poor old ARETHA FRANKLIN has cancer ☹
        The true queen of soul.
Every time her song plays *Respect I feel so good.
        Come on Aretha..... Beat it. We love you babe.
Fight back to health..

Hey! Your fucking love this. Another female screw has been sent to jail for more sex ☺
        Donna Stanton got a 2 year sentence for having it off with a prisoner in Bedford jail.
        "Another lucky fucker" ☺
        Why can't I have a bit of pussy?

Hey! Do a bit of research out there. Check it out the last 10 years how many prison screws have been sacked or sent to prison for sex and smuggling in drugs.
        Your in for a big shock... Check it out!

154

OH! THAT RAPPER "CHER LLOYD" GOT VOTED OFF OF X FACTOR
LAST NIGHT. "FUDING GOOD JOB TO"
  "CALL THAT SINGING? IT'S JUST A NOISE.

TONIGHT IT'S THE FINAL. REBECCA, MATT, AND SOME SILLY
BOY GROUP. (THEIR BALLS HAVE YET TO DROP)
  COME ON REBECCA. JOU CAN DO IT.
    SHE'S A REAL CLASSY SINGER. "PROPER".

  I SEE PAUL HILL ONE OF THE GUILFORD 4 LADS. HIS NIECE DESTINY
LAUREN HAS JUST BEEN KILLED.
  PAUL GOT CONVICTED IN THE 1970' OF THE BOMBINGS.
  HE SERVED 15 YEARS FOR A STITCH UP
  ALL 4 WERE INNOCENT.
BAD LUCK MUST RUN IN THE HILL FAMILY.

  I DONE TIME WITH ALL THE IRISH TERRORISTS.
AND EVERYBODY KNEW THE GUILFORD 4 WERE FRAMED.
  AS WERE THE BIRMINGHAM 6

"BEING IRISH WAS GUILTY IN THE 1970'...
    A BLOODY TRAVESTY OF JUSTICE...

  "BRITISH JUSTICE THE BEST IN THE WORLD ! '/
      ☺ HA! HA'
        WHAT A JOKE!

  I HAD MEAT PIE FOR DINNER.
  WE HAVE OUR ROAST DINNER AT TEA TIME ON A SUNDAY

I WAS CHATTING TO "PETER BROWN" TODAY. HE WAS ON THE YARD
OUTSIDE MY WINDOW.
  HE RECENTLY GOT 2 LIFE SENTENCES. WITH A 40 YEAR TARIFF
SO HE WILL BE 82 YRS OLD BEFORE HE IS EVEN CONSIDERED
FOR PAROLE. O͜O

  NOW THAT'S WHAT I CALL SERIOUS PORRIDGE!

BUT HE'S A TOUGH NUT... HE WILL SURVIVE.
PETE'S GOOD STUFF... A PROPER GEEZER... HE NEVER MOANS, HE JUST
GETS ON WITH IT.
   IMAGINE SERVING A 40 YEAR TARIFF?

      "COULD YOU?
   HOW WOULD YOU COPE?
      I WONDER!

   I'M WORKING ON A SPECIAL "ART" TODAY.
      A GIFT TO LORRAINE
   I WILL CALL IT - "THE BLACKEST HOLE"
         ""
         DEEP INSIDE THE BLACKEST HOLE
         ANGELS TEARS OF BLOOD
         THE SON OF LUCY GRABS YOUR HEART
         AND DRAGS YOU IN THE MUD.
         ALL AROUND THE SCREAMS OF PAIN
          A BODY CUT AND TORN
         ANOTHER SOUL RIPPED AWAY
          A NOSE BECOMES A HORN
         DEATH BECOMES A BLESSING
         FREE FROM ALL THE PAIN
          A LIFE TIME OF MADNESS
         NOW YOU ARE INSANE   JJ

   ART, POETRY, PHILOSOPHY, IT'S ALL THE SAME.
      CREATE AND COME ALIVE.

5 P.M.   JUST HAD MY ROAST BEEF, SPUDS AND CARROTS.
         FUCKING DELICIOUS.
      THE GRAVY WAS SPOT ON.
         "ALLEYUYU"
      ALLEY FUCKIN JUJU
      FANTASTICALLY DELICIOUS
   THE CHEF DINE US PROUD.
      WELL DONE MY OLD CHINA!

I DID CALL LORRAINE TODAY. AND STEVE SWATTON.
ITS ALWAYS A TREAT TO CALL ANYBODY.
   LORRAINES ALWAYS GOT SOME NEWS FOR ME.
WE HAVE A GOOD LAUGH.. I COULD CHAT WITH HER ALL DAY.
   STEVES SEEING HIS M/P OVER BEING BANNED FROM VISITING ME.
HE WONT ACCEPT BOLLACKS OFF THESE PEOPLE. WHY SHOULD HE?
      WHY SHOULD ANYBODY?   CUNTS
   WHO THE FUCK DO THEY THINK THEY ARE?
PICKING ON GOOD HONEST FOLK.   CHEEKY FUCKERS
   OH WELL ... SOON BE THE END OF X FACTOR!
         ILL FINISH THIS OFF WHEN I GET THE RESULT.

                        PROMISE
            ILL BE BACK

   I CANT FUCKING BELIEVE IT.
      REBECCA COME 2ND
   SOME PRATT CALLED MATT WON IT
WHATS UP WITH YOU VOTERS?
      I CANT BELIEVE IT
   REBECCA is A SUPERSTAR
   SHE'S THE BIGGEST THING IN U.K SINCE SHIRLEY BASSEY
      A BORN STAR
   IM FUCKING GUTTED.
   SHE'S A ONE OFF... MATTS 13 TO THE DOZEN.
      HOW THE FUCK DID SHE COME 2ND ??

157

2 OR 3 YEARS FROM NOW NOBODY WILL HAVE EVEN HEARD
OF MATT.

Rebecca WILL Be A WORLD SUPERSTAR.
A VOICE OF AN ANGEL. ȮȮ
MARK THOSE WORDS "NOW".
ON THE 12TH Dec. 2010 I PREDICT SHE WILL BE
A SUPERSTAR WITHIN 12 MONTHS FROM NOW

Rebecca - Ferguson.

ȮȮ

OH YEH! FOR ALL YOU NOSY BASTARDS WHO
ARE WONDERING IF I DID BASH THE BISHOP LAST NIGHT.

FUCK-OFF AND MIND YOUR OWN BIZZ!
WHAT'S IT GOTTA Do WITH YOU WHAT I Do
INSIDE MY FLOWERY DELL?
STAY OUT OF MY WORLD..
YOU REALLY WONT WANT TO BE INSIDE MY WORLD
BELIEVE ME "....YOU WONT BE ABLE TO STOP SCREAMING.

THIS IS NIGHTMARES OF A DAMAGED BRAIN!
THERE IS NO ESCAPE FROM INSANITY.

HEY! WHO KNOWS WHAT MADNESS LIES AHEAD.
MAYBE TOMORROW I COULD BE BACK IN THE PADDED ROOM
STRAPPED UP IN A STRAIT JACKET.

WHO REALLY GIVES A FLYING FUCK!
"MAKE SURE YOU PEEP UNDER YOUR BED"

Woke up SAM. SomeThing DISTURBED MY Sleep.
Some Fuder Woke Me up. CUNT
I LAY THere THinking 'LIFE' WHATS iT All ABOuT?
How ARE THeY Allowed To SuchK A MANS SOul AWAY?
How CAN THeY KeeP ME CAGED uP FoR LiFe?
WHAT THe FucT is GoinG ON?
THis CANT Be RightT CAN iT?

    IM ANGRY
    I Feel VeRY ANGRY.
    Plus iT's FucKinG FReezing.
I JuMP ouT of BeD ANO DROP To THe FLOOR ANO BANG
    ouT loo PRess ups. FAST Super FAST
IF THe GuARD PeePs THRough MY JuDAS Hole iN THe DOOR
He Will THiNK IM FucKinG THe FLOOR... iN THe DARK
    There is No PRiVACY iN JAiL...
You CANT even HAVe A WANK iN PRiVATe.
    iT's THAT FucKinG CRAZY...

    I SiT iN THe SiNK ANO Give MY ARSe ANO Jewells A Good
SoAP. JohNsons BABY SoAP' (ONLY THe BesT)
    AfTeR A Good BoDY WASH IM DRessed ANO BRushed THe
TeeTH. iT's ABouT 6 AM...
    I BeGiN MY WAlKing uP + DowN + uP ANO DowN
    DROP. So PRess ups. ON + ON + ON + ON
I've GoT STeve AlleN oN L.B.C... WHAT A FucKinG LAugH He is
    All He Does is MOAN ANO Rip iNTo THe Celebs
He MAKes Me LAugH.. Cuz He's So HONesT.
    CRuel. COLD. ANO TRuTHFuL.
    THeN AT 7 AM ILL HAVe A BiT of NicK FeRRARi
        He KNows His CoNKeRs. (I Do Love A DeBATe oN THe RADio)

159

I Tell The Young Cons Who Write me.
  Log onto L.B.C. or TALK SPORT RADIO, or Radio (5)
  And Listen To ALL The DeBates. News. ect.
      Keep in Touch With The Worlds News.
  Dont Be Left Behind.
          Dont end up A Cunt.
              Coz You Will if You Just Watch Telly,
  Take Your Drugs and Pull Your Cock For 20 Yrs.
      Get into The News. DeBate it
  I Follow it ALL Me.
      From The Floods And Hunger in Bangladash
  To The Salt Mines in Russia.
      It ALL intrests me.
      I Love it. Coz im Still Apart of The
  Human Race.. Yeh.. in My own Little World'

      Anyway Some Official News Now.
          Exclusive
          Red Hot of The Press   OO
                                         v
                                         O

      Only The Facts of CHARLie Bronson
      The Truth..
  I've Got Soo All To Hide!
          Now Read This Load of Shit.

      Pure. Shit,

160

FORM COMP 1
PRISONER'S FORMAL COMPLAINT

Establishment WDCM
Serial № WO400IOF

Read these notes first

1. This form is for you to make a formal written complaint under the complaints procedure. Complaints should wherever possible be sorted out informally by speaking to your wing officer or making an application. Use this form only if you have not been able to resolve your complaint this way.
2. A written complaint should be made within 3 months of the incident or of the relevant facts coming to your notice.
3. Keep the complaint brief and to the point.
4. When you have completed the form, sign it and post in the box provided. The form will be returned to you with a response.
5. If you are unhappy with the response, you can appeal on a separate form (COMP 1A).
6. Some subjects are dealt with only by the Area Manager or Prison Service headquarters. If your complaint is about one of these subjects, the reply will take longer.
7. There is a separate pink form (COMP 2) for confidential access complaints.

Your details (use BLOCK CAPITALS) : FOR SECURITY GOVERNOR.

Surname	BRONSON	First name(s)	CHARLES ARTHUR
Prison number	A8076AG	Location	C.S.C. UNIT

Have you spoken to anyone about your complaint ? Yes ☑ No ☐
If so, who did you speak to ?

S/o AND GUARDS.

Your complaint

YESTERDAY 6/12/2010 ON MY BIRTHDAY THERE WAS A STORY IN THE DAILY MIRROR SAYING I WAS TO ESCAPE FROM MY CELL WINDOW, AND THE PRISON IS ON HIGH ALERT.
YOU KNOW AND I KNOW THIS PATHETIC STORY CAN OF ONLY COME FROM ONE OF YOUR STAFF.
THE MOLE WILL HAVE RECEIVED BETWEEN 2 AND 3 GRAND FOR THE LIES! AND YOU DENY ME ACCESS TO THE MEDIA, BUT YOU ALLOW THIS SORT OF TREACHORY TO CONTINUE —
WHY IS "NOTHING" EVER DONE TO STOP THESE LIE'S ?

Does your complaint have a racial aspect ? Yes ☐ No ☐
Is your complaint about bullying ? Yes ☐ No ☐

What would you like to see done about your complaint ?

I WANT A FULL INVESTIGATION, ASK THE EDITOR OF THE PAPER WHO FED THIS STORY ?
OR IS IT ANOTHER "CONSPIRACY" TO MESS UP MY 2011 PAROLE ?
(HOW CAN I EVER WIN WHEN I'M FOREVER STABBED —
— IN MY BACK ? ? (BY PARASITES)

Signed _____   Date 7/12/2010

VF 011 Printed at HMP Kingston 4304 03/2003

161

Response to the complaint *(including any action taken)*

HAVING READ THE ARTICLE YOU REFER TO IT IS
APPARENT THAT THE MAJORITY OF THE INFORMATION IS
HISTORICAL + CAN BE ACCESSED FROM A NUMBER OF
SOURCES, FURTHER-MORE, THERE IS NOTHING TO EVIDENCE
THAT THE INFORMATION ORIGINATED FROM A MEMBER
OF STAFF.

WHILST I REALIZE THIS TYPE OF STORY MAY BE
FRUSTRATING FOR YOU, I CAN ASSURE YOU THAT ALL
INFORMATION RELATING TO ALL OFFENDERS IS MANAGED
APPROPRIATELY.

Name in block capitals ▆▆▆▆▆▆▆▆ Position S/o

Signed ▆▆▆▆▆▆▆▆ Date 9/12/10

THERE YOU HAVE IT... BUT CAN YOU BELIEVE IT?
NOW SEE WHY I REALLY DONT PLAY THERE SILLY LITTLE GAMES.
THERE LITTLE POLITICIANS .. FULL OF SHIT
THEY LIVE IN A VERY FALSE WORLD.. A LIE
ANYBODY WITH A BRAIN KNOWS A SCREW SOLD THIS STORY
SO WHAT YOU MAY SAY
WELL IF IT WAS HAPPENING TO YOU FOR 30 YRS IT WOULD SOON
PISS YOU OFF.
I'M SICK OF IT?
I'VE GOT MY PAROLE HEARING IN MARCH NEXT YEAR
I DONT NEED THIS SHIT.
CUNTS
I HOPE THE SLAG WHO SOLD THIS CRAP GETS CRABS..
CUNT.

BIG FERDI LIEVELD ARRIVED AT LUNCH.
THEY BROUGHT HIM FROM FULL SUTTON SEG BLOCK.
A MOB OF SCREWS ALL IN STAB PROOF VESTS
I'VE KNOWN FERDI SINCE HE WAS ON REMAND AT BRIXTON
BACK IN 1988.
HE'S A BIG BLACK DUDE WITH A SHAVEN SKULL.
I WOULD SAY OUT OF HIS 22 YRS HE'S BEEN INSIDE.
3/4 OF IT HE HAS SERVED IN SOLITARY
I CANT COUNT ON MY FINGERS AND TOES HOW MANY
JAILS IVE BEEN IN WITH HIM.
FERDI IS A COOL CAT.
I SALUTE THE GUY.
A GUY YOU BEST NOT FUCK WITH.
GOOD ADVICE.
(TAKE IT OR LEAVE IT) OO

163

WHAT A GREAT VISIT .. ☺

SPENCER WILDER AND HIS SON DANIEL.

These are "Two" Who Were "BANNED" For NO REASON

AND NO REASON GIVEN . COZ THERE WAS NO REASON

CUNTS ...

THIS Is How it All WORKS .... its Run BY IOIOTS·

ANYWAY.. A SMASHING VISIT ☺

DANIEL is ONLY 15½ YRS OLD

6 FEET 2. AND 14 STONE... AND A BLACK BELT AT JUDO.

I Fucking LOVE HIM. RESPECT HIM, AND ADMIRE HIM..

WHAT A SON To Be PROUD of.

The BOXING WORLD LOOK OUT ?
WATCH THIS SPACE.

ONCE iM OUT ill BE iN HIS CORNER·
WATCH THIS SPACE ..

I SHOWED HIM SOME MOVES.. AND MY SPEED PRESS UPS·

ALSO A VERY IMPORTANT EXERCISE ON How To STRENGTHEN THE NECK

"ALOT OF FIGHTERS NEGLECT THE NECK"

You MUST STRENGTHEN THE NECK MUSCLES·

Your HEAD is HEAVY BONE..

A BIG DEAD WEIGHT ON YOUR NECK

Your Be AMAZED iN How HEAVY it is

So KEEP Your NECK WELL EXERCISED AND STRONG·

(TIP OF THE DAY)

OH ! THEY SAW THERE 1st CANNIBAL TODAY

BOB MAWDSLEY ôò

The BRAIN EATER·

You SHOULD OF SEEN DANIELS FACE ☺ WHAT A PICTURE.

164

I said Quiet.. "Look through that slit in the wall,
It's the cannibal out there in the cage.

Well.. It's not every day people get to see a raving
Lunatic is it?

That dont come no.. Madder than Bob.
He even looks the bollot-
eyes Like Satan.
Scary Movie Shit!

Yeh.. Great Visit... I Really enjoyed it.

Pizza + Chips for Tea. ☺
What a Day...

Oh. And Clem McNally moved to Whitemoor CSC.
He was only up Here For Accumulated Visits
Sadly the Snow stopped most of them
Nice chap Clem...
He killed his cell mate in Strangeways some Years Back.
Why? Fuck knows... Ask Him..
Who cares" Shit happens...

I called up Mum after Tea.
Had 10 min, then called Mal Vanga..
All in All a Great Day...
And a Pile of Mail ☺
I told You im a Lucky Bastard!
I was Born Lucky
The Best Part of MY Life is Yet to Come.
I cant Wait ☺
I get excited thinking about it.
But I get Angry over Cunts Like Peter Pickering?
Who? You may well ask.

165

I Bumped into Pidgering 30 years Ago in Broadmoor Asylum
The Monster From Yorkshire.
The Media Labelled Him "The Beast of Wombwell"
He Raped And Butchered A 14 Year old Girl.

But What Alot of People Dont Know. He served 7 years For
2 Sex attacts on Girls Before That Murder.

He's Just A FILTHY Monster.

Well! There About To Let Him out.
He's Now in His 70's

I Predict. He will Strike Again!
Once A Monster Always A Monster ".

WATCH This Space.

Yeh! I Remember at Broadmoor Telling Him....
"You So Much As look at Me And I'll Rip
Your Fucking eyes out "

"He Never Did"..
Well! Them Sort Are only Brave With Little Girls.
"CUNT "
_____

I'll Leave You With Another Fact.. O O
"Proof" Honesty

And Pure Bollocks ..

When You've Read This ..
Ask Yourself The Million Dollar Question?

WHY is CHARLie BRanson still Locked up?

IN THE CROWN COURT   T19990539
AT LUTON

                                7 George Street,
                                Luton,
                                Bedfordshire.

                          Thursday 17 February, 2000

                              Before:
                    HIS HONOUR JUDGE MOSS

                          R E G I N A

                               v

                       CHARLES BRONSON
                     (D.O.B. 6.12.52.)

MR. D. MCGONIGAL appeared on behalf of the Prosecution.

THE DEFENDANT appeared in Person

(Computer aided Transcript of the Stenograph Notes of
                  Barnett, Lenten & Co.,
       (Official Court Reporters to the Crown Court)
       Cliffords Inn, Fetter Lane, London, EC4A 1LD.
                  Telephone: 0171-405-2345

                          SENTENCE

                             167

Thursday 17 February 2000

2   SENTENCE

3   JUDGE MOSS: Mr. Bronson, please stay seated; there is no need

4   to stand up. I asked you before whether you wanted to be

5   represented when it came to the question of sentence, and

6   because you changed your mind at short notice during the

7   course of the trial before I ask you again: Do you want

8   to be represented?

9   THE DEFENDANT: It is quite old. Give me some more porridge.

10   JUDGE MOSS: You also understand that given the penalty for

11   false imprisonment, which effectively is at large --

12   there is no maximum -- that I have the power to impose

13   two forms of imprisonment: One would be a life sentence

14   and the other would be a determinate sentence. You would

15   have been told about that by those that advise you.

16   THE DEFENDANT: I know all about it.

17   JUDGE MOSS: I have in mind to impose a life sentence. I need

18   to know whether you want to say anything about that

19   before I do.

20   THE DEFENDANT: Why don't you shoot me.

21   JUDGE MOSS: Do I assume from that there is nothing you wish

22   to say?

23   THE DEFENDANT: Nothing at all.

24   JUDGE MOSS: So be it. It cannot be denied that in the past

25   you have committed serious offences, Mr. Bronson. You

26   have kept your word to me that you would behave during

27   this trial, and I appreciate that, because I asked you

28   earlier on and you told me that you would not misbehave

1   and you have not done so.

2   THE DEFENDANT: My word is all I have got, your Honour..

3   JUDGE MOSS: I respect that but I still cannot shrink from my

4   public duty which is to note that these are serious

5   crimes -- the false imprisonment, the sort of things you

6   have done before, and although nobody knows what is in

7   your mind your victims all share the same views, which

8   must be that their lives are about to come to an end,

9   because it cannot be denied on the evidence we have heard

10   from your past that you are dangerous and unpredictable,

11   particularly when you are upset and angry. In those

12   circumstances, all the criteria for a discretionary life

13   sentence are in place.

14   There is no need for me to get psychiatric

15   evidence because what I have heard about you on this case

16   and in the past -- self-harm -- indicates that whilst

17   there may not be a mental illness there is clearly a

18   continuing problem and the community at large, whether it

19   is on the outside or in prison, has to have some sort of

20   protection against you.

21   I appreciate that these offences being

22   committed within the prison have a different colour to

23   them but that does not mean that they are any less

24   serious; and so because all the criteria are in place for

25   a life sentence, and because I consider you will continue

26   to be a danger in the future because of your instability,

27   I have to pass a sentence of life imprisonment.

28   The determinate sentence I would have passed in

```
 1     the alternative would have been eight years so the
 2     specified period which I have to note and announce under
 3     the Crime Sentences Act, 1997, will in fact be _four_
 4     _years_.  Thank you, Mr. Bronson, that is all.
 5   THE DEFENDANT: Thank you, your Honour.
 6                  - - - - - - - - - - - - -
 7
 8
 9
10        AGAIN I REST MY CASE!
11        WHY AM I STILL IN PRISON. ?
12
13        THIS is 10 YEARS Ago.
14
15      I APPEALED. AND GOT IT KNOCKED DOWN To 3YRS
16
17        SO BY LAW I AM NOW 7 YEARS OVER
18      THE TARIFF!
19
20        IF THIS is BRITISH JUSTICE
21        THEN SUCK MY DICK.
22
23
24              AMEN!
25
26
27
28
```

CANTEEN TODAY. :)

eggs. HONEY. CHOCCIE. FRUIT. SAME OLD TREATS.
   A MAN'S GOTTA SPOIL HIMSELF.
IF AND WHEN HE CAN.

OUR DAY IN BROADMOOR ON CANTEEN DAY — I DIVED OVER THE
SHOP COUNTER AND GRABBED ALOAD OF PACKETS OF TUBACCO.
   I SOLD THEM TO THE LOONIES FOR BARS OF GALAXY (Big BARS)
2 BIG BARS FOR ONE PIT OF BACCA.
   CANTEEN DAY IS A "MASSIVE DAY FOR ALL PRISONERS
ITS THE ONE DAY WE TREAT OURSELFS.
   THAT IS IF YOUR NOT ON PUNISHMENT.
OVER THE YEARS I'VE PROBABLY SPENT MORE TIME ON PUNISHMENT
(So CANTEEN DAY IS EVEN A BIGGER TREAT FOR ME)

   IT'S OUR SHOPPING DAY :)

ITS BEEN ONE OF THOSE DAYS WHERE EVERYTHING GOES TO
CLOCKWORK.

      "ENJOYABLE"
      PEACEFULL.
         AND
      HAPPY.

I DONE MY HOUR ON THE MULTI. GYM
      'SLOWLY'
   I USED EACH EXERCISE AS A DYNAMIC.
   I REALLY FELT THE PUMP. UP.
THE VEINS IN MY BICEPS WERE THROBBING
      IT FELT GREAT.
'GOD'- IT SHOULD BE A CRIME TO FEEL SO HAPPY.

LIVER AND ONIONS FOR TEA WITH MASHED SPUD + CARROTS.
"LOVELY TRAINING GRUB"

AT 5.30. THEY STUCK THE PHONE UNDER MY CAGE DOOR
NOW DECISION TIME? WHO DO I CALL?

MUM' MAL' DAVE' MARK' LEIGHTON' JOHNNY
SANDRA' IFTY' STEVE' LORRAINE'

I CAN ONLY CALL.. WHOSE PASSED.
I WOULD LOVE TO CALL KENTUCKY. OR MACDONALDS.
OR THE LOCAL FISH N CHIP SHOP

SO I SAY TO MYSELF "FUCK.IT" ONE CALL
IM GOING FOR LORRAINE.

NOT A BAD DECISION

WHAT A LOVELY CALL. SHE IS JUST SO NICE.
I COULD TALK TO HER ALL DAY.
I WOULD LOVE TO BE WITH HER IN THE DARK
CHEWING HER EAR...

NO HARM IN DREAMING..

GOOD NIGHT. x

IF I DONT COME BACK
"CREMATE ME"
AND SPREAD MY ASHES OVER BROADMOOR.

172

"Snows Back". 2 little Pie wag tails walking in it Right
outside my window on the Yard, and leaving there little prints.
It's cold. But Beautiful ☺

The snow brings out the Magic of Life.
It would be Nice to Die in the Snow... "Shot"
So all the white turns to Red .. Dramatic
Thats the way to Die... in a Blaze of Flory.
It Beats Cancer.
    or a Massive Heart Attack as you sit on the Bog..
The Final Shit takes you out ... What a way to go ☺☺
    Thats How Elvis went.
So Many Die on the Bog.
        You Could Be Next.
        Reading my Book... on the Bog..
        How Fucking Sad can it Get...
Of all the Billions of Books. You Chose a Branson to
Die with. on a Fucking Shit Hole.
    Your Family and Loved ones will Hate me.
        "Probally Blame me"
If you Hadn't of Read my Book You May of Survived That
Heart Attack.
        But Then again. Why Didn't You Shoot it out And
Die in the Snow?

        Its a Crazy World.
    It's Saturday.. I'm Chilling out
        I'm so Chilled I Could Be a Polar Bear.
    "I'm Going Back To Bed..
        I've Got a Beautiful Dream To Finish off.

173

"Never let go, never give in.
  Swing away the blues.
Your heart may feel heavy
  Iron your shirt. Clean your shoes!
Rock 'n' roll around the clock
Some old tart sucks your cock.
Pull your socks up. Another day
The souls ablaze so they say.
You are what you are. Don't look back
A sawn-off shotgun in the sack
Wake up laughing every day
Hell on earth is here to stay!

          enjoy it...

  The rides insane it drives you mad.
All the good turns to bad.
  Tears turn to blood and flow away,
  Nightmares baby are here to stay!
Join the circus, the freaky show
  Paint your nose and watch it glow
The journey of madness will suck you dry
Born insane until you die.

21/12/2010

Fucking SNOW   Bleeding Weather!
It's STOPPED MY FAMILY XMAS VISIT.
        I WONT SEE MUM AND MARY NOW TILL NEXT YEAR.
Such is Life.
So I CALLED MUM AND SANG Jingle Bells ONTO HER ANSWER
MACHINE.
            SHOULD CHEER THE OLD Duchess up.

The CROSSBOW CANNIBAL Killer STEVE GRIFFITHS GOT
SENTENCED TO LIFE AT LEEDS CROWN COURT TODAY.
He MURDERED   SUZANNE BLAMIRES. SUSAN RUSHWORTH AND
    SHELLEY ARMITAGE
I KNOW A BILLY ARMITAGE.   He WANTS TO START PRAYING
BILLY is NOT A RELATION TO SHELLEY.
        COZ Bill WOULD NOT SLEEP TILL He SERVED THIS evil
CUNT UP.
    He ALSO ATE THE BODY PARTS.
            Sick BASTARD.

    Hes Now Boasting He WASTED ALOT MORE!
CUNTS LIKE THIS SHOULD Be HUNG.

        You THE TAX.PAYERS ARE NOW KEEPING HIM FED
AND CLOTHED FOR THE Rest of His Life
            HURRY UP AND Die   CUNT.

    ROSALYN EDMONDS HAD A LUCKY escape FROM His FLAT
She FLED AND TOLD THE OLD Bill.
    SO 3 CHEERS FOR ROSALYN. HIP HIP HIP HIP HIP HIP HORAY.
        ONE LUCKY WOMAN She is.

175

I CAN NOW GIVE YOU AN EXCLUSIVE.
The CANNIBAL is OFFICIALLY ON A HUNGER STRIKE.
So LETS ALL HOPE He DIES SOON ☆ Yippeeee.

BUT,
The JOKE is... MR STANBURY... GRIFFITHS LAWYER
is TAKING HIS CASE TO COURT OVER HUMAN RIGHTS ISSUES IN PRISON.
Do ME A FAVOUR.
HUMAN RIGHTS. WHAT HUMAN RIGHTS?
He's NOT A HUMAN...
AND HOW is He GETTING "LEGAL AID" TO FIGHT HIS RIGHTS?
IT'S A FUCKING JOKE.
He EATS WOMEN. CHOPS THEM UP. THEN FIGHTS FOR HIS
HUMAN RIGHTS.
WHAT ABOUT MY FUCKING RIGHTS ? OO

SOMEBODY WAKE ME UP AT HOME TIME.

GOT A PILE OF MAIL.
CALLED LORRAINE... SHE ALWAYS CHEERS ME UP.
I HAD LIVER + ONION FOR TEA. ☺ LOVELY.
I THOUGHT OF GRIFFITHS EATING THEM HUMAN LIVERS. OO
(I WONDER WHAT IT TASTES LIKE }

FUCK IT ... ILL SETTLE FOR A SLICE OF PUSSY. ☺
HOT, STICKY AND DRIPPING JUICE...
GOOD NIGHT!

PS
IN A RECENT MAGAZINE SURVEY WOMEN WERE ASKED IS YOUR CUNT STILL
SENSITIVE TEN MINS AFTER SEX: 98% SAID NO He's ASLEEP. OO

BRONSON BROADCAST.. "You KNOW WHERE I AM".

Woke up with a fucking throbbing stiffy OO
    WHAT A CRUEL WORLD
ALONE.. AND NOBODY TO SUCK IT.. It's REALLY EVIL.
WHAT A WASTE OF A GOOD HARD ON.

I'm GETTING FED UP OF No PUSSY ON THE MENU.

    Hey! Let's HOPE THE CANNIBAL DIES SOON?
        WHICH ONE? THATS A QUESTION.. THERE'S THAT MANY OF
THE FUCKERS HERE IN MONSTER MANSION.

THERE'S ONE OLD BASTARD HERE IN HIS 80' OVER THE HOSPITAL WHO
KILLED A WOMAN BACK IN THE 1960'
    HE CUT HER BREASTS OFF AND COOKED THEM.

        Sick TWISTED MOTHER FUCKER.

THERE ALL HERE..
    THIS PLACE IS A HEALTH HAZARD.
    You CAN BREATHE IN THE EVIL.

I'M A CELEBRITY GET ME OUT OF HERE.

    BIG ARGUMENT WITH Bob Maudsley TODAY
        NOTHING NEW
NOT A WEEK GOES BY WE DON'T HAVE WORDS.
    THE CUNT'S BEEN PISSING IN THE SHOWER AGAIN
        IT STINKS
I'M ONLY SAD I CAN'T BREAK HIS CANNIBAL JAW.
        "CRACK" - "PROBLEM SOLVED"
"UP ON A WING.. THE CHAPS WOULD BREAK HIS LEGS.
    DIRTY BASTARD
    SUCH IS LIFE INSIDE
        ONE MUSN'T GRUMBLE.

177

I SHAKED MY HEAD. READY FOR VISIT.
  AMANDA RICHARDSON is UP TODAY.

  SHE'S A CLASSY LADY
      EX-FORCES TOO. KNOWS HOW TO USE A RIFLE.
THESE ARMY BIRDS ARE A SPECIAL BREED.
      TOUGH COOKIES.

      I DONT THINK THEY GET ENOUGH RESPECT FOR WHAT THEY DO.
      I SALUTE THEM. BRAVE WOMEN.

AMANDA DONE A FEW TOURS OF NTH IRELAND IN THE TROUBLED
YEARS.
      So SHES LIVED THE FIGHT...
NOW SHES UP TO SEE HER OLD CHINA IN THE ZOO

      IT WAS LOVELY TO SEE HER.
SHE GOT ME TWO BANANA MILK SHAKES AND SOME CHOC BARS.
I SANG HER Jingle Bollocks AND WE HAD A GOOD CHAT.
      THAT WAS INFACT MY LAST VISIT OF ZOO.

          THANK YOU AMANDA. x

      AND I MUST ADD... FOR A MOTHER OF TWO, YOU ARE
  A VERY SEXY WOMAN. WITH A BODY TO GO TO WAR FOR.
FUCK ME.

      A GEEZER ASKS THE LIBRARIAN
          HAVE YOU GOT THE NEW SELF HELP BOOK FOR MEN
              _ WITH SMALL COCKS "?

  LIBRARIAN SAYS _ " ITS NOT IN YET "

  GEEZER SAYS .. " YES THATS THE ONE '

    HEY. LAST NIGHT I WENT DOWN ON MY GIRLFRIENDS MUM AND
  MY TONGUE STUD SNAGGED HER GENITAL PIERCING.
      TALK ABOUT PANIC. I WAS IN A RIGHT OLD FLAP!

      HE. HE. HE. HA. HA. HA. HE. HE.

AFTER MY VISIT I COPPED A WHOLE PILE OF MAIL.
MOSTLY CARDS
GET ON THIS LOT   OO

JOHNNY GRIFFITHS (NO RELATION TO THE CANNIBAL) BUT HE HAS BEEN KNOWN
TO CHEW A CLIT OR SIX.

Dessy Ludwick. Denise Briely. Redd Mentlos. Ian Frost. Stu Cheshire. Iffy.
Harif Williams. Al Rayment. Harriett Mather. Buckto. Lorraine
Dee Morris and Her Girls. Tony Fear. Steve Swatton. Paul Knight Paul Massey
Loram Smith. Juanna Jarvis. Gavin Moot. Helen Probert. Dave Taylor.
Kelly Byrne. Clare Raper. Harry Holland. Andy Corbishley.
Alexandra Riel. Ryan Dubois. Mickey Dunne. Teresa Eileen. Javed Zaman
Morgan Ralph. Carol McFadyen. Terri Barrett. Rachel Tarrant

            I'M SHOWING OFF NOW
      THERES MORE..   UNBELIEVABLE.

   Dan Wilder. Micky O'Hagan. Phill Doyle. Ferdi.   Kenny Lane
 (Al Rayment Two off Him) Colin Glynn and Dave. Leanne Mayers
   My Son Mike.   Graham Earl   Big H McKenny
   Carly Mathews   Sheri Ncole   Amy Johnson
   Lady Sara Jane   Chris Power   Di Brown

      Hey im Not Making This up.

  Sadly I wish I was Making The Next one up.

      Theres Always A Nasty one
          A Xmas Kick in The Nuts

It Happens every Year..
  It's To Crucify us.
      Make us Feel Shit.

      Well.. Fuck You
       I'm Rockin + Rollin
         All The Way To The Crematorium ⟶

Community Legal Service

LEGAL SERVICES COMMISSION
Special Cases Unit
3rd & 4th Floors Invicta House, Trafalgar Place,
Cheapside, Brighton BN1 4FR   DX:94310 Brighton
Tel:01273 878 870 Fax:01273 878 990

CHARLES BRONSON   *Monster Mansion. HMP.*
5 LOVE LANE
WAKEFIELD
WEST YORKSHIRE
WF2 9AG

002338

Our Case Reference Number :

Date :   16/12/2010

Dear . Bronson

Your Application for Legal Aid

Thank you for your application. After considering the information provided by you and your solicitor, I have refused your application for the following reason(s): it is unreasonable for funding to be granted as the prospects of obtaining a successful outcome in the proceedings, assuming the case were determined at trial or other final hearing are poor.

You may apply for a review of this decision by returning the attached form, together with the reasons you feel my decision is wrong, by 30 December 2010.

The attached information sheet explains the appeal process in detail, and includes guidance to help you write your application for review. We have also written to your solicitor and you may want to speak to them before you reply to us.

If you have any questions, please contact our Customer Service Team on the number at the top of this letter.

Yours sincerely

Director, Special Cases Unit

LET0A01A
LOUI-A
34049872

DSLSC012044-M6.P02/002338/01/16334-4

180

Community
Legal Service

Application to appeal a decision of the Legal Services Commission

APP9

Name: CHARLES BRONSON

Case Reference Number:

Does your appeal need to be dealt with urgently?	✓ Yes ☐ No

If you have answered yes, please explain why *INHUMANITY . BRUTALITY . NERVE GAS .*
STARVING ME . SETTING A DOG ON ME . UNTOLD YEARS of ISOLATION
No PROGRESS . BURIED IN A CAGE . NO HUMAN CONTACT . DENIED HUMAN RIGHTS

IF I WAS BLACK, MUSLIM, OR A FOREIGNER YOU WOULD NOT DARE DENY ME LEGAL AID ?

GROUNDS OF YOUR APPEAL

Please explain why you think our decision was wrong.

Our test for whether you should get legal aid depends on: how likely you are to win; how you will benefit; how much it will cost. Please try to show us how you think we were wrong about one or more of these.

If you can, point out where you think the reasons we gave are wrong.

If there is any information we do not have, which would lead us to make a different decision, please tell us what it is.

There is no need to repeat anything you have told us before or send us any of the information that we already have. It will help your appeal if the important facts and arguments stand out clearly. But please make sure that, if there is anything more you want us and the Independent Adjudicator to know about, you send it to us now.

Unless there are exceptional circumstances the Independent Adjudicator will consider your appeal by looking at the papers you and your solicitor have sent us.

If you think there should be a hearing for you to present your appeal to the Independent Adjudicator in person, please explain your reasons here. Hearings will only be arranged where the Adjudicator is satisfied that there are exeptional circumstances why the argument cannot be put in writing and the issues cannot be resolved without a hearing.

Signed _____   Date 23 / 12 / 2010

YOUR A TOTAL DISGRACE TO BRITISH JUSTICE

LET0A02S
LOUI-A
34049872

DSLSC012044-M6.P02/002334/01163472-4

181

Well... WHAT'S LEFT TO PROVE ?
   IT'S HERE IN BLACK AND WHITE FOR ALL TO SEE. $\frac{00}{2}$
I AM NOW DENIED ANY FORM OF JUSTICE.
  THIS IS HOW THE SYSTEM BURIES CHARLIE BRONSON.
THEY DON'T WANT TO SEE ME IN COURT,
   THEY ARE AFRAID OF BEING EXPOSED.

  MY CASE EMBARASSES THEM.
MY LIFE'S BECOME A PAIN IN THERE ARSE
   THEY HAVE CREATED SOMETHING THEY NOW CAN'T CONTROL.
  THEY FEAR ME
     WHAT NEXT ?

  WHAT ELSE CAN THEY DO TO SHUT ME UP
THEY STOP MY VISITORS, MY CALLS. MY MAIL.
   NOW MY LEGAL AID !

IF I WAS A WEAK MAN .. I WOULD RIP MY SHEET UP, AND
WRAP IT AROUND MY NECK AND CALL IT A DAY.
  NO-DOUBT MANY HAVE DONE THAT IN MOMENTS OF GLOOM.
 PUSHED TO THE LIMIT. DESTROYED.
 ME .. I GET STRONGER WITH EVERY KNOCK BACK
  THE YEARS OF HOPELESSNESS SEEM TO MAKE ME STRONGER.
THIS .. I PISS ON YOUR GRAVES.

  IF THERE IS LIFE AFTER DEATH .. BE CERTAIN OF ONE THING.
I'LL BE BACK TO HAUNT YOU FUCKERS UP IN YOUR IVORY
TOWERS WHO ARE FOREVER FUCKING UP MY LIFE.

   YOUR NOT MEN.
    MEN DON'T ACT LIKE THIS.
   YOUR A BUNCH OF FACELESS COWARDS
FROM THE JUDGES. TO THE PRISON H/Q.
   YOUR POWER FREAKS .. SICK TWISTED MOTHER FUCKERS.

You Live Today - Die Tomorrow. And Your Forgetten in No Time.
Your Lifes Are No Different Than A Machine.
> "Fuct off"

MAN Picks up CHInese Girl at Party And Takes Her Home.
    She says " Me so Horny. Me Do Anything For You."
He says . Howz About A **69**?
She says , You Fuct off . Me Not Cooking Crispy
— Duck in Black Bean Sauce at This Time of Night."
                    ☺ HA HA

The Mrs Has Just Come into The Living Room Wearing
A Little P.V.C Number , Fish nets . And High Heels.
Handed Me A Cold Beer And Told Me To Chill out,
Relax And When She Returns She'll give me What She
    Does Best ☺
    " I Fucking Love SHepHards Pie ☺

Went To See A Physic Last Weekenn,
    And She Told Me I'll Be Coming into Money !
Last night I Fucked A Bird Called Penny
    " SPooky or What ?   ☺

Since The Wife Went Senile All She Does is Stare Through
The Window .....
    Maybe one Day , if its Really Wet And Cold.
        Ill Let Her in . .   ☺ HA. HA

" I BRAKED HARD BUT STILL HIT THE CAR IN FRONT!
     A CUTE BLONDE GOT OUT AND SHOUTED —
          " RAM ME UP THE ARSE WHY DONT YA ".

" THIS YOUR HONOUR is WHERE THE CONFUSION BEGAN ☺️

HERES A FUCKING JOKE ☺️
          PETER BROWN LEFT HERE ON TUESDAY
     THEY TOOK HIM TO FRANKLAND JAIL. (UP IN DURHAM)
" TODAY... 2 DAYS LATER HE'S BACK!
     (I TOLD YOU). THIS SYSTEM IS FUCKING MENTAL..

                    ☺️

     SO WHATS THAT COST TO MOVE HIM UP THERE?
     A CAT A VAN. 8 GUARDS. PETROL. WAGES.
     THEN BACK AGAIN...

          NOW SEE WHAT I MEAN
          ITS ALL ONE BIG FUCKING JOKE!

     DID YOU KNOW I HOLD THE RECORD FOR MOST MOVES
     IN A SINGLE DAY. ③
     NOW HOW DOES A PRISONER MOVE 3 TIMES IN 24 HOURS?
               I DID ☺️

     IN THE 1970's AND 80's I ALWAYS MOVED STRAPPED UP IN A BODY—
     — BELT AND ON OCCASSION ANKLE STRAPS.
               THE GOOD OLD DAYS.
     YOU CANT BEAT A GOOD OLD FASHION STRAIT-JACKET FOR A
          LONG JOURNEY... I LOOK BACK AT THESE CRAZY TIMES AND
     I END UP LAUGHING OVER IT ALL... ITS NO WONDER IM INSANE ☺️

184

Clock this drawing? A screw done it for me in Woodhill
C.S.C. unit. **MR SHARPE**

Strange enough on our first meet we never hit it off.
I actually thought he was a pratt.
But I was so wrong.

Cor he is a diamond.
A top geezer.

It goes to show we all
make bad judgements on
our journey through life.

He actually drew it
whilst I was on a
visit with
Dee Murriss.
And gave me it,
after the visit.
Cheers mate ..

Sharpe (SHARPE)

KEEP FIT CHARLY
2010

OH Well ... CHRISTMAS EVE TOMORROW
I'm watching a film tonight with GERARD BUTLER in.
Called 300.
It's supposed to be good.

I'm off.
ADIOS AMIGO

stick the legal aid up your arse! stick the legal aid up your arse.

185

"CRIMBO-DAY"

2010

MONSTER MANSION

Jingle Bollox.
Jingle Bollot. ♫
Jingle ALL THE WAY - ♫

WOKE UP AT 7AM.
FUCKING FREEZING.
I SHOULD OF SHUT MY WINDOW LAST NIGHT.
TURNED ON HEART RADIO. SOME GOOD CHRISTMAS SONGS.
IT GOT ME IN THE MOOD.
I STARTED ROCKING AROUND MY PAD. NAKED
A QUICK STRIP WASH, BRUSH THE TEETH. AND DRESSED.
AT 7.38 AM. MY OUTSIDE DOOR OPENS. ITS Ms WALKER. SHE'S
GOT A SANTA HAT ON. HAPPY XMAS CHARLIE ☺
SHE'S A GOOD SOUL... ONE OF THE NICEST PRISON GUARDS I'VE EVER
KNOWN. SHE TAKES MY FLASK AND COLLECTS THE OTHER FLASKS.
I HEAR HER OPEN THE DOORS AND WISH THEM ALL A HAPPY
CRIMBO....
AT 9AM WE ARE LET OUT ONE AT A TIME TO COLLECT
OUR XMAS BREAKFAST.
THE ONLY COOKED BREAKFAST IN 365 DAYS

OH! I, GAVE A SCREW A 6 MONTH OLD ORANGE. ITS ROCK HARD
ALMOST WHITE. AND RATTLES WITH PIPS
AN ANTIQUE FUCKING ORANGE
WROTE IN BLACK INK HAPPY XMAS BOB. C.B.
THATS THE CANNIBAL MALLOSIES GIFT SORTED....
MAKE SURE THE CUNT GETS THIS GAFFA! CHEERS.
BREAKFAST WAS, BEANS. TOMATOES. MUSHROOMS. AND BACON
(NO POXY EGG) LAZY CUNTS.
AND HERES A PISS TAKE.... SOUP. YES. SOUP

186

How The Fuckt Can We Have Soup On Xmas Breakfast?
        Tomato Soup. But it was Delicious. OO

Big Robbi sent me up Some Nuts And Pies (He Always Does)
        He's A Top Geezer
At 10-30 AM Governor Cousins Done Her Daily Rounds
    I Told Her Some Fucker In The Kitchen is Taking The Piss
Sending us Soup out For Breakfast.   "#
        She says it was A Mistake OO   Hello.

    How Can They Send Soup As A Mistake?
        It's Hot. Boiled up
    It should be eggs. Not Soup.
        Would This Happen In The Hilton? or The Ritz?
        Would it Bollocks
        The Chef Would Be Sacked.   :OO:
Oh Well..... It is Christmas   (O)
        Good Will To All Men OO

Oh! Before I Forget I Did Watch 300 Last Night
With Gerard Butler In.
            "Not A Bad Movie
    It Would of Been Alot Better If I Was In It.
"My Sort of Movie That.
        But Lets Use Real Swords And Real Blood!
    Fight Till Death"
Could You Really See Gerard Butler Doing That?
    If He Met Me Down A Dark Alley He Would
Shit His Pants And Leg it.
    "People Forget" It's All A Big Act.
Fucking Rambo. Superman. There All Actors.
    ½ of Them Are Faggotts... It's True...

187

I STARTED ONE OF MY "ART CREATIONS" AT 11AM. WHILST
LISTENING TO L.B.C. "CRISTO" HE'S A GOOD PRESENTER.
GIVE HIM A CALL 0845 60 60 973 — THATS (0845).
TELL HIM I SAID. HE'S THE DOGS BOLLOCKS. O—
YOU CAN LEARN ALOT FROM THEIR TALKT SHOWS.
    ESPECIALLY WITH George Galloway. HE'S BRILLIANT.
HE WROTE A GOOD BOOK ON FIDEL CASTRO.
    "WELL WORTH A READ."

12. O CLOCK DINNER.
    AND IF I SAY SO MYSELF IT WAS LOVELLY. ☺
THE SCREW "HODGY" WAS SERVING IT.
    I'VE KNOWN HIM A GOOD 20 YRS.
I HAD ½ A CHICKEN. ROAST SPUDS. BRUSSELLS AND GRAVY.
PLUS A BOWL OF XMAS PUDDING WITH WHITE SAUCE.
    I'VE HAD ALOT WORSE I CAN TELL YOU.
MARKS OUT OF 10. (7) THATS FARE.
    "FILLED ME UP"
I WASHED IT DOWN WITH A PINT OF SQUASH.
    ALL IN ALL. NOT BAD.

I WATCHED ABIT OF TELLY.

A GREAT PROGRAMME CALLED "ONE BORN AT CHRISTMAS"
    XMAS BABIES BEING BORN.

I STOOD TO ATTENTION FOR 10 MIN AT 3 O'CLOCK TO
LISTEN TO THE QUEEN (MY LOVELLY LANDLADY) ☺
    "FUCK KNOWS WHY.. COZ ITS ALL SHIT SHE COMES
OUT WITH THAT DONT AFFECT MY LIFE.
    BUT. I BELIEVE IN SHOWING ABIT OF RESPECT.
"I WONDER IF SHE CAN SORT OUT MY LEGAL AID?
    THEN AGAIN WHY WOULD SHE WANT TOO. AFTER I'VE

Ripped off 9 of Her Roofs 😐

SORRY MAM. (SHIT HAPPENS)

NO CALL. OR EXERCISE FOR ME TODAY
        TOTAL REST
INFACT NO CALLS TILL XMAS IS OVER FOR ME
IVE SAID ALL I WISH TO SAY.
    I DONT INTERFERE WITH THERE WORLD AT XMAS
COZ THERE ALL PISSED. IM SOBER. IT DONT MIX.

I REMEMBER ONE XMAS IN FULL SUTTON IN THE LATE 1980's
I GOT PISSED OUT OF MY SKULL AND BROKE A GEEZERS JAW.
(HE COUGHED ON ME)..
    HIS BREATH STUNK.
    I CANT HANDLE. THAT SORT OF THING.
IF HE DONE IT OUTSIDE I WOULD OF KNEE CAPPED THE CUNT.

I REMEMBER A HOSTAGE I HAD IN WOODHILL Seg BLOCK
HE BROKE WIND IN MY CELL.
    FUCK THAT- IT FREAKED ME OUT.

I THINK ALL THE YEARS IVE SPENT IN SOLITARY HAS MADE
ME VERY SENSITIVE 😐
            THATS MY EXCUSE.

MY FAV CRIMBO INSIDE MUST BE WITH THE KRAY
TWINS IN PARKHURST IN THE EARLY 1970's
        FANTASTIC
    WE EVEN HAD VODKA.
THOSE SCREWS GOT RICH ON US.
    GREAT FUCKERS CHARGED AN ARM AND A LEG!
WHEN I LOOK BACK OVER THE YEARS I FEEL VERY PROUD

AND HUMBLED TO HAVE SHARED MY LIFE WITH SUCH LEGENDS.
IF NOT 'ICONS'
I'VE MET ONLY THE BEST.
SADLY SO MANY ARE NOW LONG GONE.. :(
         THAT SADDENS ME.

4-30PM TEA

    NOTHING TO WRITE HOME ABOUT
  ACTUALLY IT WAS PISS POOR.

ILL WATCH CORONATION ST. LATER
      AND   THE ROYAL FAMILY (COMEDY)
   ENDS AT 10 PM... MY BED TIME.
   SWITCH THE LIGHT OFF
   SWITCH MY RADIO ON

      FUCK OFF SANTA..
  WHO GIVES A FLYING FUCK.

         " ALWAYS REMEMBER THIS......
    ''
        MAN IS ONLY MATTER.
        MATTER ROTS AWAY.))

    2011 SHOULD BE A CRACKER !

            00
            ᵕ

            I WONDER.

29/12/2010

BRONSON A8076AG
C.S.C.. WAKeFIELD. HMP.
W·YORKS _ WF2 9AG

1st DAY BACK IN THE GYM TODAY SINCE THE CRIMBO BOLLOCKS.

NOT ENOUGH WEIGHT ON THE MULTI GYM FOR ME! I ONCE WENT 8 YEARS WITHOUT PUSHING WEIGHTS, THEN BENCH PRESSED 350 POUND 10 FUCKING TIMES ʻOOʼ !

STRENGTH AND POWER COMES FROM WITHIN. You've EITHER GOT IT OR You AIN'T!

Your BORN WITH IT... "it's TRUE".

GARY NELSON CHINNED A SCREW OUTSIDE HIS Cell TODAY! I WAS IN THE SHOWER AT THE TIME. ' FUCK ME'. THERE MUST HAVE BEEN 30 + SCREWS RUN ONTO THE UNIT.'

ABIT of EXCITMENT '. ☺
iT LIVENED THE DAY UP.

IT WASN'T A GREAT PUNCH COZ I SEE THE SCREW WALK AWAY.

NOT A MARK ON HIM.
GARY NEVER CAUGHT HIM RIGHT.
'LUCKY FOR THE SCREW..
COZ WHEN GARY HITS YOU
You NORMALLY STAY HIT.
AND DON'T GET BACK UP.:

'He MUST Be SLIPPING ☺ OLD AGE.'

191

I HAD A LOVELLY SHOWER. 'HOT'

But I Do Miss A Soak IN The BATH AND A Rub
DOWN... You CANT BEAT A MASSAGE AFTER A WORK OUT.
{ IT WAS CHIPS BEANS AND FISH Fingers ☺ }

Bloody DeLicious.

I Covered it IN DADDY SAuce.
AND HAD Loads of Bread.

WASHED DOWN WITH A Mug of TEA WITH A Spoon of
HONEY IN IT.

I MADE 3 CALLS... Mum." Lorraine.' AND Dave Taylor.
MUM HAD A Nice CRIMBI.

SHe HAD STEAK For Xmas DAY.

Lorraine ALSO HAD A Good one, But Misses Her LATE DAD.'
SHe Loved Him To BiTS 'I Dolized Him.'

But SHe Raised A Toast For Him With Her Mum
AND 2 BRoTHeRs.

THATS BRILLIANT.

Hey! it's 2011 SATURDAY

A BRAND NEW Year

it's ALSo CANTeeN TOMoRRoW...
LiFe's HAPPY.

ANother LuNATiC BReaks FRee!
THe SHeLL CRACKS.
LiFe Begins.
THe Journey of MADNeSS

DONT We JUST Love iT?

192

"DONT FORGET" IF JOUR INTO SOME GOOD SPORTS
CLOBBER LOG ONTO MY BRONSON WEAR SITE.
it's "QUALITY GEAR" ONLY THE BEST.
VERY BIG IN THE U.S.A. AND SPAIN.
DONT GET KNOCKED DOWN BY A BUS WITHOUT MY GEAR ON.
JOU KNOW iT'S THE DOGS BOLLOCKS.
IF JOUR GONNA DIE. THEN LEAVE IN STYLE!
WE DO A NICE JOCK STRAP TO. "PADDED LEATHER" 60
WITH STUDS.
LOVELLY JUBBLY

'00'

No. Letters Today ... 😞

Holiday spells Fuckt all that up.

When I think about it, my life's been letters.
One big letter...

I remember a screw in Wandsworth in the 1970's
coming to my door and flicking a letter in through
the gap.. (it landed on my piss-pot)

I shouted.. "Oy-Cunt"

He opened the door and I sparked him out.

"Bang"

That costme 180 days remission and 56 days
punishment.

"Worth it" 😏

Coz that letter was off my mother..

You never forget things like that... "You can't"

There memories.. stuck in your head.

"Forever" 😳

Even the bad times are good ...

Roll with it.

Enjoy it.

Have some fun.

2011 should be a cracker.
Pull it and hope for the best.

Give it your best shot.

30/12/2010

BRONSON A8076AG. C.S.C. WAKTo
'MONSTER MANSION'

GREAT DAY TODAY. ✓
GREAT WORK OUT. ✓
PLENTY OF GRUB. ✓
A PILE OF LETTERS. ✓

GET ON THIS LOT.

MUM. CARLY MATHEWS. LORRAINE. EILEEN RYAN.
LEANNE MAYERS. RICKY HANSON. GRAHAM ORMESHAW
             (↑ HE USED TO DO MY LAUNDRY IN LONGLARTIN)
GRAHAM BOND. JOHN WILSON. KIEREN GRIMSHAW. IFTY.
BERNIE SLATER. COLIN DUNN. KAYLEIGH + CHARLEY MORRIS.

THE ONE THATS BOLLOCKS IS YOUNG KIERANS LETTER
HE'S IN MARSHGATE JAIL IN DONCASTER
THE FUCKING RATS WONT ALLOW HIM MY SOLITARY FITNESS
BOOK..

WHY ? O͡O

COZ THERE CUNTS THATS WHY.
evil FUCKING CUNTS.
AND THEY WONDER WHY THEY GET A RIGHT HANDER.
                                    O͡O

KIERANS A YOUNG LAD, WHOSE BANG INTO HIS
TRAINING.
        SO WHAT HARM IS THERE IN WHY HE CANT
HAVE MY BOOK ?
      ITS A BLOODY INSULT TO ALL HEALTH + FITNESS
BOOK. ITS A FUCKING LIBERTY.

195

These Pricks Go on About Rehabilitation—
and Getting Youngsters off Drugs.
They Should Encourage The Youngsters To Get Into
a Fitness Regime
There is No - Better Than Mine.

Everybody Write To The Prison Governor
H.M.P. Yoi. Marshgate
Doncaster
DNS 8UX

Give Him Your Views..
Tell Him He's An Evil Swine.
Tell Him How You Feel About Him Denying—
—Kieran Grimshaw My Body.

These People Need To Know We Are Watching. oo
There Not Hitlers.
Whats Fucking Wrong With My Body?
Could It Be Jealousy? oo

The Lad Cant Get It Out of The Library.
Cant Have It Sent In.
Cant Buy It.   ?
Whats The Matter With These Muppets
Jeffrey Archer Never Had This Bollocks
Why Charlie Bronson :
Its A Serious Case of Victimization.

Miss Barter (A Screwess) Come over on This Unit Today
Shes A Lovely Lady.
Always Smiling.
Shes Probably Been Around The World Since Ive Been Here.
She Loves To Travel.
What A Great Tan Shes Got.   Good Luck To Her.

196

I ALWAYS TRY TO HAVE A LITTLE CHAT TO HER.
NOT ALWAYS POSSIBLE WHEN I'M UNDER SO MUCH SECURITY

IT'S HARD TO BELIEVE ... BUT IN THE 1970' AND 80'z
WAS AT TIMES ON A 12 GUARD UNLOCK. WITH A DOG. OO

IT WAS AT ARMLEY JAIL I LEAPT ON AN ALSATION WHEN
I WAS CUFFED UP..

MAD MEMORIES ...
BUT VERY TOUCHING.

THATS THE STORY OF MY LIFE ... MY WORLD ... MY JOURNEY.

"PURE INSANITY AT IT'S VERY BEST.

I HAD A SALAD FOR TEA ..
"SHIT"
"RABBIT NOSH."
AFTER YOU EAT A SALAD. YOUR STILL HUNGRY.

SO I HAD 10 SLICES OF JAM SANDWICHES.
WITH A MUG OF ROSY TEA..

I CALLED MY BROTHER AT 6PM.
AND MAL VANGA ... AND BIG GARY WHITE.
JUST TO WISH THEM A LUCKY NEW YEAR..

I JUST FOUND OUT IT WAS SANDRA GARDNERS SON
WHO DONE THE CROSSBOW CANNIBALS RAGE.
HE'S A TOP CRIME REPORTER FOR YORKSHIRE.

THE BEAST IS STILL ON HIS HUNGER STRIVE
"I'LL HAVE TO SEE IF I CAN HAVE HE'S FOOD.
" I'M STARVING.

I WAS ON A 40 DAY HUNGER STRIKE
IN WHITEMOOR JAIL IN 2004. I LOST 6 STONE. (NEVER AGAIN)

197

ITS A TERRIBLE . TRAGIC THING TO DO ...
WASTING AWAY.
"Fuck. THAT...
WHY DID I DO IT ? PROTESTING

← LOOK AT THIS CUNT FLYING !!
INSANE BASTARD'.

Well!

ANOTHER DAY OVER.
ALMOST ANOTHER YEAR.
TIME FLY'S WHEN JOUR HAVING FUN

OH! I SEE CATWEASLE TODAY (BOB MAUDSLEY) ON
THE YARD..
He's LOOKING OLD NOW.
GREY HAIR. BEARD. SKIN...
THE BACKS STARTING TO BEND.
EYES ARE DEAD.
WALKING LIKE A ZOMBIE.

DEAD MAN WALKING .
— — BREATHING .
— — DREAMING .
— — THINKING .

I WATCHED AN OLD BROADMUR INMATE DIE ...
He NODDED OFF IN A CHAIR AND NEVER WOKE-UP.
THATS HOW IT ENDS FOR SOME .
BORN TO DIE . BEFORE THEY LIVE.

GRACIOUS SENOR

" DONT euer BACK AGAINST me GETTING FREED" (YOU WILL LOSE).'

198

1ST.
JAN
2011.

BRONSON·A8076AG·
MONSTER MANSION.

THEY MOVED GARY NELSON YESTERDAY!
ONE GONE... FIVE LEFT.
     WHOSE NEXT ?
  ONE THING FOR SURE... IT WAS THE LAST MOVE
LAST YEAR ☺

     We ARE NOW INTO A NEW ONE...

          FANTASTIC

   I SAW THE NEW YEAR IN WITH JOOLS HOLLAND ON BBC2!
 I LIKE HIM... "DOWN TO EARTH.
GUTTED IM NOT ON A NORMAL WING SO I COULD OF
  SORTED A DRINK OUT.
        I NEED A GOOD PISS-UP.
      ITS YEARS SINCE I HAD A DRINK

   COME TO THINK OF IT A BIT OF PUSSY WOULDN'T GO
   A MISS EITHER.
 I SEE ANOTHER "SCREWESS" HAS BEEN SENTENCED TO 2YRS FOR
HAVING SEX IN A CELL WITH A CON IN BEDFORD JAIL ●●
       "DONNA STANTON". SHE ALSO GAVE HIM A MOBILE PHONE SO
 THEY COULD TALK DIRTY...
     "FUCKING HELL". WHAT AM I DOING WRONG ●●
  WHY CANT I HAVE SOME HUMANITY ?

199

LONG LIVE INSANITY.

FREE THE SOUL.

BROADMOOR ASYLUM

I HIT THIS ROOF
THREE GLORIOUS TIMES.
A WONDERFUL HAT-TRICK
LEMONS AND LIMES.

1984.

1983.

1981.

EVERYBODY SEEMS TO BE SHAGGING
APART FROM US LADS ON SECURE
UNITS...

BUT YOUR KEEP READING IT DONT
HAPPEN...

SO WHY ARE SO MANY SCREWS
LOCKED UP?

SCORES OF THEM...

DRUGS. SEX... PHONES.

FUCK ME GUYS.

HOW MUCH FOR AN AXE?
AND A 30 FOOT LADDER.?

SOMEBODY GIVE ME A BREAK!

I SEE BILLY TREEBY HUNG HIMSELF
IN HIS CELL AT ELMLEY PRISON ON THE 12TH DECEMBER.

A SAD WAY TO END 2010.

A CELL DEATH IS THE WORST SORT OF DEATH.
(UNLESS YOUR A NONCE)

ALL PAEDOS AND SEX MONSTERS SHOULD DIE IN JAIL.
THAT WOULD BE A GREAT JOB FOR ME.
"HANGING THE FUCKERS."

WHAT ABOUT THE SCREW AT BLUNDESTON JAIL
RICHARD STEBBINGS
HE'S JUST WON 5 MILL ON THE LOTTO!!!
"LUCKY BASTARD". oo

PROBABLY GET A 22 CARAT GOLD KEY AND CHAIN
AND GOLD STUDDED BOOTS..

FUCKING RETIRE YOU CUNT.
WALK OUT THE GATE AND DONT LOOK BACK I SAY!

Hey! HAPPY NEW YEAR EVERYBODY. ☺
I GOT UP AT 6.31 AM. FELT GOOD. HAPPY. FRESH.
I GAVE ALL THE LADS A SHOUT AT MIDNIGHT.
        "BARRING THE CANNIBAL"
    I MADE A MUG OF COFFEE AND TOASTED NEW YEAR IN.
OH. I HAD A MINCE PIE TOO.
THERE WAS SOME FIREWORKS GOING OFF OVER THE WALL.
    I COULD SMELL IT IN THE AIR.
THATS THE PROBLEM WITH JAILS IN TOWNS AND CITIES
    YOU CAN SMELL THE FISH N CHIP SHOPS ON A WINDY NIGHT.
AND THE CELEBRATIONS.
        "WHO NEEDS IT?"
    "SO CLOSE... BUT SO FAR AWAY" 😖
ON A SATURDAY NIGHT YOU CAN ALMOST SMELL THE PUSSY
DRIFTING IN THROUGH THE WINDOW.
        "IT'S FUCKING CRUEL"
    "HEY" JAN 30TH THERES A MASSIVE PROTEST
OUTSIDE THIS SHIT HOLE
        A FREE BRONSON CAMPAIGN.
BELIEVE ME THIS YEAR YOUR BE SEEING ALOT OF THIS!
    "MY FRIENDS ARE STEPPING IT UP.
        TURNING UP THE HEAT.
    BE WARNED PRISON H/Q.. YOUR BEING EXPOSED THIS YEAR.
    THIS IS BRONSON'S YEAR.
EVEN THIS BOOK THEY TRIED TO STOP.
    THEY EVEN STOPPED CHRIS COWLIN THE PUBLISHER FROM
VISITING ME. AND LETTERS I WROTE HIM. AND HE WROTE ME.
        "YOU GUTLESS. FACELESS. SPINELESS CUNTS"
THEY ONLY DO IT TO STOP THE TRUTH FROM COMING OUT.
    WELL IT DONT STOP CHARLIE BOY. FUCK ALL STOPS ME.

201

THIS is WHY THEY HATE ME!
   COZ THEY CANT ever BENT ME
THEY BURY ME IN THERE DEEPEST HOLE.
   STOP ME Seeing People. That FUCK WITH MY MAIL.
THAT FUCK WITH MY CALLS.
      AND I STILL OVER COME IT.
   "EVERY FUCKER HAS A PRICE"
      "Let's Leave it AT THAT FOR NOW ☺"

   I See ELTON JOHN AND His HUSBAND HAS GOT A
BABY 'OO'

   I TOLD You THE WORLDS GONE INSANE!
THIS is WHY I FEEL LOST.
   I DONT FIT IN NO MORE.
iTS ADAM + EVE FOR ME.
   NOT ADAM + STEVE Bollocks   OO
IF Your GAY THEN ACCEPT IT. You DONT HAVE BABIES,
   WHAT A SICK WORLD We LIVE IN.

iTS 2011 ☺   YiPPeeeeee

   Let's KICK SOME FUCKING ARSE!
KICK iT I SAID — NOT SHAG IT ☺

ONE OF MY BEST NEW Years WAS IN FRANKLAND
JAIL IN THE LATE 1980' WHEN I KIDNAPPED THE
   GOVERNOR ☺ 'WHAT A WAY TO START THE YEAR OFF.
iT DONT GET ANY BETTER.
ANOTHER GOOD MEMORY WAS IN WALTON JAIL LIVERPOOL
IN THE 80s WHEN I ROBBED THE CANTEEN ☺
   GREAT MEMORIES You NEVER FORGET.
   iT'S JUST BEEN A ROLLER COASTER.

Risley. Walton. Hull. Wakefield. Armley. Albany. Norwich.
Oxford. Bristol. Garthee. Leicester. Lincoln: Fullsutton.
Frankland. Durham. Dartmoor. Winchester. Camphill. Parkhurst.
Long Lartin. Whitemoor. Brixton. Scrubbs. Belmarsh. Pentonville.
Broadmoor. Rampton. Ashworth ← used to be called Parklane
it changed to Ashworth in 1982.

   Posh eh. Parklane. For a Criminal Lunatic Asylum :

It really as been a Mad Journey!

Some of these Jails Ive Landed in a Dozen or More
Times! I used to Move every Month.

   A Dozen Moves a Year was Regular for me
Thats why My Time's Gone So Fast...

Strong Boxes! Padded Cells. Strip Cells. Solitary. Cages.
   its Been Party to Party...
More Fun than You can Dream of.

   "Fun You May Well Ask"
Yeh Im Serious - "Ive Made it My Own Fun!"
And I Dont Regret a Single Day of it.
This is the Problem with Me. And The Penal System
           They Want me to Say 'Sorry'
   "Sorry for What?
        Me Sorry?
      Fuck. off...
What Have I Got To Be Sorry About?

        Are They Sorry?
   Sorry For All The Abuse And Brutality?
   Believe me Now... They Have Denied me The Basic
of Human Rights
   At Times Along The Way Ive Felt More Like an Animal.
I went 6 Years Without even Looking in a Mirror.

MY BEARD WAS DOWN TO MY BELLY BUTTON.
I ATE WITH MY FINGERS
I WORE NO SHOES.
THEY DENIED ME BOOKS, PAPERS, PENS.
THEY EVEN FUCKED WITH MY FOOD (SMALL RATIONS)

"COME ON. IS IT NO WONDER I KICKED OFF ?
WHY DO YOU THINK I TORE OFF 9 ROOFS ?
ITS FUCKING OBVIOUS WHY.

I WAS KICKING ARSE" PROTESTING
SHOWING THEM WHOSE THE DADDY oo

THATS WHAT THEY GET WHEN THEY FUCK WITH ME !

TROUBLE

So LETS DO A DEAL ..
I DONT SAY IM SORRY ... AND YOU DONT SAY YOUR SORRY.
LETS CALL IT A DAY ... AND LET ME FREE oo

MAKE SENSE ?

NOT TO THESE CUNTS IT DONT.
THEY WANT ME TO SUFFER ALOT MORE
BELIEVE IT

BUT I REFUSE TO SUFFER ALONE.
WATCH THIS SPACE ☺

So HOW DID I START MY 1ST DAY OF 2011 ?
I WOKE UP AT 6 AM AND LAY THERE THINKING oo
HELL" ITS 2011.
ANOTHER YEAR.

THERES A NICE COLD BREEZE COMING THROUGH MY WINDOW
IT FEELS GOOD .. EVEN NICER TO A GUY LIKE ME. WHOSE HAD YEARS
OF BEING IN BOXES WITHOUT WINDOWS OR AIR. I LOVE FRESH AIR.

IT MAKES A HUMAN FEEL HUMAN.
THAT IS UNTIL YOU HEAR THE JUDAS FLAP IN THE DOOR OPEN
AND THE EYE APPEARS TO CLOCK YOU.
THEN IT BECOMES A ZOO... THE HUMAN ZOO.
BEING SPIED UPON
LIKE A FUCKING APE IN A SCIENCE LABRATORY.
HEY! YOU KIDS IF YOU EVER READ THIS...
LEARN ONE THING FROM IT.
PRISON IS NOT COOL...
ITS INSANE.
AND IT MAKES YOU INSANE.
SO STAY FREE AND REMAIN SANE. OK!
PLUS IF YOU ENJOY PUSSY...
THEN YOU REALLY DO NEED TO GIVE MY WORLD
A BIG MISS.

I JUMP OUT OF BED. ABOUT 6.30 AM
IM STILL PISSING AT 6.33 AM
ONE OF THESE ELEPHANT PISSES
"FANTASTIC"
IT FEELS SO GOOD... WHY CANT IT BE ON THE FACES
OF THEM KRAUTS UP IN PRISON H/Q
WHAT WOULD I DO TO PISS ON THEM
WHAT WOULD THEY DO TO PISS ON ME
"SUCH IS LIFE"

I SHAKE MY COCK.
THAT LAST DRIP FEELS SO GOOD.
THEN I HAVE MY BODY-WASH.
I CALL IT THE BRONCO SHOWER.
BY 6.45 AM IM FIRING ON ALL CYLINDERS
"ITS PRESS UP TIME"

7-30 I feel Pumped up

IM often Asked - WHAT Do I THINK OF WHEN I DO MY
WORK OUTS.

ILL Tell You - I DReAM, it's ALL A DReAM.

I CAN Picture MYSelf Doing it iN A Field. OR A BeAcH
I feel Free - its MY Release - MY oNe JoY iN Life-

THATs How I Survive -

Without MY PHYSICAL Powers - I Would Find it Difficult To Go oN.

'SuRe' I will still suRvive.

BUT it Would Be So HARD

IM Blessed with STRENGTH

ANd it TAKes A STRoNg Willed MiND To HANdle
ALL THis SHit.

You Have To TuRN The NegaTive iNto A Positive
ANd MAKe it WoRK FoR You.

THATs How To GeT THRough A DAY iN Hell.
Do WHAT You Do BesT
'SuRvive'.

MY Doors UNLocked At 7AM. So I SHOT out FOR
BREAKFAST (exPecTing A TRADITioNAL FRY up)
ITs SHRedded WHeat. Billed egg ANd 4 BReAd RollS
I SQueezed AN exTRA egg
GoveRNoR BRowNes was There AloNe with 10 of His GuARDs.
He used To Be The UNiT Boss SoMe YeaRs BAck
I Found HiM To Be A FAiRe MAN. So I Wish HiM well
FoR 2011.

Where's The FRY-uP GoV? THis is Piss Poor.
I Would of RiPPed A Roof off FoR Less A Few YeaRs Back.

He AGReed. It was A PoiR BReAKFAST.

PRobAbly 'CoST CUTS'

'CUTS'

How Much Is A New Roof? "SHALL I?
WHAT A START To The YeaR THAT Would Be EH. C

BACK TO MY CELL. ENJOY WHAT IVE GOT:
STICK MY RADIO ON. AND RELAX.

THATS MY MORNING OVER...... SEE NO ONE. HEAR NO ONE. "PEACE",
(PEOPLE OUTSIDE WOULD PAY GOOD MONEY FOR THIS) "PEACE" NO HASSLE, NO WORRY.

NO NAGGING WIFE. NO BILLS. NO SCREAMING KIDS.
Who SAID THERE'S NO HEAVEN ☺

I THEN STUCK ON MY AL GREEN TAPE.
THE GREAT MAN HIMSELF.

CLASSIC SONGS. LETS STAY TOGETHER. TIRED OF BEING ALONE.
TAKE ME TO THE RIVER. IM STILL IN LOVE WITH YOU
LOOK WHAT YOU DONE FOR ME

I SALUTE THE MAN. SIR AL GREEN.
WHAT A SOUL MAN.. WONDERFUL.

I COULD SHAG ALL NIGHT TO THAT KIND OF MUSIC.
(TRY ME). IM NOT JOKING !! ☺

Lunch.

THATS MY BEST MEAL ILE GET THIS YEAR. AND I MUST
SAY NOW IT WAS FIT FOR A KING.

LAMB CHOP. BEEF SAUSAGE. 2 FRIED EGGS. CRINKLEY CHIPS AND PEAS.
I HAD 4 BREAD ROLLS, AND A MUG OF SWEET TEA.
THEN APPLE PIE AND CUSTARD. (2 LOTS)
NOW THATS WHAT I CALL SPOILING ME... Lovely ☺

I THEN HAD A LAY DOWN AND DRIFTED OFF INTO A NICE
STATE OF MIND. MEMORY LANE ☺

SOME NICE ONES. SOME NOT SO NICE. SOME JUST OUT
AND OUT EVIL.

LIKE THE TIME I COME OUT OF MY CELL IN PARKHURST IN 1976
WITH A BUCKET OF SHIT. AND TIPPED IT OVER A SCREWS HEAD.
"WOW". WHAT A KICKING I GOT FOR THAT CAPER.
I COULDNT WALK FOR A WEEK AFTER.

ONE OF MY BALLS WAS THE SIZE OF AN ORANGE ☺
AND THE TIME I ALMOST HAD IT THROUGH MY OUTER CELL WALL.
BRICKS WERE CRUMBLING OUT LOVELEY, I HAD MY ESCAPE ALL PLANNED

WHAT A FETE THAT WAS. THAT WAS UNTIL A CON CALLED FIELDING GRASSED ME UP. I LOST 180 DAYS REMISSION FOR THAT. HE LATER COPPED A 100 STITCHES IN HIS BOAT. "CUNT"

There's ALWAYS SOMEBODY WHOSE PREPARED To SELL YOU DOWN THE RIVER. "BE CAREFUL"
SOME WILL SELL THERE GRANNY FOR A SPOT OF PAROLE!

TEA WAS SHIT. "BACK To NORMAL".

I MADE A FEW CALLS.

AND THAT'S MY START To 2011.
HERE WE GO FOR ANOTHER YEAR OF MADNESS.
DON'T WE JUST LOVE IT.

FOR WHAT IT'S WORTH
TAKE THIS ONE BIT OF ADVICE, COZ IT WILL
SAVE YOU A LOT OF PAIN AND HEARTACHE.
IF YOU END UP IN JAIL OR THE ASYLUM, GO WITH THE FLOW.
DONT FIGHT IT. RELAX AND CHILL OUT.
COZ IT'S THE ONLY SURE WAY To WIN YOUR FREEDOM!
"IF YOU CANT OR WONT DO THIS...
THEN BEST YOU DO WHAT I'VE DONE.
KICK SOME FUCKING ARSE!
AND
"ENJOY THE RIDE To HELL...
BURN-LAUGHING.'

CAN YOU BELIEVE IT! FORD OPEN PRISON IN WEST SUSSEX
HAS KICKED OFF. 'A FUCKING RIOT'

IT'S A POXY CAT. D OPEN JAIL 😮

YOU DONT HAVE TO ESCAPE FROM THERE. YOU JUST WALK OUT !

THERE IS NO SECURITY.

THERES ABOUT 400 CONS THERE

ALOT OF THEM ARE LONG TERMERS. LIFER'S FINISHING OFF THERE
SENTENCES.

IT'S FUCKING CRAZY 😮

"IAN FROST" TOLD ME ABOUT IT WHEN I CALLED HIM UP
TO WISH HIM A LUCKY NEW YEAR.

IAN'S DOING ME A BIG FAVOUR IN MARCH
HE'S GOT A BOXING SHOW COMING UP.

I'VE SORTED IT FOR YOUNG DANIEL WILDING TO FIGHT
ON THE SHOW 😊

WATCH OUT FOR THIS YOUNGSTER...

I PREDICT HE WILL BE A CHAMPION LATER.

I ALSO CALLED LORRAINE..
SHE WAS OUT WALKING THE DOG.

I CALLED MUM. SHE WAS OUT. SO I LEFT A MESSAGE

I CALLED IFTY!

AND MY BROTHER MART.

(THEN MY UNITS RUN OUT)

IT'S BEEN A GREAT NEW YEARS DAY FOR ME..
ESPECIALLY THE LUNCH.

LET'S JUST SAY.. I'VE HAD ALOT WORSE!
AND NO DOUBT ALOT MORE WORSE TO COME 😳

'HOPEFULLY NICER ONES TOO 😊'

Well..
    it's 9.30 PM.
        IM CALLING it A DAY 🙂
    But ILL Leave You WITH one THought!
"
    Would You RIOT IN AN OPEN JAIL ? "

        "ONLY A COMPLETE CUNT Would!
    WHY RIOT WHEN You CAN WALK OUT!

        Believe me NOW
        (IT Would of ONLY Been A HANDFULL)

    CONS serving A Long sentence Would Not of
    Wished To Get Mixed up IN THAT.

        Something Like THAT Would Put THERE Release Back
    Years..

        THe Lifer's WILL Suffer over THAT.
    AND THAT's WHAT I Keep on SAYING To THe LADS.

        Be PREPARED
        (ANYTHING CAN HAPPEN ANYTIME. ANYPLACE)

    Fudt Me... it's ONLY 1st JAN 2011 AND we Have
    A RIOT ALREADY 🙂
        YiPPPPeeeee! YARHHHooooo!

6.1.2011

BRONSON A8076AG. CSC.
MONSTER MANSION

I TREATED MYSELF TO A TIN OF STEWING STEAK
£2.8sp A Fucking Go.
The SCREWS HEATED IT UP FOR ME, AND I HAD IT FOR TEA
"BLOODY DELICIOUS"

I CALLED MY BROTHER UP... SAD NEWS.
TRACEY His ex WIFE'S GOT A BRAIN TUMOR.
He's BEEN UP THE HOSPITAL ALL DAY.
WHAT A START TO THE NEW YEAR

TRACEY + MARK USED TO VISIT ME IN ASHWORTH ASYLUM
BACK IN THE 1980'
SHE'S A LOVELY SORT.
The MOST BEAUTIFUL eyes THAT SPARKLE When SHe SMILE
I Do HOPE SHe WILL PULL THROUGH IT.
I BELIEVE SHe WILL.
{ JUST A FEELING }

Rocky EGG"
EXTRA HARD BOILED

Rocky

IT's WHY I ALWAYS Tell feople.
Live Your LIFE LIKE ITS THe
LAST DAY.
"ENJOY LIFE."
Coz TOMORROW IT CAN ALL STOP.
A FLICK OF A SWITCH ...
"DARKNESS".

211

MARKYS Re Booked OUR Visit FOR FEB 1st
So ill SEE HIM AND MUM THEN.
SOMETHING SPECiAL FOR FEB... ☺

I ALSO CALLED MAL VANGO. He DOes A GREAT JoB ON THE
BRONSON WEB Site.
He TELLS ME THERE'S LOTS OF PEOPLE NOT HAPPY ABOUT THE
LATEST BOLLOCKS ON MY LEGAL AID KNOCK BACK.
ALL SAY WHAT I SAID ... IT'S A DISGRACE
AN UNJUST ACT.
THERE CAN BE <u>NO JUSTICE</u> WithOUT LEGAL AID.
Fucking HYPOCRITES.

I TOLD MAL MY NEW YEARS RESOLUTION.
To Go ON MARGARINE.. LURPAKS To EXPENSIVE ☺
SO MY NEXT RUMBLE WILL BE MARGE...

HEY... "FANCY A READ OF A REPORT THATS FOR
MY PAROLE HEARING iN MARCH?

Your Love THis oNe ..
ONCE YOu've READ IT ASK YOURSELF ONE <u>QUESTION</u>!!

" WOULD You TRUST A PSYCHOLOGIST?
ESPECIALLY ONE WHOSE PART OF THE PENAL SYSTEM.

<u>OO</u>

I WOULD SOONER Go 15 ROUNDS WITH ROCKY EGG.

I GUESS IM FROM THE OLD SCHOOL OF MANKIND.
" DON'T TRUST OUTSIDERS
AND
STAY WELL CLEAR OF HEAD SHRINKS   OO
                                    n

212

SENTENCE PLANNING AND REVIEW REPORT BY PSYCHOLOGIST	SPR E

HMP Wakefield	12th November 2010	
Charles ARTHUR	BRONSON	LiFE

BT1314/A8076AG	Category A

I am a Senior Forensic Psychologist at HMP Wakefield and have worked for HM Prison Service since July 2000. I am a Chartered member of the British Psychological Society and a Registered Psychologist with the Health Professions Council. I have over 10 years experience of working with high risk sexual and violent offenders and am a nationally trained facilitator and supervisor in the Core, Adapted, Extended, Better Lives Booster and Healthy Sexual Functioning Sex Offender Treatment Programmes. I am also trained in a number of risk, cognitive and personality assessments, including the WAIS-III assessment, the HCR-20 tool (Webster et al 1997), the Violence Risk Scale, including Sex Offender version (VRS and VRS:SO Wong and Gordon), the Psychopathy Checklist-Revised (PCL-R Hare) and the International Personality Disorder Examination (IPDE Loranger 1999).

KNOWLEDGE OF THE PRISONER

I have been working in the Exceptional Risk Unit of the Close Supervision Centre (CSC) at HMP Wakefield since August 2003 and am currently the Lead Psychologist for the unit. Prior to this I was the designated Psychologist for the Healthcare and Segregation units. Since 2005 I have been the designated psychologist for Mr. Bronson whilst he has been located at HMP Wakefield. Within this role I attend multidisciplinary reviews and regularly discuss Mr. Bronson's case and observed behaviours with wing staff, wing managers and departments such as Education and Probation. I also have knowledge of Mr. Bronson's case through one to one intervention work, which Mr. Bronson has engaged in at various times, although this engagement has fluctuated, and as yet no specific assessments or intervention work have been conducted. I have compiled various reports for Mr. Bronson over this period, including Sentence Planning reports (e.g L. Homer 4th October 2007), Category A reports and previous parole reports (February and October 2008). I will seek to provide a summary of the information contained in these reports below, as well as providing an update on Mr. Bronson's behaviour since his return to HMP Wakefield.

Mr. Bronson was convicted of the offences of threats to kill and false imprisonment at Luton Crown Court in February 2000. Whilst at HM Prison Hull, he took an art teacher hostage because of comments he had made about a poster Mr. Bronson had designed. Mr. Bronson was originally sentenced to a tariff of 4 years; however on appeal in May 2001 this was reduced to 3 years.

Mr. Bronson has previous convictions recorded against him dating back to 1964, beginning with offences of stealing. He was initially dealt with by way of community orders, although in 1974 he received a 7 year prison sentence for offences of robbery, aggravated burglary, assault with intent to rob and possession of firearms. It is noted that during this sentence Mr. Bronson received a consecutive period of 9 months imprisonment and was detained at Broadmoor following another offence of violence. He was released in 1987 and then again sentenced in 1988 and given a further period of 7 years imprisonment for an offence of robbery. Mr. Bronson was again released in 1992 but was arrested in 1993 for further offences of grievous bodily harm and carrying a firearm. He received a custodial sentence of 8 years, which is when his index offence was committed. During this sentence he has also accumulated additional sentences and adjudications for incidents of attempted and actual hostage taking and aggressive and disruptive behaviour, including staging rooftop protests. As such he has spent a significant amount of his prison sentence in Segregation and Special Units. In February 1998 Mr. Bronson was received into the Close Supervision Centre (CSC) system, and in May 2002 was accepted into the Exceptional Risk Unit at HMP Wakefield.

RISK ASSESSMENT

Triggers for Mr. Bronson's violent behaviour have previously been identified through activity assessments using the risk assessment principles of the HCR-20 as a framework (L. Homer 14/11/05) as well as a functional analysis of a specific incident when Mr. Bronson attempted to take a Governor hostage in1994 (completed as part of individual session work with Mr. Bronson). The identified triggers include;

> Perceived rebuffs/knock backs/inability to get his own way
> Unrealistic expectations of the system/perceiving that the unit is stopping him from progressing   *IT Is AND HAS DONE FOR YEARS.*
> Perceptions that people are disrespecting/insulting/criticising/humiliating/ridiculing/taking liberties
> Perceived challenge to status and identity
> Perceived lack of response to requests/demands
> Seeing self as the victim and blaming 'the system' for this
> Situations that trigger feelings of upset, anger, disappointment, annoyance, frustration, tension, stress, anxiety, paranoia
> Disturbances to routine, e.g sudden regime changes, visits delayed, cancelled, delay in mail, no access to gym/exercise
> Association with other prisoners, particularly those he fears/does not like

THE ONLY HUMAN I FEAR is MYSELF."

Static risk:
As indicated above, due to Mr. Bronson's fluctuating level of engagement, no formal assessments of risk have yet been completed. Mr. Bronson has consistently been encouraged to engage with the CSC Forensic Psychological Risk Assessment process, which will assist in identifying static risk as well as assessing his current risk and specific personality traits. *EVERYTHING I SAY THEY TWIST.*

Dynamic risk:
A number of factors known to underpin use of violence that are relevant to Mr. Bronson have been identified and are documented in previous reports. These include;

- History of previous violence, including history of hostage taking
- Personality disorder   *YeH: AFTeR 36 YRS OF BOLLOCKS WHO WOULDN'T*   *?*
- Lack of insight
- Poor emotional control

- Hypersensitivity/over reaction to events/circumstances/individuals
- Negative rumination/brooding
- Instrumental use of violence
- Need to exert control
- Attention seeking/media interest . *You Fuckers Need To Stop That.*
- Violence supportive attitudes
- Hostile bias/perceived disrespect
- Difficulty inhibiting aggression

Further assessment and exploration of Mr. Bronson's thoughts and feelings and lifestyle has been deemed necessary in order to understand more about his beliefs and motivations for using violence, and identify specific areas of treatment need. *Fuck off*

In addition, his previous behaviour and presentation suggest that there may be underlying personality issues that could potentially heighten Mr. Bronson's risk. The ongoing assessment process that has been recommended will assist in providing further information about such factors. *I will never divulge where I buried my loot*

Protective factors

Consideration has also been given to factors that may prevent or reduce the risk of Mr. Bronson behaving violently. These have included at different times;

- ➢ Good relationships with certain staff
- ➢ Engagement in physical activity
- ➢ Appears settled on the unit
- ➢ Wanting to progress/'change his ways'
- ➢ Clear structuring of expectations/definition of progress
- ➢ Current environment – no association with other prisoners/high staff: prisoner ratio *And 30 years of isolation in a coffin.*

EVIDENCE OF RISK REDUCTION/CONTINUED RISK

As detailed above, Mr. Bronson's engagement with Psychology has consistently fluctuated. An analysis of his pattern of engagement indicates that he initially expresses motivation to engage with assessment work/reports, continues with this engagement for a relatively short period of time, then withdraws from this engagement when he has not liked the content of sessions or feedback from reports, citing it is "not for him". He subsequently re-engages, usually following a specific incident which has tended to involve risk-paralleling behaviours. This pattern is also consistent with his engagement with Psychology at other establishments, as well as other agencies including Probation and the Mental Health In-Reach team. *OO*

Examples of previous risk paralleling behaviours whilst located at HMP Wakefield are well-documented in previous reports and include;

- Going out on exercise and refusing to return inside. During this time Mr Bronson smeared himself with butter, tore his T shirt and made a bandana and wrist straps, and had to be removed by Control and Restraint teams.
- Spitting at a member of the Dedicated Search Team
- Continuing to 'goad' another prisoner on the unit by whistling/shouting inappropriate comments *Fuck me. Britains Most Dangerous Man is whistling OO*

143

- Responding to 'goading' behaviour by another prisoner on the unit
- Shouting/inappropriate behaviour towards unit staff and Governors, e.g during CSC Care and Management plan reviews and parole hearing
- Asking for another unit to be opened for him and other Exceptional Risk offenders
- Negative response to Probation reports/feedback
- Responding negatively when things are not as he wants/expects, *OO*

In addition, Mr. Bronson's profile within the media has been maintained by both himself, e.g release of books, sending out of artwork, and his family/supporters, e.g dedicated website, staged protests etc. In 2009, a feature film was released about Mr. Bronson, which had been approved by him, and which he had contributed to by meeting with the actor portraying him in the film. This indicates a continued need for Mr. Bronson to achieve status. *No¯. it's ABOUT EXPOSING You PARASITES .*

Following the release of the film, and consistent requests by Mr. Bronson to be allowed the opportunity to demonstrate he had changed, Mr. Bronson was relocated to HMP Long Lartin, and subsequently HMP Woodhill. Following initial periods of compliance, there were significant further risk-paralleling incidences, including; *PROGRESS MOVE DONT TAKE THE PISS .*

- refusing to leave his cell, and having a Control and Restraint team enter his cell, and remove him from the exercise yard (Long Lartin). During this time he also engaged in an incident of self-harm, cutting his upper arm with a blade, which staff then entered the cell to remove *THE ONLY WAY To GET THEM To UNLOCK MY DOOR*
- assaulting the Number One Governor at Woodhill, *He DESERVED IT .*
- destroying and damaging property in the CV room at Woodhill
- attacking a prison dog and the dog handler at Woodhill *THE DOG ATTACKED ME .*
- making threats to take a hostage and 'get' several Governors at HMP Woodhill, including threatening to cut the Unit Governor's eyes out.
- exercising naked in his cell. *So WHAT ? I'M A NUDIST .*

There were also concerns that his behaviour with staff fluctuated between him being agitated and calm depending on who he was talking to. For example, overall he was observed to be interacting well with wing staff, laughing and joking with officers, and focusing his frustration on unit managers and Governors. Other behaviours included him ripping up his OASys report, and reacting negatively when told he could not pass newspapers, which resulted in him trying to isolate Senior Officers from the staff team.

Due to the seriousness of the above incidents, Mr. Bronson was returned to the Exceptional Risk Unit at HMP Wakefield, where he acknowledged to unit staff that he *OO* thought he might be "ill" and "it might be time to think about going back to Broadmoor". This suggested some ability to reflect on his behaviour and initially Mr. Bronson appeared to be accepting some personal responsibility for his behaviour and presented as contrite and willing to engage with the multidisciplinary team to explore his behaviour.

He initially attended initial Care and Management planning meetings and engaged positively, expressing a desire to 'change his ways and get help'. He attended the first session with Psychology with a list of assessments, asking for them to be completed "as soon as possible". When we explored that these were the same assessments Mr. Bronson had previously given informed consent to undertake in 2006, he expressed surprise, saying "so I've wasted all this time (not doing them)". It was agreed that we would begin

144

with a cognitive functioning assessment, as Mr. Bronson had been engaging with the Mental Health In-Reach team, and it was felt that this would complement the work/assessments he had been discussing with them. However, despite asking questions in passing the day before and telling me he was "ready for it, bring it on", when I attended the unit to administer the WAIS-III assessment, unit staff informed me that Mr. Bronson had changed his mind, and did not want to engage. The reasons for this remain somewhat unclear, as staff observed some apparent anxiety from Mr. Bronson on the morning of the assessment, from the way he was asking questions of them about what it involved. However, when seen at his door by myself, Mr. Bronson did not acknowledge this, saying "it's just not for me" and citing other issues he was having on the unit, including feeling that his visits/mail had been "messed with". Since this time he has subsequently withdrawn from other members of the multidisciplinary team, and his Care and Management planning meetings. *You cant even sort your own lifes out let alone mine* ☺

His behaviour on the unit has also deteriorated, with him continuing to perceive that his visits and mail are being "messed with", and being verbally abusive to another prisoner on the Exceptional Risk Unit over the issue of phone calls and visits. He also behaved in a verbally aggressive and challenging manner when interviewed by the police over the incidents of violence whilst at HMP Woodhill. Most recently, on the 12th November 2010, following a period of time when Mr. Bronson had challenged the Director of the High Security Estate when he visited the unit, and told staff that he "wanted a rumble", he proceeded to enter the gym enclosure as part of his daily regime, tell staff that they "had a problem", and engaged in very similar behaviour to previous incidences, e.g producing some butter and smearing it over him, taking off his T-shirt and ripping it to make a bandana and wrist straps, and telling staff to 'come and get him'. Prior to him being removed by the Control and Restraint team, Mr. Bronson was overheard making threats to take a hostage, and "the next one (I take) I'll kill".

This all suggests that Mr. Bronson's triggers to violence and ability to manage his emotions and use of violence remain relatively unchanged, and that there is a high level of continued risk. This concurs with previous observations and assessments of Mr. Bronson's level of insight and motivation which have placed him largely in the 'precontemplation' stage of change (Prochaska and DiClemente 1982), in that he does not really see the need to change his behaviour, and his awareness and insight into his risk factors is limited. It should be noted that these continued incidences of violent behaviour are occurring in controlled environments that are designed to reduce the likelihood of individuals behaving violently by limiting their exposure to potential situations that could trigger violence. It should also be noted that other known ameliorating factors for violence such as age are not impacting upon Mr. Bronson's capacity for violence, something that he himself acknowledged on his return to HMP Wakefield.

RECOMMENDATIONS

Further work on exploring the factors that underpin Mr. Bronson's behaviour, particularly his use of violence and aggression, and developing his insight into these factors continues to be needed in order for significant reduction in risk to be demonstrated. An integrated way of working involving a multi-disciplinary team approach has previously been recommended and in my opinion remains the most appropriate way of working with Mr. Bronson alongside ensuring he is appropriately located in an environment that can effectively manage his level of risk.

145

It is anticipated that this will assist in developing Mr. Bronson's motivation and readiness to engage in assessment and intervention work and eventually address risk factors associated with his use of violence. Mr. Bronson is encouraged to re-engage with the CSC multi-disciplinary team and the CSC Forensic Psychology assessment process in order to be able to explore and address his use of violence and identify the most appropriate intervention work to develop alternative ways of dealing with risky situations. Given Mr. Bronson's continued engagement in violence and other risk-parallelling behaviours over the last reported period, in my opinion he is appropriately located in the Exceptional Risk Unit of HMP Wakefield, and therefore not suitable for open conditions or release.

	Signature	Date
Senior Forensic psychologist (Manager E)		29/11/10

IN THe FRee WORLD I WOULD NOT ACT THiS WAY.
COZ I WOULD Be FRee OF ALL THiS SHiT.
NOBODY OUTSIDE WOULD Be WANTING TO CONTROL MY LiFe.
MY MiND. MY SOUL.
    I WOULD Be iN CONTROL OF Me!

MY PROBLEMS ARE THe SYSTEMS DOiNGS...
    iT'S A FuckiNG Big GAME TO THEM..
        MY LiFe is BeiNG SUCKED iNTO OBLiViON.
        ANOTHER DiMENSiON.
        ANOTHER WORLD..

THESE PSYChOLOGY FREAKS DONT eXiST iN MY WORLD.
    'ReAL MeN'. DONT eNTERTAiN THEM.
    'ReAL MeN'. MOVE ON ALONE.
    THEY BLEED iN THe DARK
        ROLL ON TO THe NEXT CHAPTER
    PSYChOLOGiST'S CANT HELP A MAN LiKE Me.

THEY JUST MAKE THINGS WORSE ..

There only good AT WORKING WITH PAEDIS . AND SEX BEASTS
AND SILLY PEOPLE ..

I'M NOBODYS PLAY-TOY .

I BELIEVE IN PUNISHMENT .
The Birch .
Hanging
AND ONCE A WEEK Hidings .. OO ' BRING IT ON !

LOCK US UP . AND GIVE US FUCK ALL .
We DESERVE NOTHING

ONLY A RELEASE DATE ..
I HAVE SERVED MORE THAN ENOGH TIME
IT'S NOW HOME TIME ...

YOU CUNT'S HAVE HAD MORE THAN YOUR POUND OF MEAT
FROM ME ...

WAKE UP AND SMELL YOUR OWN SHIT . OO
The WRITINGS ON THE WALL .... IN BLOOD ..

CAPITAL LETTERS ...

BRONSON IS N0 . LONGER A DANGER TO THE LOVELY
BRITISH PUBLIC ..

HE'S AN ARTIST . POET . AUTHOR . SINGER . WHO THE FUCK
ARE YOU ? OO (I KNOW WHO I AM)

YEH .... WHO ARE YOU FUCKERS ?
GO PLAY GAMES WITH THE MONSTERS .
DROP ME OUT OF IT .

219

AFTER THAT PILE OF SHIT - LETS MOVE ON TO BETTER
THINGS.
MY SISTER LORRAINE IS MOVING BACK TO ENGLAND FROM SPAIN. :)
SHES BEEN OUT IN THE SUN FOR A GOOD 5 YEARS.
     SO SHES BACK IN MARCH FOR GOOD :)
NOW THAT'S GOOD NEWS....
     COZ IT'S NOT BEEN THE SAME WITHOUT HER.
          PLUS WE DRIFTED APART
     SHES A GOOD SOUL..
WE WAS LIKE TWINS AS KIDS.
I USED TO LICK HER FACE AND SUCK HER TOES :)
  ONLY LORRAINE COULD SHARE MY PINEAPPLE CHUNKS
AND BITE INTO MY TOFFEE APPLE.

          SO IM WELL CHUFFED MY SOUL TWIN IS BACK IN
     MY LIFE.
ON THE COUPLE OF OCCASSIONS I'VE COME CLOSE TO DEATH.
     IT WAS HER FACE I SAW THAT SEEMED TO BRING ME BACK.
     WE HAVE A VERY EERIE BOND.
        A TRUE SOUL SISTER IN MY HEART.

          SO THANK'S FOR RETURNING TO LIGHT UP MY WORLD
                                        :)

     I DONT MISS ALOT.. BUT ONE SMILE FROM HER SETS
ME UP BIG TIME :)

        ALSO MY OTHER LORRAINE IS UP TO VISIT ME ON
     SATURDAY :)
        SHES ALSO SPECIAL TO ME.
IVE JUST HEARD ON THE NEWS LONDON TRAINS ARE ON
ALERT FOR TERRORIST ATTACKS :)
        ' FUCKING WANKERS '.

220

Lorraine has to get the Kings Cross train see!!

Let it be known now ...

If any of my family or close friends were to be blown up by a bunch of fucking cowardly terrorists

I would go on a mission in prison and take out as many of the scum I could ..

That's a promise.

Cuz prisons are full of the fuckers.

Gutless. spineless cunts .

Hey! and they all get legal aid to fight for there human rights

They bomb our country and people up
Then the tax payers cough up for there rights.''

You fucking mugs
It's time you British people wake up.''

Jeff ...
Times flying ..

Coronation St. is on in ½ hour ☺
So ill sort a mug of tea out ready
And I've a cheese roll ☺

'Never had it so good have I?

Adios . Amigo

I WAS UP AT 5 AM .. FUCK KNOWS WHY.
I LAY THERE TILL 5.30 AM 'THINKING'
    JUST DEEP IN THOUGHT.

Life ... WHAT THE FUCK AM I SERVING LIFE FOR?

5.35 AM I HAD ONE OF THE BEST SHITS I'VE HAD FOR AGES
'WHAT IS IT ABOUT A SHIT?'
WHAT A WAY TO START A DAY.
I FELT LIGHT, FAST. READY FOR ANYTHING. ANYBODY.
        'BRING IT ON'

BY 6 AM I WAS STRIP WASHED, DRESSED. AND BRUSHED THE TEETH.
BY 6.30 AM I HAD POLISHED OFF 800 PUSH UPS AND 200 SQUATS.

    LORRAINES UP TODAY ☺
I FUCKING LOVE HER.
        SHE'S SO SPECIAL.

    TALL. ELEGANT. SMART. FUNNY. CHEEKY AND SO LOVELY TO
LOOK AT.

    IT WAS SNOWING LAST NIGHT.
    SHE ALWAYS COMES WHEN IT'S SNOWING
            'SNOW WHITE'
FOR FUCK SAKES DONT BRING THE 7 DWARFS.

222

AT 2.15 PM I'M ESCORTED TO THE VISIT ROOM "THE ZOO"
LORRAINE'S IN THE NEXT ROOM AT 2.18 PM.
   SHE LOOKED SMART. LIKE A BARRISTER.
3/4 LENGTH SKIRT. STOCKINGS WITH A SEEM DOWN THE BACK
A LOVELY WHITE SILK SHIRT.
         SHE HAD MY WHITE GOLD RING ON.

   OH! DID I NOT SAY
        I'M GETTING MARRIED ☺

   I'M SERIOUS... WE ARE TO MARRY..
   I JUST TOLD HER STRAIGHT.. "WE ARE TO MARRY.
      IT'S FATE.
      IT'S MEANT TO HAPPEN
      IT WILL HAPPEN..

   NOT YET! IT CAN'T HAPPEN YET.
   I WANT OUT OF THESE CAGES. ✓
   I WANT OUT OF THESE C.S.C UNITS ✓
   I WANT TO BE IN A LOW CATEGORY PRISON ✓

         "THEN WE MARRY FOR REAL"

      I CAN'T FUCKING WAIT.
         I LOVE WEDDING CAKE." ☺
   AND OUR CAKE WILL BE AWESOME.
            "BELIEVE IT"

      I LOVE HER.
      I LOVE BEING WITH HER
      I LOVE EVERYTHING ABOUT HER
         SHE'S A VERY SPECIAL LADY.....

223

Guess WHAT?
LORRAINE'S GOT A 5½ INCH TONGUE..
AND I've SUCKED IT THROUGH THE BARS.
    IT TASTES LOVELLY. ☺
LIKE A FRESHLY BAKED APPLE PIE.

'ANYWAY'.. YOU NOW KNOW WHO MY FUTURE WIFE IS..
ALL YOU BIMBOS WHO SEND ME YOUR NAKED PHOTOS AND FILTHY
LETTERS PLEASE STOP.

    YOU KNOW HOW I AM.

    ONE WOMANS MORE THAN ENOUGH FOR ME.
MY WONDERFUL LORRAINE LOOKS AFTER MY NEEDS.
                    ⁻ THANK YOU ⁻
                    ⟍⟍⟍⟍⟍ X

    DO YOU KNOW SOME WOMEN RUB THERE PUSSY FLAPS ON
THERE LETTERS TO ME "
    AND TELL ME TO LICK IT?
WHATS THE PROBLEM WITH GIRLS TODAY?
    THATS NOT LADY LIKE is it?
                    " OR IS IT?

    MAYBE IM OLD FASHION...

AND WHILE im LICKING IT ·· WHAT ARE THEY UP TO?
        SUCKING SOME COCK...
    THERE SURE NOT WAITING LOYALLY FOR MY COCK.'
" ANYWAY ' IT STOPS NOW ··

        IM A MARRIED MAN ☺
        IM TAKEN... THANKYOU.

224

A GREAT VISIT. A MAGICAL DAY
   ONLY GUTTED I CANT HAVE LORRAINE IN
MY BED FOR THE NIGHT.
     "FUCK ME. SHE'S HOT.
   LOVELLY LONG LEGS.
   SHORT BLACK HAIR.
     SLIM NECK.
     LONG FINGERS.
   A 5½ INCH TONGUE.

          "COME-ON"
WHOSE A LUCKY GEEZER? ☺

CHEESE SALAD FOR TEA.
   I ATE IT WITH A SMILE.
IM HAVING AN EARLY NIGHT TONIGHT.
     IM CUTTING OFF
IM LISTENING TO HEART RADIO WITH MY WOMAN.
   (AFTER IVE CREATED HER AN ART)

     ADIOS . AMIGOS .

   Long Live SANITY

225

COPY

Dated 31/12/2010

To: THE DAILY MIRROR

Sent via email: iftkhar@live.co.uk

jeremy.armstrong@mirror.co.uk

Without Prejudice

Dear Jeremy Armstrong
Re: Daily Mirror Publication 06 12 2010 'Bronson's Monster Mansions Escape Bid'
Since reading the above article, we the extended family of Mr. Charles Bronson has been in a state of disbelieve and shock, deeply offended and distraught by its inaccurate fictional content.

It is my opinion that eighther, you have not took in to consideration, the detrimental impact, this could have on many lives or you have no consideration, for the many consequences of your actions, least of all given the already difficult visiting rights been restricted or altogether stopped.

To this end I am very keen to ask for a detraction of your report together with an apology.

This type of article serves no other purpose but to make the lives of many people increasingly more difficult.

To make up story's about a human being who is unable to voice his side of the true facts, is not conducive of fair journalism.

Has a reporter you do have a duty of care and no one is immune to liable actions being taken and proved. Certainly at the very least reputations for delivering factual reports could may well suffer has a result

I can not express enough the consequences of your inaccurate report, upon the already difficult and strict procedures with which we have to contend with.

I am led to believe that mine and my children's human rights, may well be infringed upon should it come to light, that rejections of my children's visiting rights have resulted based upon your report.

Given the massive knock on effect that could possibly arise from your article I once again ask you to withdraw your comments

Awaiting your response in this regard has a matter of urgency
Yours Sincerely

Mr. M.Iftkhar
11/1 2011

BRONSON A8076AG CSC
MONSTER MANSION

I GOT THIS SENT iN TODAY FROM IFTY.
He NEVER LETS ME DOWN. (IF) ONLY 'EVERYBODY WOULD DO
THIS SORT OF THING.... THE LiBERTiES WOULD SOON STIP.

226

THANKS IFTY MY BROTHER.
"SALAAM"
BY THE WAY. He's A 'REAL MUSLIM
A TRUE SOUL.
MOST MUSLIMS ARE DECENT People.
REALLY GOOD TO KNOW.
They HAVE GOOD QUALITIES.
I HAVE MANY MUSLIM BROTHERS.
ESPECIALLY OUT IN PAKISTAN.

ASK IFTY WHY?
He WILL TELL YOU.
NOT MANY People KNOW WHAT I DO.
YOU'D BE AMAZED IN WHAT I HAVE ACHIEVED
FROM INSIDE THIS COFFIN.
"TOTALLY AMAZED"

IT EVEN SHOCKS ME AT SOME OF MY FETES."
(IT'S REALLY NOT FOR ME TO SAY)

BUT I CONTINUE TO DO WHAT I DO
FOR THE PAKISTANI People.

COZ I LOVE THEM. OK!

I CALLED 'IAN FROST' TONIGHT.
He's PUTTING MY FIGHTER DANIEL WILDER ON HIS FIGHT
NIGHT IN MARCH ☺ DOWN IN BRIGHTON.

I'M BUZZING
IT'S OUR 1ST FIGHT ☺ MY LAD IS FIGHTING UNDER ME
"HOW PROUD AM I?"
IT'S ON... READY TO RUMBLE ☺☺

227

I GOT A PILE OF MAIL..
AND LOTS OF NEWS.
THERE'S ANOTHER MOVIE BEING SHOT ABOUT MY LIFE.
    MICKEY DUNNE HAS JUST CONFIRMED IT
  " I KNOW FUCK ALL ABOUT IT"
     SO I HOPE I'M GETTING A SLICE OF THE DOSH !
IF NOT ILL BE KNOCKING ON SOME DOORS LATER . OO
        " DON'T BE GREEDY LADS.
      REMEMBER I'M AN OLD DUCHESS OUT THERE.
    AND A WIR TO BE
     PLUS THINK OF MY PENSION ? 'OO' NOT FAR OFF .

LOOK AT THESE DAFT CUNTS

    WHAT SORT OF CUNTS LET A MAN WRAP THEM UP ?
      THERE ONLY BRAVE HIJACKING A PLANE FULL OF
      WOMEN AND KIDS.
            IN MY CELL THEY SHIT-IT

NOT SO BRAVE NOW.
YOU FUCKING SPINELESS CUNTS..
ANY FUCKER CAN HIJACK A PLANE
FULL OF WOMEN + KIDS
NOW YOUR UP AGAINST
      ME...

SADDAM HUSSEIN
WASN'T SO BAD.
THIS GUY IS NUTS.

WHY
ME

PRISON PROPERTY

HMP BELMARSH

PROPERTY

BELMARSH
1996.
" THE IRAQI
HIJACKERS
ARE
HIJACKED.

YOU COULDN'T MAKE
THIS SHIT UP.

MY SON Mike WROTE .. HE's WRITING A BOOK HIMSELF ..
SHOULD BE A GOOD READ..

Coz HE's BEEN TO HELL AND BACK ON SMACK.''

SADLY HE ENTERED INTO THE DRUG WORLD AND GOT CAUGHT.''

MAYBE HIS BOOK CAN HELP THE KIDS STAY CLEAR OF IT.'

LETS BE HONEST -- DRUGS ARE FOR MUGS''
            " DRUG MUGS"
            Fucking IDIOTS ..
LAZY, GUTLESS. TREACHEROUS, LYING CUNTS ...

MY SON is CLEAN NOW
        So HE's NO LONGER A CUNT.
            I LOVE HIM x

        GOOD LUCK SON.

LEANNE MAYERS" is DOING OKAY.
        SHE's A LOVELY GIRL.
        NEARLY FINISHED HER SENTENCE NOW.
    I DO HOPE SHE CAN TURN HER LIFE AROUND
        I ONLY WISH I WAS OUT FOR HER RELEASE.
        Coz I WOULD SORT HER OUT INTO SOME BIZZ
        SHE NEEDS A BIT OF SUPPORT ..

MUGGY PROBATION PRATTS DONT DO IT.''
    THEY DONT BUNG HER A FEW QUID WHEN SHES SKINT
            I FUCKING DO'

IM ACTUALLY ALL SHE's GOT.
        ITS FUCKING TRAGIC.
All SHE's EVER HAD IS ABUSE FROM PEOPLE.
                            CUNTS.

229

STEVE SWATTON POSTED ME IN SOME POSTCARDS.
CHEERS BUDDY.

AMANDA SENT IN SOME LOVELY PHOTOS OF HER HOUSE.
SHE'S EVEN GOT A PIANO.

YEP... I'VE HAD A CRACKING DAY.

APART FROM HANIBAL CANIBAL SHOUTING THE ODDS
I HAD TO PUT THE EVIL CUNT IN HIS PLACE.

OH. PETE BROWN HAD THE HOMICIDE MOB UP TO QUESTION HIM
ON MORE MURDERS FROM NOTTINGHAMSHIRE.

"AS IF PETE GIVES A FLYING FUCK...
HE'S SERVING 40 + YEARS..."

WE'VE HEARD A WHISPER DANNY SONNEX MAY SOON BE
COMING HERE FROM LONGLARTIN
HE IS CHARGED WITH TAKING A SCREW HOSTAGE.
"FUCK ME". HE'S ALREADY SERVING 2 LIFES...
"YEH... HOW DOES ANYBODY SERVE 2 LIFES?
DO YOU HAVE TO DIE... AND RETURN?

HEY. YOUR FUCKING LOVE THIS...
DAVID CHAYTOR THE M.P. WHO COPPED 18 MTHS JAIL
LAST WEEK.
HE'S IN WANDSWORTH JAIL... AND CRYING ABOUT
HE CAN'T HAVE A CHINA CUP TO DRINK HIS TEA...
THE CUNT FIDDLED 22K OF TAX PAYERS MONEY AND HE'S

Moaning over a china cup ...... "Cunt"
I'd give him one ... "in his face.
I'd cut his nose off and make him eat it.

"What a prick"
I bet all I've got he gets out in no time!!
He won't serve it all...

He looks what he is ... "A snake"..

Oh well. I've had my lot for today!
Time for bed ..

"One last thing." Stay well clear of my Lorraine –
or face me later. in a very dark alley.

when you hear the –
– chain saw start up.
Your legs will be off
2 seconds later..

Amen.

R.I.P.

Charlie Bronson.
aka
Mickey Peterson.
aka
Ali Charles Ahmed.
aka
Robin Banks.
6.12.52 ..... ?

Who was he.?

Then I'll
bash your
skull in
with your
legs.

Stay well clear
of my wife.

Amen

231

13.1.2011

BRONSON A8076AG
C.S.C.
MONSTER MANSION

I'M STANDING AT THE WINDOW. HAVING A CHAT
TO ROBBIE STEWART WHOSE ON THE YARD.
JUST PASSING THE TIME OF DAY.
I SLUNG HIM OUT ONE OF MY "ECLAIRS"
SO WE ARE BOTH CHEWING ON A LOVELY SWEET.
    MY OUTSIDE DOOR OPENS..
    THE SCREW SAYS...
        "MR MCALLISTER IS HERE TO SEE YOU."

YES YOU MAY WELL ASK WHO?
    I'LL TELL YOU..

HE'S THE EVIL CUNT WHOSE BEEN MAKING MY LIFE
A STRUGGLE "OO"

I CALL HIM. THE PIG WITH NO ANSWERS

HE'S COME UP FROM PRISON H/Q.
    HE'S IN CHARGE OF ALL MAX SECURE PRISONERS
        HE'S GOD
HIS DECISIONS BURY US.. OR FREE US.

ME.. HE BURIED ME LONG AGO.

I WALKED UP TO THE CAGE BARS..
    CHEWING ON MY ECLAIR
I LOOKED HIM IN THE EYES.. AND LET HIM HAVE IT.
    A MOUTH FULL OF SWEET JUICE AND SPIT.

I watched the brown liquid drip down his face.
Into his mouth.
    Into that evil lying mouth of his
        Thats all he's worth to me. "Spit"
If I had known he was outside my door I would of
    shit in a marvel tin and covered him with it.
    I lost 3½ stone down to him in one dungeon.
    I almost lost my sanity "again" down to him in another
    dungeon.
        Its pure fucking hate between him and me.
    I could easily pour acid into his eyes and laugh as
    he screams in agony.
    I could rip out his heart and feed the crossbow
    killer it.
            I fucking hate him.

    He's like most MP's. "Smug cunts".
    Hiding from the truth.
            Lying through there teeth.

        Teeth (if) only this cafe door was open.
                I would smash the fuckers out.
    What a day.
            My fucking head is bursting

                    "Cunt"

F1127A - NOTICE OF REPORT
COPY FOR PRISONER

Charge number 403134

First name(s) .... CHARLES .... Surname .... BRONSON ....

Number .... A8076AG ....

You have been placed on report by .... SENIOR OFFICER ....

for an alleged offence which was committed at .... 10:20 hours on .... 13/01/11 .... (date)

at .... CELL 06 CSC .... (place)

The offence with which you are charged is that you:

RULE 51, PARA 1
COMMITS ANY ASSAULT

Contrary to Rule .... 51 .... Paragraph .... 1 .... Prison / ~~YOI~~ Rules

(Delete as appropriate)

The report of the alleged offence is as follows:

AT APPROX 10:20 ON 13/01/11 AT CELL 06 ON THE CSC YOU, CHARLES BRONSON A8076AG, SPAT THROUGH YOUR CELL DOOR INTO THE FACE OF MR [REDACTED]. IT WAS AT THIS TIME THAT A SMALL AMOUNT OF SPIT LANDED IN MY LEFT EYE AND DOWN THE SIDE OF MY FACE. THIS CONCLUDES MY EVIDENCE.

Signature of reporting Officer ....

Your case will be heard at .... AM .... hours on .... 14/1/11 .... (date)

You will have every opportunity to make your defence. If you wish to write out what you want to say you may ask for writing paper. You or the adjudicator may read it out at the hearing.

You may also say whether you wish to call any witnesses.

This form was issued to you at .... 17:30 .... hours on .... 13/1/11 .... (date)

by .... (name of issuing officer - block capitals)

OR016 Printed by HMP Albany

234

F1127 C   What happens when you are put on report

1. The Prisoners' Information Pack and the Adjudication Manual (Prison Service Order 2000) give guidance on report procedure. You may ask to see a copy. If you think you need more advice, ask an officer. You will find paper attached to this page. Think if you want to call any witnesses. You may also ask to see any statements submitted in evidence.

2. The person hearing the report (adjudicator) will ask you if you have received this form showing the charges against you and if you understand what will happen during the hearing.

3. The adjudicator will read out the charge(s) and ask if you understand them.

4. The adjudicator will then ask you:

- If you have made a written reply to the charge(s) (see over the page)

- if you want any additional help at the hearing. This could be legal representation, legal advice or a friend. The adjudicator decides whether or not to allow you to have any of these. If s/he refuses the hearing will go ahead and you should be ready for this. If s/he agrees the hearing will be adjourned while you contact a solicitor. The Legal Services Officer can help you;

- if you want to call any witnesses, and if so whom. You can ask for witnesses later but if you give names now the adjudicator will have more time to find them and call them to give evidence. Remember that other prisoners cannot be compelled to give evidence.

5. The person who reported you will give evidence. You can ask relevant questions.

6. Any witnesses in support of the charge will then give evidence. You can question them. Do not argue with witnesses. If you cannot ask the right questions to bring out your point ask the adjudicator to help you.

7. The adjudicator will ask you to explain your behaviour. You can do this by speaking to him and you can also read out any written statement or ask the adjudicator to read it out.

8. If you wish to call witnesses, ask to do so and say who they are, even if you have already named them. Say what you believe their evidence will prove. If the adjudicator thinks they will be able to help to explain what happened they will be called.

9. You and other present can ask the witness relevant questions.

10. Whether or not you have called witnesses, you can now say anything further about your case, comment on the evidence and point out anything you think is in your favour.

11. The adjudicator will tell you if s/he finds the charge proved or is going to dismiss it.

12. If the adjudicator finds the charge proved (guilty) s/he will then ask you why you think you should be treated leniently. You can ask for someone to support your plea for leniency.

13. A report on your behaviour in prison and your adjudication record during this time in prison will be read out. The adjudicator will ask if you have anything to say about the report and any questions.

14. The adjudicator will announce the punishment(s) for each charge. If you do not understand how the punishment will affect you ask the adjudicator to explain.

15. The adjudicator may adjourn the hearing or bring it to an end at any time, for example, to await the results of a police investigation or for a key witness to be present. You will be told why.

16. You will be handed a form F256D at the end of the hearing or soon after. This will give you details of your punishments and tell you how you may ask for a review if you think you have not been treated fairly. You will then be returned to normal location unless you are being segregated under Prison Rule 45 or YOI Rule 49.

PRISONER'S STATEMENT

You may use this sheet if you wish to make a written reply. **Please ask** for more paper if you need it.

FRIDAY. 13TH. JAN 2011

IT WAS A BRILLIANT SHOT.
IT GOT McALLISTER SMACK IN THE BOAT
ALL He DESERVED.
IM AS GUILTY AS ADOLF HITLER.

"SADLY"

I AM GUTTED SOME FLEW OFF HIS SPECS
AND HIT SENIOR OFFICER CURRIE

I FEEL VERY BAD OVER THIS. COZ I WOULD NEVER
EVER HARM ANY FEMALE

I HAVE TO MUCH RESPECT FOR WOMEN.

SO FOR THIS . I TRUELY APOLOGIZE.
I HAVE SPOKEN TO HER. AND SAID SORRY.

SHE KNOWS IT WAS A TOTAL ACCIDENT.
(IT WILL NOT HAPPEN AGAIN)

BEST McALLISTER STAYS AWAY FROM MY CAGE DOOR.
COZ I HATE HIS GUTS.
AND He HATES MINE.
(ITS PERSONAL)

HOW TO ASK FOR A REVIEW OF YOUR ADJUDICATION

If your Adjudicator was a District Judge

If you, or your solicitor on your behalf, wish to apply for a review of the punishment a written request must be sent to the Governor within 14 days of the completion date of the adjudication.

In all other cases

If you are not satisfied with the outcome of your adjudication you may:

Complain about the findings and/or punishment by completing an ADJ1 Complaint form.

You may also contact your solicitor for advice.

You should note that if your case is taken up by your solicitor, MP or any special interest group it will still go through the same complaint procedure although you do not need to complete an ADJ1 complaint form.

You may write to the Prisons and Probation Ombudsman when the Complaints procedure has been completed.

If you have recieved a punishment of additional days you may subject to conditions apply to have some of them given back.

Note: You must make your complaint within 6 weeks of the completion date of the adjudication.

I WONT BORE YOU WITH WHAT PUNISHMENT I GOT
I ONLY WISH IT WAS 6 OF THE BIRCH.
"REAL PUNISHMENT"
BLOOD.
PAIN.
SCARS.

I FUDTING LOVE IT..
BRING IT ON..

PRISON TODAY IS FOR FAIRIES.
"BELIEVE ME".

"HEY". NOW FOR A LITTLE TREAT :)
HERE'S SOME RECENT 1ST TIME CORRESPONDENCES.
JUST TO GIVE YOU A TASTE..
MY BROTHER MARKS GOT SACKS FULL OF THEM.
"THOUSANDS". FROM ALL OVER THE WORLD.
FROM ALL DIFFERENT WALKS OF LIFE.

IM VERY HUMBLED... AND... GRATEFUL.
MY APOLOGIES I HAVE NOT REPLYED
HOW CAN I ?
IM IN PRISON ... NOT A POST OFFICE.

ADIOS. AMIGOS

"ENJOY" :)

238

Conrad ▓▓▓▓
A0259AF / (RC9034)
HMP Sudbury
Ashbourne
DE6 5HW

Charlie Bronson A8076AG / BT1314
HMP Wakefield
Love Lane
Wakefield
West Yorks
WF2 9AG

Dear Mr Bronson

With deep regret I am very sorry to read about your continuing struggle with Zionist in this & previous so called governments of the people I say that in words only for the people more like for there own personal agenda for us serving prisoners & the ones that have gone before us your personal memorial that has helped so many within the prison caged estate Governments have come & gone yet you have been unlawfully kept within there cage. Your name & followers live on when they have left this world The purpose of my letter is to seek your help? Please read enclosed letter I seek your support fundraising to acquire me the means to search a section of the moors that I located in 2006 but unfortunately I was sentenced to IPP within 3 months of the find (Oct 2006) My first time imprisonment under section 224 (Reckless Arson) nobody received any kind of injury only property damage to a night club that I had forcible been ejected from by Zionist doormen under the instruction of the owner that was not big enough to carry it out his self yet order others to carry out his dirty work what's done is done cant turn back the clock? Yet I personal believe that if I hadn't received this IPP I would have made & carried out that promises I made on the very day to return to the lost sprit Keith Bennet soul on that day I was on the moors & the only time I have been on the moors

> Some kind of art done by your good self (*lost Boy-Moors wasteland grave*) that I will be able to auction to provide founds to hire a mini-digger to search just one location that I found items buried I don't have the founds available or the means to raise such founds to hire equipment needed to carry out *one final search* of just one location I have been able to achieve resettlement release & planning to return in April 2011 (over-night ROTL) if I can some how raise the funds? I intend to hire equipment needed for search around £300-£500 all money left over will go directly to Winnie Johnson/Help find Keith-Found I made a personal promise that one day I would some how return & find the remains one-day?. Now that I am receiving day release & over-night release it may just come true. I have contacted Winnie myself letting her aware that GMP have held this evidence since 2006 that has not ever been made public I believe its stuck on the shelve in the GMP store room (cold murder case) never even been DNA tested that's my personal view & when I do locate Keith in April & bring closure for Winnie & many others I will make it public knowledge that I couldn't of done it without your help & offer I would dearly love to get one over GM Police but more importantly retrieve Keith before the good lord take her away I have waited all my sentence just to return to one spot on the moors that the Police was feet away from previous searching years ago they left coffee plastic cups scattered only feet away from location if only they would of carried out detailed search inside the circle soil hillside I believe Keith leg is trapped behind his back? Somehow can you please help in any-way in increasing any founds to undertake search? Can you help in anyway?

Yours Sincerely
Conrad ▓▓▓▓▓▓▓▓   7th January 2011

239

DEAR MR BRONSON, CHARLES

I HOPE YOU ARE WELL.

PLEASE FORGIVE ME, BUT THIS IS THE FIRST TIME I
HAVE WRITTEN TO SOMEONE WITH SUCH A HIGH PROFILE.
MY NAME IS CARLY AND I LIVE IN BIRMINGHAM (GOD,
THAT SOUNDED LIKE SOMETHING FROM 'BLIND DATE') I
    WOULDN'T BLAME YOU IF YOU STOPPED READING THIS
LETTER RIGHT ABOUT NOW.

TO BE TRUTHFUL AND STRAIGHT TO THE POINT, THE REASON
FOR MY LETTER TO YOU IS TO DO WITH A FRIEND OF
MINE, TO WHOM I HOLD VERY DEAR, HAVE SUCH HIGH
REGARD FOR AND RESPECT. I RESPECT HIM BECAUSE OF
WHAT HE HAS ACHIEVED AND THE THINGS HE HAS
SACRIFICED TO GET WHERE HE IS TODAY. I AM TRUELY
PLEASED FOR HIM BECAUSE THE SACRIFICES ARE
    BEGINNING TO PAY OFF AND WILL CONTINUE TO DO
SO.
MY FRIEND IS AN ACTOR AND HE HAS LANDED HIMSELF
AN ABSOLUTELY AMAZING ROLE. HIS NAME IS LOUIS
MURRALL AND HE IS TRUELY A GREAT GUY AND HE
CERTAINLY HAS A HIGH REGARD FOR YOU. HE IS
EXTREMELY DEDICATED TO THE ROLE HE IS CURRENTLY
PLAYING AND I RESPECT HIM SO MUCH FOR THAT AS
THE CHARACTER HE IS PLAYING IS NOT FICTIONAL.

I REALLY HOPE YOU DON'T MIND ME WRITING TO YOU
AND I HOPE I HAVEN'T BORED YOU OR THAT YOU FIND ME
CHEEKY, BUT I REALLY WANTED TO TRY AND DO

SOMETHING SPECIAL FOR LOUIS. A SURPRISE TO LET
HIM KNOW HOW PROUD I AM OF HIM.
I THOUGHT A SMALL LETTER OR NOTE FROM YOU TO HIM
OF GOOD LUCK OR WHAT EVER. YOU COULD EVEN TELL
HIM HE'S GOT A MAD FRIEND WHO WRITES RANDOM
LETTERS BUT THAT SHE THINKS A LOT OF HIM!
(OK - MAYBE NOT THE LAST ONE) I JUST KNOW HE
WOULD LOVE IT.
I HOPE YOU DON'T THINK I'VE BEEN TOO CHEEKY IN
ASKING, BUT I WOULD LOVE TO BE ABLE TO GO UP
TO HIM AND SAY 'HEY LOU! GOT SOMETHING FOR YA',
HAND HIM SOMETHING FROM YOU, TO SEE HIS FACE WOULD
BE PRICELESS AND WOULD MAKE MY DAY.

I'M SURE YOU GET THOUSANDS OF LETTERS, SO I'VE TRIED
TO KEEP MINE SHORT AND SWEET.

I LOOK FORWARD TO HEARING FROM YOU.

THANK YOU AND BEST WISHES

CARLY

Charles
BRONSON

Jack ████ A4400AE ROCHESTER
KENT 1 FORT Road
ME1 3QS

tO BRONSON' im a FREIND ov dave Paul' he said
you and him had Been wRiting to eachoveR' and
uRe good FREINDS wiv Spara' arent ya' I
feel like a mug writ'n to Sum1 i dnt No
But' wen i Read vRe Book' i felt like i new
you 4 MANy years' So even dave said
he was in contact wiv ya' and said
u could drop him a letteR' i felt it
would B a oppvRtunity' to get to No ya
PeRSoNLy Not JUST Readi'n your Book.
Well anyway im 20 yeARs old FRom
South London' WIMBLEDON SW20' and
im Banged up at the moment' in sum
mugy youth oFENDERS iN Kent' i dnt
Reli Relate to the Boys in heRe theRe
to imature' ive gRown up wiv the old a
age sinse i was young so ive got diffRenc
moRals' and a diffeRent level ov acting
in company ive u No wat i meAN' I
got 2 yeARs and 5 months' 4 takin sum
ones caR oFF them' PRoPh mugy im
imBARASED aRouk' it Reli' i didnt do
it to make money oR anyFing' i was
dRvNk and in a mad State ov mind
it's oNly a small Sentence anyway' But
pointless' so u No that dave is ill yeh
Sad Reli' hes a Nice old fellat' BAD
fiv9s do hapeN to good people 4 SuRe
im Not Religovs But i Ave Been Praying
4 him it's worth a try tho. I Bet alot
ov people have said this But' u Remind
me ov myself in a sense' even tho

im a young boy to u' But the last 5 years
its Been me against the world 'I just
got fed up wiv all these people who fink
there this and that' ive just rebeled
from young' and fought my way through
the ranks' wen i was 15 i was scared
ov alot ov older men' so I just started
fightin them all' now im 20 there like
30+ none ov them would ever disrespect
me' or my freinds' all tho alot ov my
so called freind s' aint helped me out
But wen i was on the outsize' id do
anyfing to help any 1' But people started
dependin on me to much' wen I was
doin well they was all there' hangin
off my boloxs' But wen ure down on
ure arse they nowere to B seen' But
my mums Been there for me regardless
so i have felt guilty 4 all the times
ive had' firearms police kiccin off
my door' and I had murder squad
showin my mum nasty pictures ov
sum one who got hacked up wiv a sword
or sumik' the cunts will do anyfing to
get at me trust they hate me' But my mum
has stayed strong through everything'
family is the most important thing
i wana make my mum proud But im so
heavaly in the lifestyle wiv the Big
people' its not easy to jump out ov it all
listen Bronson its down to u ive u want
to reply mate ask me anyfing u want to
no' hope to hear from u soon, Stay strong
                                    Jack

10th of Jan
5·35pm Monday
HMp peterbrough
saville Road
westwood
peterborough
pe3 - 7pd

C2 - 19.
(female side)

Dearest Charles
x

Smiling so much
+ writing this
letter!

Hello & finally I get to fore fill my dream
to write to you. I have dreamt of
this day for a while I was just to
frightened to write but I plucked up the
courage & thought stuff it go for it eb's.
well I have read most of your books &
loved them all & I have also heard you
have been on TV from your cell Room wow.
even when I was on the outside I have
always admired you because your strong
willed take everything in your stride &
handsome if you dont mind me saying
sorry if you have a mrs. well as you
guessed I am inside just done 11 month's
& still have another 3 to do not long left.
The whole time I have been here I have
been trying to get your newest prison
address & today I finally got it whoop
whoop. well a little about me but first
I was going to put a photo of me in
this letter but was not quite sure if you
wanted one or if you had a mrs because

I dont want to step on her toes if you do
well I love my music always listening to
my 80's & love songs 24/7 I Read books
so fast I have to have a sack of them
a week laugh out loud my star sign is
The Ram Aries I was born in April & my
Name is April-May what a joke. I am
5'2 curvy & proud size 12 long black hair
dark eyes & olive skin No-one calls me
by my Real name (April-May) because I
hate it so everyone knows me as easy my
Nickname. had a Real Rough & sad up-
bringing I am lucky to be alive. I have
seen & done things No-one at my age
should of seen though & done but what
has happened to me makes me who I am
a little fighter, strong willed & gobby laugh
out loud. Oh yeah my age is 29 I am
The Big 30 This April. I never had the
chance to go to school so I self taught
myself to Read & write out of a
Stephen King book in the library. I still
love learning new things & will try most
topics on anything & everything well enough
about me charles Before I go I would love
to Recieve a letter from you would make
my week, month, year & my whole life
But I do understand if you dont write
Back as I expect your a busy man with
all your fan mail & writing & what not
I am going to sign off now all the Best

245

To you & Take care & Charles your a amazing fella Their are alot of people out There who Think The same as me. Sorry if my spelling aint to great but you know why & all. Happy New year & I wait with baited breath on your Reply. Thank you.

Love from.

TGRY
x x

25ᵗʰ DEC 2010
Merry christmas lad.

Mark ▮▮▮▮▮▮
HMP Forest Bank
AGE CROFT Road
Salford, Manchester
M27 8FB.

Dear Charlie
HEllo mate, I hope this letter finds you
IN good health.
Firstly I must admit that I feel a bit shitty Not writing to your
good Self a lot sooner because Ive read your books and tried to
do them "workouts", Ive even bought your film (which WAS FUCKING AGE)
anyway better late than never aye!
Im FROM LiverPool and Im HERE IN Forest bank doing a little 8
year Streach for Hi-Jacking wagons IN Bolton, (conspiracy to RoB)
I'll Be out IN 2014 some time, Just after you mate (Hope so),
Ive Been reading your books Since you began writing them and
Im always gobsmacked, usually read them twice then give them to
a pal or con to read, (NEVER Get them BACK) cunts! I'vE Just
finished your loonyology book' Super reading, I always Said
you were a Genius but they didnt believe me, h.
Im working IN the kitchens at the minute oN £17 50 a week.
Fucking pittance. I reckon you've gotta keep Moving and using
your head though So working keeps me off the Bed, I love the
gym aswell, Im Benching 80 kg Now and I can do six reps without
help which is good for Someone OF my size, Im Concentrating on
c/v aswell getting on the Rowing machines and tread mills as much
as possible.
do you Still do your pad workouts or do you get anytime in the
gym (probably not getting gym) I can See it Now, you on the
Bench press surrounded By Ten Screws pissing themselfs ha. "Cunts"
I hope your daily routine is better Now also, I havent read about
you IN the papers latley so I asume you've chilled out, oh shit.
you was in the paper a while BACK, Im a forgetfull shit Sometime

I Totally forgot mate, if I remember right you gave a
guvnor a sore head (nice one).
maybe they'll let you come here and sort some of these
clowns out. this jail is A joke, its not like jail used to be
now its full of dirty smack heads and nonces who need to
pick on weak people and lick screws Arses. Im on the same
thinking as you mate, Bring them to my cell for ten minutes
and let me talk To them with my fists, makes me sick to
think that they are in the same place as me.
any way charlie I hope you had a good christmas mate,
and a good new year, I hope you can write Back and we
can have a good old cuppa tea or fish and chips one day
that sounds a bit ginger beer but you know what I mean
I prefere a good hot Ruby Murry myself and maybe a pint
of stella. look After yourself lad.

any way Ive drawn you a picture of what I think best
describes you mate. dont forget charlie, us scousers salute you!

SAUSAGE DINNER...
- WINNER.

All the best
charlie.
Scouse mark.

DEAN

BAKEWELL
DERBYSHIRE

Dear Charlie

I hope everything is alright for you.
I have read 2 of your books and I have got
your film. I thought tom hardy played a very good
part. I found your books and film very intresting. Just
a small look at some of the things you have
bean through in prison and some of the other places
you have been. I Like your artwork Charlie its
all got a meaning to it. I think you will get out
one day Alot of them in prison should do the time
you have done. When you think of some of
the things they have done. I think the system is
is all wrong Well Charlie im not very good
at writing Letters oven when I was locked up.

249

Charlie I have Put a £10 postal order in with letter so you can buy your supplies So Charlie when or if you have the time please write back. I will write to you again soon.

Hope to hear from you soon

Dean
S

Charles Bronson
5 Love Lane
Wakefield
West Yorkshire
WF2 9AG
UK

Dear Charles:

My name is Michael ████████ I am 35 years old and I live near Toronto, Canada, which is about 2 hours away from Buffalo, NY and 4 hours from Detroit.
I am married and have one child, a son who is 6 months old.
I am familiar with your crimes but I am not writing to you in hopes of you telling me details about them. I find people who can do what you did to be very fascinating and interesting. I think a lot of people have the same thoughts but there is a fine line between keeping them in your head and acting on them.
I also want you to know that in no way am I looking for fame or to profit from our correspondence. If you want to correspond with me we can talk about whatever you want.
I have taken the liberty of including a self addressed envelope and some stamps so you can send me or anyone else you want a letter. Thank you for taking the time to read my letter and I hope to hear back from you.
Before I finish this letter I thought I would end on a joke. At the very least I hope I can put a smile on your face and make you forget about where you are, even if it is for just a couple of seconds. Anyway here goes......
A new teacher was trying to make use of her psychology courses. She started her class by saying, "everyone who thinks you're stupid, stand up", after a few seconds, little Johnny stands up. The teacher said, "Do you think your stupid, little Johnny? "No ma'am but I hate to see you standing there all by yourself".

Sincerely,

M. Mc Naught

Michael ████████
████████

CANADA

251

To mr B

Hows it going mate.

my names adam [redacted] im from
a place called bracknell its in
berkshire.
I'm in Hmp reading at the moment
Just got transferd from Hmp portland
for another 2 cases iv got (death buy
dangorous driving and supply of class B)
im serving a 5 already so hope it
goes well in court.

I read a book of yours in portland
when i was on basic for beating
up a nonce, its a cushty book and
your done a lot of mad shit. IV
come close to kicking of lately at
these screws i came out the block
on x-mas eve for conspiricy to supply
Hmp with drugs and went for a visit
yesterday to find out i was on closed
visits and my last visit they sent my
dons on there way and said you aint
coming in. If there was more charles
bronsons out there then these people
would think twice about how they
treat us so i aploud what youv done
to defend your pride and to defend oar
rights you deserve a pat on the back.

I was reading the paper last night
and sore that people on the out are
doing a walk in your name to raise
awarness of you being stuck in
the system and them not letting you
out. you served your time for
the robbery and youv served more than
enough time for the Hostages and strikes
youv done so wot are you still doing in
Jail. In my eyes the parole board dont
no the real ~~meane~~ meaning of Justice
theres dirty rapists coming in and out
of Jail all the time not even doing
a Quarter of wot youv done its a
complete discrace to are country how
they treat decent people like your self
compared to murderes, rapists and
forenors who get more privaleges then
you. (its wrong)

Im only 19 and iv only been in Jail
15 months, iv done a few months down
the block nothing to what youv experi-
anced but wanted to let you no that
even the younger generation are
thinking of ya and we hope you
get your release soon! take it
easy bruva 4rm murphy. p.s if you
wana wright back this is my adress.

Hmp reading
Forbury road
reading
berkshire
Rg1 3Hy

adam ▓▓▓▓▓▓▓
▓▓▓▓▓▓▓

To Mr Bronson

Hello my name is alex I'm in 3 PARA, currently in Afghanistan. I hope you don't mind me writing to you. Me and the blokes here recently watched your film and we loved it, I've also read your book. The amount of press ups you can do is very impressive plus the amount you train. We've got some strong lads here but none that could match you for press ups. How is life with you at the moment? I read that one of your paintings went for £1,500. That's not bad at all. Hope your keeping well and fit, take care. No worries if you can't write back probably got loads of mail.

alex

Nikita ████████
Hmp Bronzfield
Woodthorpe Road
Ashford, middlesex
TWI5 3JZ

"Happy Birthday!"

a over due letter, i know it was your birthday
a few days ago, i also saw what they wrote about
you in the paper, i think the papers talk alot of
shit, hence the headline "butter Nutter" well let
me start off properly, im Nikita keetley, iv been
in for 5 months, im in for firearms, i got 15 months
for it, im from Nottingham and have a son called
malachi, im Not a bibel Nut, Nore am I a person to
claim they know too much im Just me, i love to write
and love football, im Not a tom boy, Not like the strange
lookin women in hear, people say i'm good looking but i
dont see where there looking at, I love artwork and
id love to be able to be as good as you but some people
have it some people dont, i saw the film that was
made (about 12 times) and love everything about it!,
your Just one of the most loved men in briten! well i'll
say you ask any-one who charly bronson is they will
know, well i dabt i'll get a Reply i bet you get loads
of mail from all Random people, but i wish you
the best xmas you can have concidering the curcomstances
and a Nice New year, who knows you cold be
some place Nice soon,
        Take care
        Nikita
        X

255

DEAR MR BRONSON,

I have recently watched your film, and following that read a couple of your books, which is why I'm writing to you. I wanted to thank you for Inspiring me to do something with my life, I feel selfish that I do nothing with my freedom wasting it just working and watching telly like a slob. I read of a man trapped within four walls who above all odds keeps himself fighting fit, writes and is a talented artist. I'm overweight and smokes or did, im trying to give up and thanks to you put myself on a strick fitness regime from your book. I've ~~alt~~ always wanted to be a boxer so hopefully with hard work I ~~with~~ will achive this. Anyhow enough of the soppy bollocks stuff I know you like a joke so heres my favorite:

A Panda was sat on the side of the road mending it's own buisness when along came a prostitute, The prostitute says "Hi what are you doing? fancy coming round for ~~the~~ dinner? The panda agrees and says thanks. After the meal the prostitute asks if he wants to have sex! The panda couldn't belive his luck and says yes.

After dinner the prostitute says thats fifty quid!
The panda Says "fuck off! what Do you MEAN?
prostitute Says 'thats my job, if you dont believe
me look in the dictionary, So he does and its
Says

PROSTITUTE — DOES SEXUAL FAVOURS
FOR MONEY.

The panda says your right, fair enough
look up Panda, so she does. it says

Panda — EATS, SHOOTS AND LEAVES!

Hope that put a smile on your face, feel
free to keep in touch you'll always have a
friend in me. Your a LEGEND!

All the best
KEEP STRONG!

Danny

14.12.2010   Morgan ▓▓▓▓
▓▓▓▓▓▓▓▓▓▓
▓▓▓▓▓
▓▓▓▓▓▓▓▓

                         South Wales.

Dear charlie,
                 Im in the middle
of reading your book "Diaries
from hell". I've also read a
few other books of yours and
i do intend to read all your
books. I hope you like the
christmas card. I do hope
this card and letter reach
you and that you actually
do hold and read this
letter. Your a true warrior
charlie and i do hope you
walk out to freedom sooner
rather than later. Anyway

Im not very good at ~~right~~
writing letters so i'll leave
it here. It would be
amazing to get a letter
back from you even if
it's just a short one to
say you recieved the card.
So take care, look after
yourself and i no you'll
never give up.

Yours faithfully

Morgan ███████

Hi Charlie
    Just wanted to write you
and wish you a happy Christmas.
I am Helen, a friend of Dave Taylor
I've met him through Bronson Wear,
Plus he, came to our Gym to do
a seminar on Whin Chun, it was
Fantastic, He did the Chop Stick move
there. He is a great Person.
let me tell you a Bit about myself,
I am an aerobics/fitness instructor, I
also teach Pole Dancing/Fitness.
Iv been teaching about 24 years now.
I Love it, Im 42 years old next month
But I still have many years left to
teach yet Ha Ha!
I teach Kettle Bells too, they are
weights with Handles, and a fantastic
workout, 20 mins Burns so much
fat and Tones up. I do ladies
Classes, But I have taught Men,
I used to take Wednesbury Rugby Club
every Saturday, the guys loved it,
he did it out on the rugby Pitch!
Iv seen many of Your drawings, they
are Brilliant, I know you have a
shit life in the Charlie, But its
Clear Your Mind is Strong and I Know
you train every day, its good you have
your Humour, it Shows in Your drawings
Hoping You will write me Back,
    Take Care, Helen x.

261

JAVED ▮▮▮▮▮

Birmingham
▮▮▮▮▮

HELLO MR BRONSON

Firstly i hope that this letter reaches you
in the best of health. How are you? im
fine i thought id write you a letter after
reading most of your BOOKS in H.m.p
while serving a prision sentence of 5 years
in H.m.p winson Green The thing is ive
been Released from custody as im from
Birmingham my name is JAVED Zaman i
am 30 years of AGE i thought id
write you a letter asking if the home
office has any news on Releasing you
following your time in jail The thing is that
ive also seen some of your clips on
the internet to do with your Release you see mr
Bronson at this moment i am reading
your Book solitary fitness which is helping
me with my Training Regime at the gym
its a useful book and its giving me a
guide on fitness mr BRonson im writing
you this letter today ive received
a postcard from your self Today
very funny its about cheese & wine
nice one the thing is that mr
BRonson you are a remarkable man

262

The thing is that good idea mr Bronson. Im going to be looking out for that book "Diaries from hell" you mentioned it came out in 2009 the thing is mr Bronson i was wondering if you could do me a drawing because in most of your books you have drawings. The thing is that mr Bronson if any way i can help you please let me know by the way meery Xmass i hope you have a good Xmass me im o.k just training hard at the gym charlie after doing my sentence the thing is that im a reformed character especially after doing a course E.T.S things are looking good at the moment ive got my car and am looking for work but there is not much work for me at the moment. after sending me this postcard i thought id say keep it up im now a supporter of your campaign ive got a friend who is a solicitor im going to ask him if he could give me some info about your release just a general inquiry. in to your release

any way thought id write back
saying Thanks for the post card
and if you have a meery
xmass and a happy new
year i hope 2011 brings you
some Joy and good news.
also mr Benson i was
wondering if you could do me
a little drawing Just so i
can have a picture so it will
keep me strong.

yours Thankfully

Javed

P.S ENOUGH RESPECT Thanks for
writing back

Lee ███████ H.M.P
STRANGEWAYS
1 SOUTHALL ST
MANCHESTER.
SALFORD M60 9AH

15/12/10.

"Hi Charlie"

how's things with you?
i fort i would send you this to let you know
i finialy got to read diaries from hell but it was
worth waiting for its fuckin brilliant i read it in
too days its a piss take whot people do with your
drawings you know with e. bay (fuckin tramps)
i feel a cunt as ive asked you for a bit of your
art but its only for my cell and to treasure
myself theirs one or two in the book whot
are the dogs bollocks i sent you a christmas card
the other week its fuckin mad whot people send
you and how much mail you get ill be gratefull if
you give my address and number to one of your girls
but not a fatty ha,ha, have you had a xmas card off
your next door (maudsley) ha,ha, only jokeing but you've
really seen some loons in your time away but its
time to be with your family so fingers crossed for
you this new year is yours (2011 BRONSON)
sounds good that but even better to see you walk
out id tell every screw to watch the news.
their faces ha,ha, (cunts) anyway if i send
you a picture of my son with his brothers
boxing gloves on could you please sign it for
us he's only three but loves a fight and who
else better to sign it yours truely ive put
a stamped address envelope in with this but i
was after a little pic or art but you've got my
word im not an e,bay man ive more respect mate.

265

but i'll be really gratefull if you could do the
photo of my son please i understand you
get bizzy with your art but try your best
to let me know and i'll send it to you soon
As hope your christmas is As good as it can be
All the best to your family remember this 2011
is yours. please write back soon with A little
picture And to let me know over my son photo
cheers All the best Charlie

p.s can't beat that 95 press ups in 30 seconds.
ho could you show me or tell me haw to
do your croc press up cheers Mate.

"Yes Charlie B

This is my Second letter to You
DID You get it? Well I JUST Thought
I'D WRITE You A Script again.

Well C, B I'AM A LIFER
LIKE You AND been IN 5 Year now
should be Geting out soon?

I'VE been meaning to write to
you fer time because ME + You
have some thing in common Ano
that's WE Dont GIVE A FIYING Fuck!

Yes Charlie B I've been Long Lartin,
FRANKLAND, (MANCHESTER STRANGEWAYS)
There Fucking shit brother. What's it
LIKE there! What's the room services
LIKE? :)

I need to ask You a Qestion
C, B AR You A Fighter of this
MOTHER FUCKING SYSTEM that's tried to
Fuck AR head up fer Years?

When AR You out? there was
a rumor of You geting out IN
2012?.

Hey C, B Listen You sexy
man send ME A Picture of Your
self so I can Put it on the
internet so You will be never
Forgotten.

PRISON No.
B
3
2
9

H.M.P LANCASTER CASTLE
LANCASTER CASTLE
CASTLE Hill
LA1 1YL

A

GANG MEMBER OF THE PURPLE HACK'E TEAM :)
LIVERPOOL

ꞌHAPPY X MAS LADꞌ

In replying to this letter, please write on the envelope:
Number .... Name ....
Wing **B**...

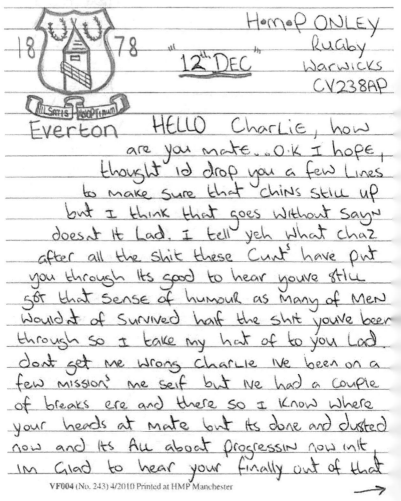

18 78

Everton

"12ᵗʰ DEC"

H·m·P ONLEY
Rugby
Warwicks
CV238AP

HELLO CharLie, how are you mate...O·K I hope, thought id drop you a few Lines to make sure that chins still up but I think that goes without sayn doesn't it Lad. I tell yeh what chaz after all the shit these Cunts have put you through Its good to hear youve still got that sense of humour as many of men would·nt of survived half the shit youve been through so I take my hat of to you Lad dont get me wrong CharLie Ive been on a few missions me self but Ive had a couple of breaks ere and there so I know where your heads at mate but its done and dusted now and Its All about progressin now ink Im Glad to hear your finally out of that

VF004 (No. 243) 4/2010 Printed at HMP Manchester

→

fucked up cage aswell, Lets hope they put a proper Animal in there now hey. Cuntleys a good candidate in he Lad, not half, Ive Just finished my prison diary, a bit different from the rest of your books but a decent read tho and make sure you make that Crimes N punishments happen as that will be a Belter that Lad. as you can see im in some snide cat C now which is full of arse lickin screw boys but I sopose yeh get them everywhere now, I Landed here a few months ago after spendin 3 months in my Local on G.o.a.d, "WALTON", Its the same old shit hole from when you was there only the Blocks now on B1, so theyve sent me up here, Just to fuck me aboat but it will take MORE than this to get a Scouser down init Charlie. FUCK EM, im goin home in a couple of months time now so Ill Just take a back seat for the time being init mate. I was with your good pal CLIFF moody back in 08 in Buckley HALL he's chilled right out now and should be on his way back to the North east Just soon; He talks Highly of you aswell and told me a few storys of back in the day. Good stuff, oh well charlie Ill get off now Lad, Id be Over the Moon to hear Back from you but if not then not to worry as I know how it is Lad so you

take good care of yeh self chaz and
dont let these cunts get you down as your
worth 10 of these lad and Its All about
gettin ont there for your old dear and the
rest of the family now, the Jokes Over now
init,
TAKE it EASY Soldier.

JASON.

LEGENd.!

FREE BRono.

NORWICH,
NORFOLK ▓▓▓▓▓
8ᵀᴴ Jan.

CHARLES BRONSON,
Dear MR. BRONSON.

I would be very grateful if you could
autograph the enclosed cover for me please.
I very much enjoy the paintings I have
seen of yours and have a copy of one
of your paintings on my wall. Turner is
my favourite painter, and I would be
very grateful if you could autograph
it.

Thanking you very much.

Yours Sincerely
RICHARD ▓▓▓▓▓

JoNo ▓▓▓▓▓▓▓

▓▓▓▓▓▓▓
Maltby
Rotherham
▓▓▓▓▓▓▓

Charles Bronson

Thought I would drop you another letter,
been having a look around your website &
Seen the free Bronson protest next year found
it really interesting, me & my partner are
going to be going

Also the Bronson 30 mile challenge my partner
is a firm supporter of breast cancer too so its
win, win.

But first I got to get my partner in shape
She's not fat just really unfit. I'm an
expara & with your Solitary fitness book we will be
going hardcore although she doesn't know that
part just yet.

Have the best x-mas you can
Sent you a card hope it got through

Take care
JoNo.

When writing to Members of Parliament please give your previous home
address in order to avoid delay in your case being taken up by the M24 0UG

In replying to this letter, please write on the envelope:
Number ▓▓▓▓▓▓ Name NOEL ▓▓▓▓▓▓
Wing A4/ 24

Mr Bronson.

My Name is Noel ▓▓▓ I'm
Currently in Prison waiting trial for armed
Robbery on a Post office.
        I was reading the Sun the
other day and read about its Sponsord Run
form Dartmoor thats were I got your
address. This sparked a Convo off between
me and my mate "Dibble" he was on about
your film and we were on about
how come the law keeps people like
your self in here and give Rappenty
an 'Nonce' little Sentances. Not right
at all. Your original offence is Robbery
for fuck sake. AnyWay This Sparked
the reason for my picture of me
Sick to the tooth of Judges. I've been
told that you are a bit of an artist
as well and hope you like my atempt.
                Well my mate Said
that you would'int write ad I was a

dick head but I thraught fuck it your
a person Just as anyother and every
one likes letters so hear I am
Writeing.
Do you Still held a record for
push ups or was it Commandos? I Suppose
you get all kinds of Werdos Writeing letters.
to you but if you would Just pop me
a quike Saympto back it would be much
appresheated, on even one of your pieces of
Art for my Wall
                                    Look forward for a reply
        Your a legend

    F.T.S   Noel ▨.

        You might be lost in the System
        But you will never be forgotten
                Remeber I told you
                        Ths.
Bronson   out.
No.1
BOXER

1·1·11·   Kevin (Kevo)
                               H.M.P. Liverpool
"All THE BEST"   68 Hornby Road
                               L9-3DF
                               F4-18

alrite charl,
            Hope you don't mind me
writin' it's Just that am in walton
& I got talkin' to a friend of yours
"Mark lilliot" he's writin a book & he
told me you went to Stay with
him when you got out wick I thought
woz cool i've Read youe book &
watched youe film & am a fan I've
been away 7 times Now & I'M
sick of it obviously am no good
at bein a crim coz I always get
caught haha I've Just had another
christmas away from my family &
it breaks my heart not bein with
them so am gonna go Straight &
Join the Rat-Race when I get out
Normal 9-5 crap!! am not puttin' me
Mam through anymore of this, do you
know the Nightclub "Chelsea Reach" New
brighton prom, well they've been turned it
into luxury apartments we were all gutted
we had some crackin night's in there
i even got a piece of the dancefloor
(how sad am I haha) sentimental I suppose
it was made famous by the film
letter to breshnev about a Russian

275

Sailor who falls in love with a
Scouse girl, a bit of useless info
for you haha well Mate it's the
1st of Jan I have no Resolution's
only dream's haha hope you're gettin'
treated Well & I hope to god 1 day
you get to go back home I Mean
that mate you take Care am
gonna go & get a Shower highlight
of the day haha

yours Sincerely
Kevo.

thats about as
good as my
art get's haha.

Jeff
HMP Liverpool
62 Hornby Road L-9-3DF.

Alright.

Charlie mate how's
it going. Happy New Year. An
Wish you all the Best for
the years to come. Am Current
Serving A Sentance in Her
Magisties Walton Prison. It's
my first ever time in the
Big House! An A really eye
opener. I Bumped into a
close friend of mine An
your's Mark Lilliot in which
I Got Talking to Him An even
He said About his Book.
which Ave Read. An you
Were Mentioned in it An
Which We Got Talking An
thats How I Got your Number
I Like my Ant Charlie
An Am Doing my Best to
improve on it But I only
Get the Bare Essentials. in
this Dump! HaHaHoHo Charlie
Ave Seen Bits of your.
Ant in your Books An text
An Am Obsessed with that
Ave Seen its Just Down my
path. So Charlie I would
Like to See More of your
Ant. It Would Be Much Appreciate
Ave Sent you a Little sketch
It A Woman Bent over An
A Woman Kneeling Down you
P.T.O

277

Will (noBenly) Work The Rest
out For Youself. Well Charlie
Going to close Now Because
Its Feeding Time. I Look
Forand to hearing From You
An Seeing Gour Aut. So
Pls Charlie Send me A Couple
of Giggles Thanks Mate
An All the Best

Yours Sincerly
Jeff ▒▒▒▒▒.

Peace out ←.

Dear Charlie,

I hope you are well. And despite your circumstances I hope you are making the most of this time of year.

I will start by saying Merry Christmas and I hope you have a good new year.

Charlie, you may know who I am by now as Dave has mentioned me to you. I just wanted to say its been an absolute journey for me to learn all about who you are. It has been a very interesting part of my life. I can safely say I have never known anyone as strong minded as you. The way you have put up with what's happened to you is a true inspiration from a fellow none quitters point of view. It just shows no matter how hard things are in life you can overcome them and fight any odds.

Its been an adventure for me to learn all about you, it's been a pleasure and this is certainly something that will stick with me for the rest of my life! And to say that I am very proud. I just hope what I have done helps you in the long run, as I do believe you have been through too much over the years and its time people knew the real story. Just from reading your books I can see you are a very warm, friendly and naturally humorous gentlemen.

Which brings me to my next point, I don't think you are treated like a human being, some of the things you have shared with the world in your book should no doubt be raising eyebrows and questioning if you have been failed. I do truly believe from the bottom of my heart you have been failed. You are a perfect example that human rights stand for fuck all!

Obviously there are always 2 sides to a story, but I believe what has happened to you and others could have been avoided.

I don't really know what to put in this letter so I thought I would tell you a little bit about me.

My full name is Louis Anthony Peter Murrall and I was born and bred in Birmingham. I love my roots and what my city is all about. Its important to me that people remember that I am just a lad from Birmingham with a dream of success. I grew up with a loving and caring family and I was named after my great great great grandfather Louis Pankhurst who was a direct descendant of Emily Pankhurt the suffragette as my grand mother always told me. I have been acting since I was 11, I'm now 27 and my desires of becoming a professional actor have never died down. Its a want and need and too me its the only thing I feel good at! I am a pretty useless at everything else! haha! I support Aston Villa and I am originally from the same place as Ozzy Osborune (who I long to play in a film). I have 1 brother who is my rock and my best friend. Growing up myself I was never the most behaved of lads and often found myself sitting in a custody suite at my local knick for being a prat! As I got older my brother became my wiser, he guided me into a path of peace and acceptance. I also love my boxing, I have had 3 fights, won none, lost one and drew two - bit chit ent I Charlie??? hahaha! Nothing creates an adrenaline rush thou like getting in the ring to go toe-to-toe with someone!!

Charlie, I feel really cheeky asking, but I am organising my second boxing event for April next year. It would be an honor if you could possibly donate one of your drawings to this cause as the entire purse from the event is going to kids with cancer. I put a similar event on last year for my little cousin Mikey who has been told by the doctors he would never walk and never talk - last week he spoke his first words and stood up all by himself - what the fuck do these quacks know eh mate?? Tossers! I raised over £10,000 for the children's Birmingham Hospital. So 2011 I intend to make double that and put on an even bigger event for the kids with cancer. One of your works of wonder would go down a treat at this event and showing your support would be such a pleasure.

I can't help but being cheeky and asking for a picture of my own Charlie. Your pictures are incredible. I went to see Dave last week and he showed me a small part of your collection. They say a picture can say a thousand words......I say have you fucking seen Charlie Bronson's pictures then??? Yours speak a story, a story I can't work out but each one is more interesting than the last! There incredible Charlie and I would love nothing more than to have one framed hanging on my wall?

Anyway Charlie, I have ran out of things to say, but I hope this letter reached you well.

I have a nice saying for you if you don't mind me saying so....

"THEY WILL MAKE ME....BUT THEY WILL NEVER BREAK ME!!!"

Charlie, thanks again for taking the time to read this and thank you for providing me with such a challenging accomplishment. It truly has been an honor.

Take Care Charlie and make the most of this joyful time of year,

Your new friend,

(BRONSON 2011)

Louis ▮▮▮▮▮▮

Mpika Relief Fund

Working for the relief of hunger and suffering in the heart of Africa

Registered charity No:1106841

Chair: Mrs June Martin,

Trustees: Rev Marguerite Mower, Mrs Tina Watkin, Mrs Shirley Burge, Mr Robert Ford, Mrs Helen Hooper, Mrs Jackie Wilkinson.

FOR MORE INFORMATION PLEASE CONTACT: June Martin, 2, Commercial Street, Denholme, Bradford, BD13 4AD. Tel: 07737731077 e-mail: mpikarelief@yahoo.co.uk web: www.mpika.org

Charles Bronson,
A8076AG
HMP Wakefield,
5, Love Lane,
Wakefield
West Yorkshire
WF2 9AG

14th December 2010

Dear Charlie,

I am just writing to say a big THANKYOU for the three original drawings that I have received for our charity, via your friend Jack Binns, who has been a customer of our little charity shop for a number of years. He brought them to me and told me that you had expressed a wish for them to raise money for children in need.

I can assure you Charlie that EVERY PENNY we raise from these drawings will go directly to help children in Africa. We are only a small charity and we are run entirely by volunteers. I am sure you would be touched if you could see these kids and what a difference we have made to their lives Charlie, many have been brought to us as babies, suffering and near to death. With love and care they are all growing up with beds to sleep on, proper meals and an education.

I have enclosed our latest newsletter for you to read, I hope this reaches you safely.

To give the drawings the best chance to raise money, I am going to frame them up nicely, ask Jack to write an accompanying note, try to get an article in the paper and then put them on e-bay.

I will let you know how much they have raised for the children.

Thanks again Charlie,
Best Wishes,

June Martin

(Mrs) June Martin (Chair and co-founder of Mpika Relief Fund)

281

Well I Hope You enjoyed All THAT, As Much As I
Do Reading Them.

There WONDRFUL, INTRESTING People.

The CHARITY ONES I ALWAYS TRY To Help.

BUT The Powers THAT Be —

— Like McALLISTER even STOP THAT

The CUNTS HATE To See Me Doing ANY Good.
Cuz it's NOT Good For There "LABEL" of
Violent Thug.

They WANT Me SCREWED DOWN Big TIME.
IM To Be Made AN exAMPle To others.

"Fuck WITH us — AND Your end up Like BRONSON"

I've Been "UNOFFICIALY" Told BY A VERY High RANKED SCREW
(WHO Will ReMAIN NAMELESS)

I Will NEVER Be ReleASED WHILST IM FIT · STRONG AND
HEALTHY.

Cuz IM Seen As A DANGER To EVERYbody.

THEY WANT Me ZIPPED UP IN A BODY BAG.

Well... We SHALL See

ONE Sure THING I Do KNOW...
MY FUTURE Wife LORRAINE LOVES Me.
AND ALL MY FAMILY AND FRIENDS KNOW THE TRUTH.

So Fuck You PRICKS WHO Seem
DETERMINED To BURY Me.
AND Fuck You McALLISTER....

20/1/2011

It's getting cold again. I can smell the snow coming .. Feel it in the bones.
I always piss alot in the cold 'OO'
     Could Be old Age creeping in.
It's when the bones start rattling the problems start up. And the brain shrinks, and You forget if You've wiped Your arse or not...

I'm on a visit later today with Jack Binns and Ryan DuBois. Last time they came the fucking sniffer dog had them.. And both are Anti-Drugs.
     So I hope the dog gets it right today

Rice Krispies for Breakfast 'OO' A real mans grub
This is how it's all ended up...
     The worlds a fucking big faggot.. Run by faggots..
I cut myself shaving.
     Talking of That.. I knew a copper in Luton who was so stupid, he couldn't even nick himself shaving :- Ha Ha.

There's some daft old Bill.. Fuck knows how they ever pass the test, or be trusted with a truncheon and a pair of cuffs

     Dinner was Mushroom Soup.. 6 bread rolls. And a cheese pie.
          Fucking Lovely
A nice mug of cha to wash it down :-
          with a spoon of honey in it.

283

Galloway's
Society for the Blind

91 Balmoral Road
Morecambe
LA3 1SS
Tel: (01524) 414846
Fax: (01524) 414846

13-01-2011

Dear Mr Bronson ,

My name is Christopher Pitt and I work for Galloways Society For The Blind, in May this year we are holding a Art Exhibition and Auction to raise funds and awareness for blind and partly sighted people in our area, I am writing to ask you if you would please be interested and willing to donate a piece of your work or a sketch to help us continue our work. May I take this chance to thank you for your consideration and for reading this letter. I enclose a S A E should you need it .

Yours Faithfully

Christopher Pitt

Area Manager for North Lancashire Region

SORTED CHRIS ! ON IT'S WAY MATE. Keep up The Good WORK. Coz Them PARASITES in The House of COMMONS Wont Go out of THere WAY To Help You

I Get Scores of These Letters every Year. I Do MY BIT.. IT Gives Me A Bit of PRIDE.

nalsvi   **Supporting visually impaired people**   Charity No. 526088

website: www.galloways.org.uk

FundRaising
Standards Board

284

Plus its Nice To Be Nice,
    If You CANT Be NiG. THen Fuck oFF —
            Go cHew oN A LeMoN —
                        "CUNT"

I've HAD No Telly All weelt —
    MY PUNisHMenT eNDs MONDAY.
            Dont Suppose I've Missed AloT ?
        BuT I've CReATeD SoMe CRAckTing ART AnD CAusHT uP
    wiTH SoMe LeTTers, ☺
            So iTs DoNe Mr Good.
            BARe iN MiND I HAD No T.V FoR 3 DecAdes
    So iM oNe oF THem SoRT oF MeN WHo ReAlly DonT Give
    A FlyiNg FuckT.

2. 15pM — MY Visit ARRives ☺
        GReAT To See THem — BuT SADly THe CANTeeN WAs
    CLoseD. "Fuck kNows WHY"
        So I HAD No CHics oR Milk sHAkes ☹
            "Fuckting LiBeRTY"
    THATs SHow Bizz FoR You ᵖ

        FARe PlAY To THe ScReW. MR WHoleN.
    He SoRTeD us SoMe T BAgs ouT
                        ToP FeeTcR
    So AtleAst we HAD A Cup oF Rosy.

    I TRieD JActs Suit JAckeT oN —
        He SliPPeD iT THRough THe BARs
    Hes A SMART olD FuckeR is JActT.
            ONe TRue LegeNd

        I Love His old StoRies —
            WHAT A cHARAcTeR.

He was a Mercenary Years Ago.
A crack shot.
A man you dont fuck with.
Its Wrote all over His Beat.
"Dont Fuck with Me
I'm Jack Binns.

Ryan Looked Smart in His Black Suit.
He Looks Alert Alive my Brother Mark.
Top Geezer is Ryan
He Itmins a Few of my Buddies From Leeds

Both Jack + Ryan Will Be on the Protest
Outside This Piss Hole on the 30th This Month
"Watch This Space"
My Supporters Are About To expose it All.

The Sun, 20 January 2011:

BRONSON TO MARRY WIFE NO3

BRITAIN'S most violent prisoner is to get married for the third time.

A pal announced Charles Bronson's engagement on his website.

A statement said: "Love is in the air. Charles Bronson is engaged to be married. I can't reveal who the lady is."

Bronson, 58, who is in Wakefield Jail, West Yorkshire, has been behind bars for 37 years — 33 of them in solitary confinement. He was originally jailed for seven years in 1974 for armed robbery, but the sentence was extended after attacks on prison warders and kidnap bids.

His first wife divorced him soon after he was jailed. Bronson converted to Islam for his second marriage in a 2001 jail ceremony, but that lasted just four years.

The Sun. Today 20th Jan 2011

See How They Pick my Worst evre Photo -- To Make Me Look Crazy.
This Snap Was 10 yrs Back Through a Security Van Window Taking me To The London Appeal Courts.
I Got 3 years Knocked off.
I said To The 3 Appeal Judges
You Tight Fuckers
"I Hope You Choke on Your Xmas Lunch.

They Looked At Me As If To Say
"You Ungrateful Bastard
(Some Judges Just Cant Win)

286

The TWITTERING, TWATTERING, TWOTTERING TWITTERS HAVE
STARTED UP ON MY RECENT STATEMENT.
I AM TO MARRY.
GUTLESS, SPINELESS, SOUL-LESS, FACELESS, TWITTERERS !!

IT ALL GETS BACK TO ME. WHO SAYS WHAT.
You CUNTS.
SOME PEOPLE JUST CAN'T BE HAPPY FOR OTHERS !!
THEY HAVE TO BE NASTY
YOU TWITTERING NOSY CUNTS ! ○○

CHARLIE'S AT IT AGAIN.
IT WON'T LAST.
WHO IS SHE
SOME BIRD OUT FOR FAME.
GOLD DIGGER.
HOW CAN ANY SANE WOMAN MARRY BRONSON
HE WOULD TAKE HER HOSTAGE.
TWITTER, TWITTER, TWITTER
FACE BOOT FUCK FACES.

WELL HERE is 10 GOOD REASONS WHY I WILL BE
GETTING MARRIED TO MY LOVELY LORRAINE.

1/ SHE MAKES ME SMILE AND FEEL GOOD. ✓
2/ SHE HAS NO BAGGAGE. YOUNG FREE AND SINGLE ✓
3/ SHE IS A VERY ATTRACTIVE AND SMART LADY ✓
4/ SHE'S A BRILLIANT ARTIST ✓
5/ SHE LOVES LIFE. A VERY PURE SOUL ✓
6/ SHE'S NOT INT. GLAMOUR OR FALSENESS OR CRIMINALITY ✓
7/ I TRUST HER WITH MY LIFE ✓
8/ THE MOMENT I SEE HER I KNOW SHE WAS SO SPECIAL ✓
9/ SHE ACTUALLY UNDERSTANDS AND ACCEPTS MY STRANGE WAYS ✓
10/ I LOVE WEDDING CAKE. :'

287

OKAY TWITTERERS...
GET THAT FINGER TWITTERING
Wheres Your 10 Reasons Why Its A Joke.
And Put Your Names Down You Cunts.

Coz one Day I Could Well Kick Your Doors iN And
Do Some Serious Twittering on Your Head With A 14 Pound
Lump Hammer...
Never Doubt It

I Got A Pile of Letters Today
Some Right Silly ones Too.

Ive Got To Let You See A Couple.
Seeing is Believing.
otherwise You Wont Believe it
It Makes Me Laugh Anyway

Theres Some Sad Fuckers iN This World...
Some Great Actors.

This Cunt - "Luke Harper" Should Get
A Golden Oscar.
Who The Fuck Does He Think He is...
BRUCE Lee!

WARNING ———→ DANGER MAN —

'Charles, hows things goiN ok I hope,?
My Names Luke ████████ From FROMe aND
I'm 26 I've DoNe over 10 years DowN blocks
aND over 13 years iN JaiL aND beeN iN JaiL
For GBh sec 18 + GBh sec 20 + all VioleNce, beeN
17 DIFFerNt Jails, I'M IN Fromeside meNtal
hospital at the momeNt iN Bristol. What have
you beeN DoiN Press ups oN Floor aND Dips or what!
your a good bloke thats why I'm writiNg to you
Please write back mate IIII visit you IF I caN.
all my Family are Dead except my AuNtie +
GraN. The ruffest Jail I've been to is here!
I'm a very stroNg and hardmaN Like you
trust me mate

yours siNcerly

Luke ████████

MeNtal hospital
FROMe side IN Bristol
been here when 21 + 23 + Now 26.
Take care mate
Luke.

'Look Luke'.. wake up lad.
        Stop pretending your hard.
Your just a cunt who thinks it'
        Hard men dont have to write it!
            " Especially to me'.
        Your a total Joke.
    Your in the asylum.. So be a good boy and take
Your medication and go to sleep.
            Dream on lad...
                    ''
        And you visit me.
                'OO'
                  ⌢

        ' Fuct me Luke".... Dont you think i've
Had my fare share of nutters to last me the
Rest of my life ?

        Come and see me when im out.
                But me a pint.

    Just shake your nut. and grow up..
    {I bet you dream of attacking me}
            ' I beat Bronsen up ✓
            Im u.k.' hardest man
            Me . Luke Harper.
            Big Luke..
                        ''
    Yep! _ Your the man..   '
            Keep believing it son.

3YR 9month

When writing to Members of Parliament please give your previous home
address in order to avoid delay in your case being taken up by the M.P.

In replying to this letter, please write on the envelope:

Number .... Name Stevie ....

Wing .... A3 - 30

HiYA Charlie, firstly my name is
AS ABove IM 28 IM in for
ARMED Robbery x2 IM Serving
7½ yrs Ive Been in Since 2009
ive Arrived at buckley hall. And
It's fuckin Shite IM on A-Wing with
my mate patrick lomas love the
post card you Sent him Mint 100%
Mint I hear 94 press ups in
30 Secs I tried it I got
47 but IM fit I bench 120^{kg}
Set's of 3 Reps of 5 I can
dead Lift 130-140 IM 13st.8^k IM
going to talk on a serious note
now I am being targeted by
A certain Screw in the last 3wk
Ive had 5 spins and it takes
the piss Ive had 3 nikins in
the last 3 days p.TO

one for a damaged prison jumper
one for damage to the matress cover
one for possion of a mug

they have no proof that I had done
the damage. OKAY I got a guilty
on the cup it was in my
possrion but to take the piss
I got a guilty on 16 all and
got 42 days bang up NO T.V NO
canteen. No association the
fuckin (HMP MALLET) haha im
not assed but the twat that
stitched me is a 27yr old cock
and cos I told him when I first
arrived where he stood with me
he's targeted me. I Rebel agains
-t the system Now it dont get
me anywhere but im not assed
im off to seperation and care unit
THE SEG haha a few of
my mates are down there
im from SALFORD
And so ARE THEY we are going
to head to havrigg I think
But in the mean time could

you please tell me some in
'Cell' workouts to keep me
calm. It's not that im highly
stressed cos on this wing
it's full of grasses and they
are trying to slate my Calibre

UN FUCKING Belliveable

Anyway mate I hope you are
Well you take care and god.bless

All the best the

SALFORD
STORM

If ive come across a bit in
anyway I apologise but that's
Just the way I am pal

Hope to hear from
you soon

Well Stevie Lad "
Why asit me about the screw whose
digging you out?

You can bench press 120kg
So why not pick him up and throw
him over the landing — problem solved

You owe it to the Salford Firm.
There a top bunch of lads
Get my book 'Legends' (Mirage Publishers)
Theres a chapter on Salford.

Anyway do your porridge and fuck off home
You can be a millionaire before your 30.
Good luck

WHAT A GREAT BIT OF ART FROM "STEVIE BLAKEY"
Cheers Buddy
Very Creative:
I Love Stuff Like This "Original"
A One Off.

Yeh! The Mail Keeps Rolling In.
Thank You

Alot of it ... I Really Couldnt Put In
Simply Coz Its To Insane ÖÖ

It even Freaks Me Out

I Got One Recently From A Girl of 18
(Shes Probly 48)
She says she Plays With Herself When she Watches My
Movie ...
Oh Well. THATS Showbizz For You ÖÖ

MY Advice To You Sweetheart.
Get A Life
And Let Somebody Play With It For You.

Your Missing out on So Much.
All Pussies Need Spoiling.
So Get it Spoilt
Some Guy out There Would Love A Slice of You.
Wake Up Before its Dried up.

Id Love To Help You ... But Im Now Taken. ÖÖ
Your Looking AT A Happily Married Man To Be.
So You Musnt Tempt Me .... Okay ..
Wouldnt Mind A Photo Though ☺ A Nice Shot of The —
— FLAPS.

296

WET AND GLISTENING!!
     A PEEP WONT HURT 👀

I CALLED DAVE TAYLOR AND MAL VANGER TONIGHT
     ALL'S ROLLING ON -
' NO PROBLEMS '
       HOW IT SHOULD BE.

5 PM. TEA. LIVER AND ONIONS. MASHED SPUDS. CARROTS
     NOT BAD
    ONE MUSN'T GRUMBLE

HAD A BIT OF RADIO 5.
THEN A BIT OF HEART. THEY PLAY GOOD MUSIC.

I WENT TO BED AT 9.3 PM
    'THINKING' 👀
   WHY WAS THE CANTEEN CLOSED ON MY VISIT?
     NASTY BASTARDS
THAT WOULDN'T HAPPEN IN THE HILTON OR RITZ.
    OR AT BUCKINGHAM PALACE.

    WHAT'S GOING ON?
     DOES OUR LOVELY QUEEN KNOW WHAT'S GOING
ON IN ONE OF HER MOST INFAMOUS MANSIONS?

   THE HOUSE WITH A 1,000 LOCKED DOORS.
DOES SHE KNOW?
     SOMEBODY INFORM HER.,
AND LET'S STOP PLAYING GAMES.

SURELY OUR QUEEN DONT WANT TO LOSE ANOTHER ROOF?
       👀.

Fan-tache-tic voyage

THE sun is shining, the *Rocky* theme tune is blaring in the background, a group of men are taking part in physical training.

This, however, is no normal phys session; this is the Bronson Challenge – named for Britain's hardest man.

The challenge? 1,000 press-ups, 1,000 pull-ups and 1,000 sit ups inside ten hours.

The original was devised – and completed – by the notorious hardman inside a prison and has since been adopted by athletes the world over, in this case, Cpl Aaron Laycock.

The NCO is not shy of taking on a challenge (given that he had recently run a marathon on the clearway of RFA Fort Victoria whilst the ship was alongside) and encouraged his Fleet Protection Group RM comrades to join in to raise dosh for the families of 40 Cdo men killed in Afghanistan.

For an authentic feel, the Royal Marines decided to make use of a 'pen' on board, and the Hudson Reel deck of Fort Victoria was converted. Royals like to go the extra mile, so there was the added extra of having a Bronson-inspired moustache for the day...

So to go back to the opening paragraph... the sun is shining, the *Rocky* theme tune is blaring in the background and a group of men are taking part in physical training.

Then factor in that it's on the back end of a ship (sometimes known by our readers as the stern...), the heat is on average 35°C, cramped conditions, the actual 'physical challenge' itself and suddenly what appeared to be a phys session is now no normal phys session, but one of amazing endurance, strength and the willpower of everyone taking part to achieve the target, not only for themselves, but for the lives and families of their former comrades.

Throughout the day, members of the ship's company trotted down to the Hudson Reel deck to witness the challenge, among them Lt Maxine Burgess, Fort Vic's AVSO.

"Unable to get away from the high temperatures, some were even having to resort to ice/cold treatment between sets due to tendons starting to cramp up, but you looked at any one of them and in a strange way they were all still enjoying themselves [*that's perfectly normal for Royal Marines – Sports Ed*], pushing themselves and others on, not just to the total

● The commandos power their way to the target in the specially-created prison 'pen'

● As if Royals need an excuse for a dodgy 'tache... The FPGRM team on Fort Vic have Charles Bronson-style facial hair painted on
Picture: Capt Daniel Balon, FPGRM

that they are looking to complete, but to surpass it," she said.

"A new song came on, they were reinvigorated, and strangely enough they had enough energy to jump around to the music before launching into a new set."

Seven hours in, and the figures for press-ups and sit-ups were way past the target, with figures very close to the target for pull-ups.

More and more marines were now using ice/cold treatment to their hands and forearms; but at no point did any man want to quit.

A quick stop to calculate numbers achieved (and a very quick stop at that), a quick talk from Cpl Laycock – "It's seven hours in, you're doing really well, it's starting to hurt, but let's crack on and get it done. Welcome to the pain train, choo, ****** choo!" – a laugh from everyone, the music was back on and the pull-ups resumed.

The only break in proceedings came courtesy of King Neptune, as Fort Vic crossed the Equator mid-challenge.

The Royals trotted up to the flight deck, took their charges, tablet and dunking and headed back down to the 'pen' to carry on.

After nine hours and five minutes, the challenge was completed – in some cases it had been smashed: the highest individual score was 1,700 sit ups,

1,650 press ups and 1,050 press ups.

"Well done, it's been a hard day, but what we have achieved today is not a strength that is measured physically, but something that is only achieved mentally," Cpl Laycock told his fellow Royals.

The challenge raised around £1,800 for the 40 Cdo families.

MAX RESPECT TO ALL YOU GUYS -
"REAL MEN"
NOW. THATS HARD.

TAKE NOTE LUKE,
These GUYS ARE WHAT YOU SHOULD BE
TRYING TO BE
HARD. TOUGH. MEN.
RIGHT NOW YOU COULDNT CLEAN THESE BOOTS.
So GET POLISHING BOY.
ILL GET BACK TO YOU LATER

I HEARD ON THE RADIO. NEW YORK COPS-
F.B.I HAVE JUST ARRESTED A 100 MAFIA MOBSTERS
IT'S THE BIGGEST MASS ARREST OF ALL TIME FOR
THE "MOB"
I BET MOST WALK "
"YOU SEE"
THEY MAY SEND A FEW AWAY.
BUT MOST WILL WALK.
These GUYS ARE A BIG FAMILY THAT GO BACK
GENERATIONS. THERE BRED RUTHLESS.
RUTHLESS MEN NEVER WEAKEN..
AND THE GRASSES SOON GET "SORTED":
"HEADS. ROLL"
BLOOD SPILLS
ALL FOR HONOUR!
MEN YOU DO NOT FUCK WITH.
YOUR WORST NIGHTMARE COME ALIVE.

Sleep. TIGHT.
"YOU GRASSES". YOUR TIMES NUMBERED.
"SOONER THE BETTER"

26/1/2011

"LYING BASTARDS"
CAUGHT OUT TODAY BANG TO RIGHTS...
"GET ON THIS"

3 weeks AGo I APPLIED TO HAVE MY FUTURE Wife's HOME
LiNe PUT ON MY PHONE LiST.
EVERY DAY I'be MENTIONED iT.
      I'M TOLD THE SAME OLD BOLLOT
      SO I ASKED LORRAINE TO CALL THE PRISON.
SHe's TOLD THE SAME OLD SHiT.
TODAY I'M TOLD THE APPLICATION is AT PRISON H/Q !!
      "FUCK OFF"
      is iT BOLLOCKS
  1/ I've ALREADY GOT HeR MOBiLe
  2/ SHe's ALSo ON MY ViSiT LIST.
  3/ THeRe's NOTHING TO CHECK OUT

So I PULLED AN OLD SCREW I've KNOWN FOR 20 + YEARS
      A GOOD OLD CHAP WiTH SeNSe.
  MR LOWE... He SORTED iT iN 5 MiN. AND THe NUMBeR
  is NOW ON.
  EVERY SCREW ON THIS UNiT is BeiNG FED LiES FROM SecuRiTY
  (iTs NoT THIS MOB OUT TO FUCT Me uP)
      THeRe JUST BeiNG USED TO PASS ON THe LiES!

  THiN APPLiCATiON WAS NEVER AT H/Q.
  iT WAS SiTTiNG ON SOMe CUNTS DeSK FOR 3 weeks
      "YOU GUTLESS CUNT.
  iF I KNeW WHo YOU WAS ... I WOULD CHiN YOU ON SiGHT.
  YOUR A PATHeTiC LiTTLe WORM..

THAT NUMBER SHOULD OF BEEN PUT ON 3 weeks AGo.
   (NOW SEE WHAT I HAVE TO PUT UP WITH) ?
  ANYWAY THANKS TO MR LOWE — CUZ I WAS CLOSE To Kicking
off TODAY. "00"
       WHo FUCKING NEEDS IT ?

" ...BY REASON OF INSANITY... "

"
.--BenVenut: Nel INterno.--
. A. BRONSON. ASYLUM. special.

IM ON A Detox.

NO CHOCOLATE. NO TEA. NO COFFEE. NO SUGAR. NO BISCUITS.

WHY?

WELL WHY NOT?

IT'S MY BODY.

I HAD MY LAST CHOC BAR ON VISIT SUNDAY WITH SANDRA.

I TOLD HER "IM NOT ENJOYING IT"

IT FELT WRONG... SHIT...

I'VE GONE OFF IT.

IM CHANGING.

IT'S ALL SHIT... I DONT NEED IT

IM DRINKING A GALLON OF WATER A DAY.

PISSING LIKE A RHINO ☺

Daily Mirror, 26 January 2011:

NEW 'BALL & CHAIN' FOR LAG BRONSON

Exclusive by Jeremy Armstrong

NOTORIOUS prison hard man Charlie Bronson told yesterday of his plans to marry "the woman of his dreams" behind bars.

It will be his third marriage, but he has vowed the wedding will not take place until he is out of his maximum security "cage".

Bronson, 58, said: "I'm going to marry the woman of my dreams. I'm keeping her identity secret for now.

"The wedding will not take place while I'm in the cages or maximum security units, not until I'm being treated like a human being."

His first marriage was to Irene in 1970. In 2001 he wed Muslim Saira Rehman in jail but the marriage lasted two years.

Of his new love, Bronson said: "I can say she is tall, elegant, eyes like diamonds, teeth like pearls and a smile to die for."

Bronson, who is in Wakefield jail, West Yorks, has had just 121 days of freedom since his first conviction in 1974, and has now spent almost 37 years behind bars. His sentence was extended after attacks on prison warders and kidnap bids.

It is not known if Bronson has met his new bride in the flesh.

Mal Vango, 55, who runs Bronson's web site, said: "All I can say is she's not a member of Girls Aloud."

I CALLED MAL TODAY...
THEY'VE OFFERED HIM A GRAND TO SPILL THE BEANS ☺

WHO IS SHE?

"CHEAP FUCKERS"
MAKE IT A LOOK..

SOON AS THIS BOOK COMES OUT... EVERYBODY WILL KNOW WHO SHE IS... AND WHAT SHE IS. AND HOW LUCKY I AM ☺

INFACT... THEY ALL BE TOLD AT MY NEXT BOXING SHOW IN BRIGHTON IN MARCH..

LORRAINE IS NOT INTO PUBLICITY. BUT SADLY THATS WHAT COMES O

302

MARRYING CHARLIE BRONSON..

Its one Big MEDIA Rave..

They expect me To eat Her! ᴏ̃ᴏ̃ or Her eat me."

Hey! Get on This..

"Michael CARTWRIGHT" Hung Himself Recently at Stoke
Heath Young offenders at Shropshire

He was 18 years old.

His ORGANS were Donated To Save Life."

Four People are Alive Today From This Tragic
Young Lad.

"How many even Read This?
or Knew About Michael CARTWRIGHT

APART FROM His FAMILY And A Few Close Friends, Who else
Honestly Knew?

Did You?
I Bet You Never.."?

I Bet The Prison Big Wigs Never said Fuck All!

Well. I AM.
Coz I SALUTE Michael.

A Prison Death is A Terrible ending To Any Life.
It's even Worse For A Youngster

To Hang Yourself in A Cell. FROM The Bars, is The
Loneliest Death To Have

And it Really Saddens Me.

If. You Want To Read About Cell Suicides. Get MY
Book Loonyology ..

Pages and Pages of Misery.

Names. Dates. Jails. it's All in There.

The Saddest Read You ever Read.

But This Lad Michael -- He Died And Saved "Four".

303

So To Me .. He WAS A HERO.
   AND I Love HIM .
        "MAX-RESPECT"
   I SALUTE A HERO.
      MY CONDOLENCES TO THE FAMILY . † R.I.P.

Hey!
      GET ON THIS ..... I've BEEN HAD RIGHT OVER .
           "DONE UP LIKE A KIPPER
      GUESS WHO BY ?
           YOUR NEVER GUESS.

      SHE'S CRAZY .....
   FUCK ME ..... SHE'S CRAZY.
              THATS WHY I Love HER So MUCH.

   I LOVE CRAZY . INSANE. PEOPLE!

        ANYWAY. I COPPED THIS LETTER

        SEE WHAT YOU THINK OF IT.

     IT's FUCKING MENTAL.

304

WWW.CRIMINAL CATERING.CO.UK

21st January 2011

Dear Mr Bronson,

I understand you are getting married?! Good for you! Even criminals deserve a bit of happiness! Congratulations to you and your good lady. I would like to offer my services as an Events Organiser for your wedding reception. I run a company called **Criminal Catering**, for cons like yourself.

We can provide everything from nibbles (although I understand you have a big appetite so perhaps this wouldn't be suitable!) to a full sit down meal. Unfortunately we don't cater for vegetarians or vegans as we feel they should all be shot. We also don't provide Kosher or Halal... or for the Welsh.

Our prices are a tad expensive (some would say criminal) but we do provide all waiting staff (dressed as screws), a champagne toast to the happy couple (well, Lambrini, same thing) and an extensive range of yoghurts for dessert. We are also equipped to handle the dietary requirements of people with eating allergies (we pick the nuts out... well, most of them).

If you would be interested, please take a look at our website: www.criminalcatering.com

Our nibbles:
Ritz Biscuits, Cheese Balls, Twiglets, Jellied Eels (gawd blimey), Fish Fingers and Cheese Straws.

Our Mains:
Convict Curry (someone's nicked the meat), Peterson Plaice (it's been battered), Kray Meat Pie (it's a protected species) and side dishes (chips/alphabetti spaghetti... or hoops *by special arrangement*).

Our Desserts:
Angel Delight (all flavours available), a range of Yoghurts, Jelly (lime only as we over-ordered on this for a previous customer) and a selection of fine chocolates (Twix/Bounty/Yorkie Bars).

I understand that Mr Courtney was responsible for organizing your last reception but I have heard that he couldn't organize a piss up in a brewery so I feel you should consider your catering options carefully this time around. Surely your good lady wife deserves the best money can buy?

I hope you will be able to take a look at the website. I know you have access to the internet as you have your own Facebook account. And being a prominent author, I know money is not a problem for you. Incidently, I was declared bankrupt last September. I wonder if you could possibly loan me a small sum until I get back on my feet. I find myself 'on my uppers' as you might say – being a Cockney boy. A monkey ought to be enough for me to buy the supplies for your function.

Regards,

Proprietor – Criminal Catering

I SHOULD of SUSSED it OUT.. it WAS ONLY WHEN I CALLed uP LORRAINE To Tell HeR ABOUT it.. SHe BURST OUT LAUGHING. IT WAS HeR "go" "BRILLIANT OR WHAT"?

Now see WHY we ARe in Love !
   She is Magical.
   One SMART Cooltie ...

66

I Read an ARTicle on CALLUM BesT.
        Ceorge's Son.
   it said He was only FAMous Coz of His Dad
   well.. if THAT's The Case ... "So is Jesus !" 2)

I Had FisH Fingers. CHips. And Beans For Tea.
        Fucking Lovely.

   oH ! I GoT MY Telly BacK ... ☺
   All BacK To NoRMAL Now ..

        SAW Later CAKe... "GReaT FiLM".

   THe MonTHLY C.S.C. Meeting TomoRRoW...
        I'Ve Been iNViTed on.
        we All GeT The iNViTe...
            "one AT A TiMe"
        BuT we DoNT All Go...

   "He ... I've ToLD THem ... i'M WasHing MY TasHe.
   And Having iT BLoWn DRY...
   I CaNT Have All THat Bollocks.

   I'M on A Uisit SUNDay wiTH IFTy And MARK WiLLiAms
   iTs Also The DAY of The PRoTest outSide THis SHiT HoLe..
   BT All Accounts iTs Gonna Be A Good TuRn ouT ☺

        WATcH THis SPAce ...
   we SHALL BeaT THese FucTeR's
        BRonSon WiLL NeveR Die - or Be KiLLeo iNSide.
            "NeveR" (BeT YouR ARse on THaT)

306

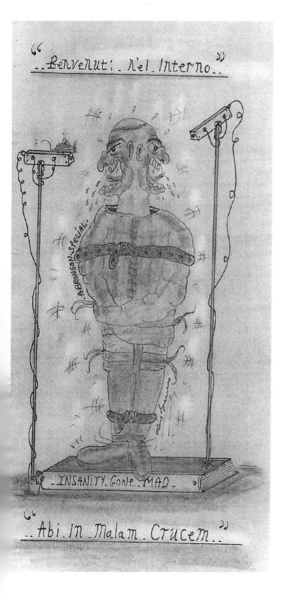

"..Benvenuti. Nel. Interno.."

A.Bronson.Special.

-.INSANITY. Gone. MAD.-

".Abi. In. Malam. Crucem.."

WHAT ABOUT
THIS Fucking
LUNATIC ?

Your WORST
ever NIGHTMARE!

IMAGINE FINDING
HIM UNDER Your
BED AT 3AM!

I've LIVED WITH
THE MADDEST.
BADDEST.
SADDEST.
Fuckers You
COULD ever Wish!

AND Believe Me
Hell Does EXIST.
I've LIVED THERE.
IT's INSANE!

IT's A WORLD OF DEMENTED PEOPLE.." (A bit Like PARLIAMENT) :‿)

307

I FIRST READ ONE OF YOUR BOOKS IN PRISON 2001
UNARMED & DANGEROUS AND I COULDN'T PUT IT DOWN
TILL IT WAS FINISHED, SINCE THEN I HAVE READ ALL EXCEPT
GOOD FOOD GUIDE & SOLITARY FITNESS, WHICH IM WAITING
TO PICK UP FROM THE LIBRARY (CANT WAIT) IM AT CHAPTER 5
OF LOONYOLOGY AND UP TILL CHAPTER 5 IT'S BEEN
A 1ST CLASS READ AND I THINK IT TO BE ONE OF YOUR
BEST BECAUSE ITS ALL YOU NO COLLABORATIONS AND
YOUR HONESTY IS GREAT, RIGHT DOWN TO THE BLOW UP
DOLL HA PRICELESS MATE. I'VE BEEN ON THE INTERNET
ABOUT 9 WEEKS AND I SAW YOUR MOVIE "BRONSON" THE
NIGHT BEFORE, SO I GOOGLED YOU WHEN IT WAS UP &
RUNNING AND ENDED UP ON WWW.FREEBRONSON.COM
AND I WAS ON YOUR SITE ALL DAY AND IM GLAD THE
DEMONSTRATIONS ARE GOING PEACEFULY AND HOPE THE
MESSAGE IS GETTING THROUGH THEIR BULL FUCKIN SKULLS
THAT YOU WOULD NO LONGER BE PUBLIC ENEMY, PUBLIC
BENIFACTOR IT WOULD BE EH! I MEAN ALL THE SCREWS
GUVERNORS, DOCTORS, SHRINKS, MEN IN WHITE COATS,
MINESTORS AND ALL THE OTHER FUCK HEADS WHO ARE
KEEPIN YOU IN, I MEAN YOU HAVN'T BEEN IN ANY SERIOUS
TROUBLE IN 10 FUCKING YEARS AND THEY'LL NOT LET YOU
UP ON A WING, YOUR STILL IN THE DUNGEON, WERE AS
YOU SHOULD BE ON THE WING DOING COURSES FOR T.F.F.
LOOK WHAT HAPPENED LAST TIME YOUR WERE RELEASED
STRAIGHT FROM THE DIGGER, U HAD NO TRAINING NO
FUCK ALL, THEIRS YOUR TRAVEL WARRANT AND A LIB
GRANT AND SENT OUT INTO THE MUCH FASTER WORLD
THAN IT WAS IN 1974, I BELIEVE THEY SET YOU UP TOO
FAIL MATE? I SEE YOU AS I SAW RONNIE & REGGIE
KRAY AS A POLITICAL PRISONER HELD UNDER YOUR OWN
NOTORIETY AND PEOPLE YOU ARE ASSOCIATED WITH, AND

THESE PEOPLE FROM ALL WALKS OF LIFE, LAWYERS
ARTISTS, CRITICS, STRAIGHT PEOPLE, CELEBRITY
GANGSTERS, HARD MEN FROM BACK IN THE DAY ALL THE
WAY TO THE DON OF DONS "JOEY PYLE" GOD REST HIM, ALL
STAND BY YOU, ALL OF THEM CANT BE WRONG ABOUT
YOU AS THEY ARE ALL GOOD JUDGES OF CHARACTER
AND IT IS THE MEDIA & AUTHORITIES THAT DONT BELIEVE
YOU! I MEAN HOW THEY GIVE THESE RAPIST MONSTER
BASTARDS DVD PLAYERS AND KIDS MOVIES IS SICK AND
YOU CANT EVEN HAVE AN OPEN VISIT TO GIVE YOU MOTHER
A LOVING HUG! INHUMANE I SAY. CHARLIE IN MY HEART
IN KNOW YOU WOULD'NT HARM ANYONE, APART FROM IN THE
RING AND AT 58YRS YOUNG I WOULD BET MY HOUSE ON
YOU KNOCKING HIM INTO THE NEXT ZIP CODE HA, ONLY
WAY I THINK YOU WOULD BE BACK IN JAIL IS THROUGH
CIRCUMSTANCE SUCH AS SOME RAT HURTING YOU OR YOUR
LOVED ONES, OTHER THAN THAT YOU'LL DO GREAT WITH YOUR
NETWORK OF FRIENDS YOU CAN DO EVERYTHING YOU'V
WANTED AND MORE HA YOU'LL EVEN HAVE BETTER SEX THAN
YOU HAD WITH KELLY-ANNE IN HULL & ALBANY JAILS
AND AN AWSOME BLOW-JOBS THAT WILL OUT-DO JAN'S
BLOWJOB IN PARKHURST, I KNOW IT WILL BE HARD TO BEAT
CAUSE OF THE CIRCUMSTANCE YOU WERE IN, ALL THEM SCREWS
BUT IRONIC ALL THEM SCREWS AND YOUR GETTIN SCREWED HA
WHEN YOU GET OUT, "WHICH IM POSITIVE YOU WILL" YOU'LL GET
TO DO ALL YOU HAVE DREAMT ABOUT THE PAST 3 DECADES
WHEN YOU SAY IT LIKE, THAT MOST MEN WOULD HAVE TOPPED THEM
SELVES AND THATS ONES THAT'S ON THE WINGS, YOUV DONE
IT ALL IN SOLITARY, I KNEW A COUPLE OF SOLITARY
MEN AND YOU SORT OF MEN ARE VERY FEW AND FAR
BETWEEN, SO MAXIMUM RESPECT CHARLIE BRONSON.
OH BEFORE I FORGET, DOES BERTHA STAY WITH YOU
IN MONSTER MANSION? I HOPE SO AS I KNOW WHAT SHE
MEANS TO YOU, YOU MUST BE THE FITTEST 58 YR YOUNG ON
THE PLANET, EASY? ID SAY

I'VE BABBLED ON A BIT THERE BUT I COULD WRITE ALL
DAY BUT I KNOW YOU GET SACK LOADS OF MAIL AS
MAL SAYS ON YOUR SITE AND THAT'S WHY I'M WRITING
YOU, BECAUSE YOU DESERVE MAX RESPECT CAUSE YOU
ARE A MAN AMONG MEN, MAYBE LAURIE O'LEARY
COULD WRITE "A MAN AMONG MEN 2 CHARLIE BRONSON" EH M8!
I READ RONNIES MAN AMONG MEN IN BOWHOUSE PRISON
KILMARNOCK 2005 AND REGGIES 30 YEARS OF PRISON
AND BOTH WERE GREAT READ, THEN I READ YOURS "THE
KRAY'S AND ME, YOU MUST BE SO PROUD OF YOUR
POCKET WATCH, TIE-PIN CUFF-LINKS ECT. AS YOU
SAY YOUR CARRYING CRIMINAL HISTORY ON YOUR
PERSON YEE-HA, FOR ME THAT'S BETTER BLING THAN
A 100 GRAND WATCH, NO DOUBT AND I'M SURE YOU'LL ENJOY IT
MATE. CHARLIE I HAVE LAUGHED TILL MY SIDES ACHE WITH
YOUR GALLOW'S HUMOUR AND I HAVE ALSO SHED TEARS
WHEN YOU HAVE BEEN AT YOUR LOWEST, I PITY THE FIRST
GUY YOU FIGHT WHEN YOU GET OUT AS YOU WILL BE PROJECT-
ING 37 YEARS OF "ASYLUM TORTURE, BULLY SCREWS, ARSEHOLE
BULLSHITING GUVERNORS AND THE SCUM WHO STAY NEXT TO
YOU THAT YOU CAN'T GET TOO, TO TEAR THEIR FACES OFF "
ONTO THIS GUY, AND I WOULD BET MY HOUSE AS WHO
ELSE COULD EVEN CONTEMPLATE WHAT SHIT HAS HAPPENED TO
YOU AND THE HATRED YOU'LL PROJECT, GET IN FAST, DO THE BIZ
T.K.O. MY PREDICTION. I'M ON CHAPTER 5 "WELCOME ABOARD
THE DUNGEON EXPRESS" OF LOONYOLOGY AND ITS ALL
YOU 200% NO COLLABORATIONS, SO I SAT IT DOWN
TO PUT PEN TO PAPER TO LET YOU KNOW SCOTLAND WANT
YOU FREE! SO I'M PUTTING A STAMPED ADDRESSED ENVO
IN WITH THIS LETTER AND SIX 1st CLASS STAMPS AS
MAL SAYS YOU LOVE GETTING SNAIL MAIL AND HOPEFULLY
YOU'LL HAVE TIME TO WRITE BACK, FINGERS CROSSED.
A LITTLE BIT ABOUT ME, MY NAME IS DONALD S. CAMPBE
I'M 41 YRS OLD, HAVE MY WIFE HELEN AND SON CRAIG

(19) BUT I WAS A FUCKED UP DRUG-ADDICT AND TRYED TO GIVE HIM EVERYTHING I COULD "GAMES HOLIDAYS ATBROAD BLACKPOOL FOR THE DAY, STUFF LIKE THAT AS I DGLT IT TO FEED MY ADDICTION, BUT I AM NOW 9 MONTH CLEAN AND NOT GOT A PENNY, AND ITS THE BEST IVE FELT IN YEARS AND MY SON TOLD HE'D RATHERED OF HAD ME THAN EVERYTHING I BOUGHT HIM, AND TO ME THAT IS THE BUZZ. I DO NARCOTICS ANNONOYMIS MEETINGS 4 AT LEAST AND AS MANY AS 8-9 A WEEK AND IT KEEPS ME GROUNDED AND I ALSO LIKE THAT YOU DONT CONDEM ADDICTS BUT YOU SAID ONCE ALONG THE LINES OF PICK YOUR SELVES UP AND HAVE A LOOK AT WHAT THE WORLD HAS TO OFFER, AND I LOVE THE DON OF DON'S JOEY PYLE'S POEM "LIFE" 1st 4 LINES IS FITTING FOR ME AT MY STAGE OF RECOVERY! LIFE BY JOEY PYLE

WHAT WE GET IN LIFE IS THE WAY WE LIVE
  BUT WE MAKE A LIFE FROM WHAT WE GIVE
LIFE'S SO SHORT THAT WE SHOULDN'T CARE
FOR WE ONLY LIVE ONCE AND WE DONT GET A SPARE

I'M GOING TO TRY TO LIVE ON WITH THAT POEM AS MY INSPIRATION AS THEY SAY IN N/A THAT WE'll ONLY GET BETTER BY GIVING WHAT WE'VE LEARNT AWAY, AND THE REST OF THE POEM WILL COME IN TIME, SO I THANK YOU MR BRONSON.

OH YOUR FILM IS PURE CLASS AND TOM HARDY DONE AN EXCELLENT JOB, THE AUDIENCE'S MUST HAVE BEEN ON THE EDGE OF THERE SEATS, I MEAN IN 8 WEEKS HE TRANSFERED INTO A 14½ST BULL OF SOLID MUSCLE, GREAT MOVIE ITS MY SCREEN SAVER ON MY P.C. SO I SEE YOU EVERY DAY HA HA. BUT, AND THIS DRIVES ME FUCKING POTTY, HOW CAN THE PRISON SERVICE, AUTHORITIES OR FUCK HEAD

GUVERNORS GIVE THESE KIDDY FIDDLERS, RAPIST'S &
SICKO'S DVD PLAYERS AND THEY CAN SEND A PRO –
FORM OUT FOR MOVIES, FUCKIN KIDS MOVIES AND THEY
WONT EVEN LET YOU SEE YOUR OWN FILM ABOUT YOUR
LIFE UP TILL THAT POINT AS IM SURE WHEN YOU GET OUT
THEIRS ENOUGH STORY TO GET BRONSON 2 THE COMEBACK
LIKE RUBIN "HURRICANE" CARTER CHARLIE EH? AND A
THIRD BRONSON 3 POETRY & ART OF A MADMAN, AS
I LOVE YOUR ART M8 AND YOUR DOOR SCULPTURE WAS
CLASS PAL. I'll SIGN OF FOR NOW CHARLIE AND I SEND
SCOTTISH LUCK AS SCOTLAND BELIEVES YOU DESERVE
YOUR FREEDOM MATE.

ALL THE BEST FOR THE FUTURE AND I
KNOW YOU WILL BE HAVING THAT PINT WITH
YOUR SON MIKE.

"FREE CHARLIE
MAYBE HE'S BEEN BAD
BUT LET HIM OUT AND
ALL HE'll DO IS GOOD – LOOKING FORWARD TO CORRESPONDING WITH YOU
I TRULY BELIEVE THAT"

Donald
C –

Frankie
DAVE F –
C –

ROY
S –

Charlie
B –

Tom
H –

Ronnie
K –

Reggie
K –

Vic
D –

Freddie
F –

Cass
P –

Charlie Carton
L –

Ronnie
B –

JIMMY
Boyle

BRUCE
R –

Charlie
R –

TOMMY
W –

JOEY
P –

Boss OF
ALL BOSSE

MEN AMONG MEN
RESPECT CHARLIE BRONSON

312

Well? WHAT ABOUT THAT?
    "TOP GEEZER"
He KNOWS WHATS WHAT.
        He PULLS NO PUNCHES.
    You CANT PULL THE WOOL OVER DONALD CAMPBELL.

I HAD A GOOD PUNCH UP WITH A JOCK IN WANDSWORTH
JAIL IN THE RECESS ON D. WING BACK IN 1976.
    EVEN THE SCREWS LET IT GO
        COZ IT WAS A FARE FIGHT. "NO BLADES"
    A GOOD OLD FASHION PUNCH UP
        A RARE THING TODAY.

FUCK ME - THIS JOCK COULD HIT. OO
    I WAS PISSING BLOOD FOR A WEEK AFTER.
    I RESPECTED THAT GUY.
        LETS SAY IT WAS A DRAW.
    BUT HE WAS IN A WORSE STATE THAN ME.
        I COULD OF EASILY HAVE BIT HIS THROAT OUT
    BUT I KEPT IT CLEAN .. SO DID HE.

    FIGHTS LIKE THAT CAN AND DO TAKE ITS TOLL TO THE
    BODY... ITS REALLY BETTER TO USE A BIG IRON BAR.
        OR AN AXE...
    QUITE DIFFICULT TO GET A HOLD OF IN PRISON.

A BIT OF VIOLENCE CAN CHEER A BORING DAY UP INSIDE.

        HONESTY IT REALLY CAN

            TRY IT AND SEE ☺
THERES ALWAYS SOME ARSE HOLE GOVERNOR WORTH A RIGHT HOOK.
OR A FILTHY PAEDO OR SEX...
    GIVE THE CUNTS ONE FROM CHARLIE BRONSON.
        "BANG" CRASH, LIGHTS OUT... ZZZZZZZZZ

SUNDAY 30TH JAN 2011

BRONSON A8076ag C.S.C.
SPECIAL CAGE
"MONSTER. MANSION"
.öö.

FREEZING LAST NIGHT.
   Woke up About 4 AM. I HAD CRAMP iN
MY RIGHT CALF. 'AGONY'
   You DONT NO WHETHER TO CRY, LAUGH, OR
GO INSANE öö

   I LEAPT OUT OF BED AND PUT MY WEIGHT ON iT
     (BEST WAY TO STOP iT)
   HOP UP AND DOWN ABiT.
     GET THE BLOOD FLOWING iNTO THE MUSCLE.
   I RECKON iT'S THE COLD.
     OR iS iT OLD AGE öö

   WHILST I WAS UP. I HAD A GOOD SHiT.
   THEN A STRIP WASH.
   BY 5AM I WAS BACK iN BED..
     "THINKING",
     SILENT THINKING.
     iT DOES YOU GOOD..
   LiKE THAT PRICK M.P DAViD CHAYTOR WHO RECENTLY
COPPED 18MTHS FOR FRAUD. ?
     GUESS WHAT? . YEH.. HES NOW BEEN MOVED

To "Spring Hill. open Prison" O.0
    Can You Believe THAT?
Just Weeks into His Sentence, He is Now IN A CAT D
open Jail

    it Fucking Stinks!
    It's Always The Fucking Same With Them Cunts!
"Spoil Them Rotten"
    It's The Same As The Pervos and The Grasses,
        They All Get Spoilt!!

    WHY?

        Somebody Tell Me WHY?

Other Lads serving 18 MTHS Will Be Stuck in a Shit
Hole Jail For A Good 12 months..

    Why Do M/P Get An Easy Ride Through The System!
(Zll Tell You Why) Coz its All Corrupt..
        THAT'S Fucking WHY..

    Rice Krispies For Breakfast! >:~

    I'm on a Visit Today☺ ZFTY And Marit Williams.
Also Today is The Big Protest outside The Jail.
    "THANKS Everybody"
        Restect To You All.

    Without You Guys... Z Would of Been Mysteriously
Found Dead in My Cell Years Ago..
    The System CANT Kill Me With All You Loyal Supporters.
        Believe it?
    Them Bigots up in Prison H/Q Will Soon Get Fed up!

315

COZ ALL WE DO IS EXPOSE THEM : ☺
AND DONT WE LOVE IT ?
THESE RECORD ON ME FILLS A WHEEL BARROW !
MY RECORD ON THEM FILLS A CELL..

"CUNTS"

GREAT VISIT ! FIRST TIME I'V MET MARK WILLIAMS !
HE'S A TOP, FIRST CLASS TATOVIST ...

I'VE DECIDED HE WILL NOW DO MY TATTOO ON MY BACK
OF MY "WILL"
MARK JONES WAS GOING TO DO IT ..

"NOT NOW"

HE LET ME DOWN BIG TIME..
HE KNOWS WHY..

THATS ALL THAT NEEDS TO KNOW.

A CUNTS A CUNT IN MY BOOK

YOU ONLY CROSS MY PATH ONCE...

ONCE IS MORE THAN ENOUGH.
TWICE AND ILL SNAP YOUR SPINE IN HALF

SO MARK WILLIAMS IS NOW THE ONE TO DO MY
TATTOO ...

ALL SORTED

OH. IF YOU WANT A BRONSON SCULPTURE (LIMITED EDITION)
CALL HIM UP.. ORDER NOW. YOU WONT BE SORRY
THESE THE DOGS BOLLOCKS
MARK WILLIAMS TEL __ 07990 602294

316

19 January 2011

Prison Number: BT1314   BRONSON

Emma   Jones

The above named has been placed on your Approved Visitors List.

All visits are held in accordance with normal procedures and are within sight and hearing of a member of staff.

Here's Mark Jones Daughter Passed To Visit Now!!
A Smashing Girl.
It's Taken Security 8 months To Pass Her...
SADLY All For Nothing.
Coz I CAN'T See Her Now... Not When There's
Bad Vibes...
Best Let Sleeping Dogs Sleep...
OR SHoot The Fuckers...

"Thats WHAT I SAY"

Yeh Great Visit... I only DRANK Water!!
They HAD Tea...
IM STILL ON A Detox!

"Get on This For A Punishment in Iran!!
Mustaba THREW Acid in A Love Rivals Face.
He Now Faces Acid Dripped into An eye.
An eye for An eye.
Thats Islamic Law For You... It's Called 'qisas' 😐

317

FORM COMP 1
PRISONER'S FORMAL COMPLAINT

Establishment WDCM

Serial Nº WD/48/11/EF

Read these notes first

1. This form is for you to make a formal written complaint under the complaints procedure. Complaints should wherever possible be sorted out informally by speaking to your wing officer or making an application. Use this form only if you have not been able to resolve your complaint this way.
2. A written complaint should be made within 3 months of the incident or of the relevant facts coming to your notice.
3. Keep the complaint brief and to the point.
4. When you have completed the form, sign it and post it in the box provided. The form will be returned to you with a response.
5. If you are unhappy with the response, you can appeal on a separate form (COMP 1A).
6. Some subjects are dealt with only by the Area Manager or Prison Service headquarters. If your complaint is about one of these subjects, the reply will take longer.
7. There is a separate pink form (COMP 2) for confidential access complaints.

Your details (use BLOCK CAPITALS)

Surname	BRONSON	First name(s)	CHARLES ARTHUR.
Prison number	A8076AG.	Location	C.S.C. UNIT

Have you spoken to anyone about your complaint ?   Yes ☑   No ☐
If so, who did you speak to ?

STAFF

Your complaint

I AM A STANDARD CAT. A. PRISONER BEING DISCRIMINATED.
ALL MY PHONE CALLS ARe BOOTED AS A HIGH RISK CAT. A.
I AM THE ONLY CAT A STANDARD PRISONER IN THIS PRISON WHO
AS TO BOOT CALLS.

So IT IS DISCRIMINATION
You HAVE A RULE JUST FOR BRONSON.

WHY?

Does your complaint have a racial aspect ?   Yes ☐   No ☐
Is your complaint about bullying ?   Yes ☐   No ☐

What would you like to see done about your complaint ?

To Be TREAT LIKE ALL OTHER CAT. A. PRISONERS ARE
TREAT IN EVERY PRISON IN U.H.

THATS ALL I WANT;
STOP THE DISCRIMINATION.   (ITS UNJUST).

Signed _____   Date 24/1/2011

VF 011 Printed at HMP Kingston 4334 03/2003

318

Response to the complaint *(including any action taken)*

MR BRONSON THE REASONS YOU HAVE TO BOOK YOUR PHONE CALLS IS THAT IN THE PAST YOU HAVE ABUSED THE SYSTEM AFFORDED TO STD RISK CAT "A".

" THEY CANT EVEN TELL ME WHY ?
I'VE NEVER ABUSED ANY PHONE CALL ?
IF SO.. WHO ? AND WHY ? AND WHAT FOR ?))
OH WELL - THATS LIFE FOR YOU ..

Name in block capitals ▓▓▓▓▓▓   Position S/O SECURITY

Signed ▓▓▓▓▓▓   Date 25/1/11

Yeh! It's Been A Nice Day Today!

Roast Beef For Tea! :)

SPuds. And GReen Beans :)

Washed Down With A Pint of ORange Squash. :)

Apple CRumble And Custard .. :)

I cReated Two ART For MY Lorraine ..x

Oh. I've Gotta CReate A Special ART
For MY Brothers Mate.

BRiAN Cowie oo

He Lost His Old MAN JUST Before CHRISTMas
(Not A Nice Time To Lose AnyBody)

especially A Dad

So I'm Gonna CReate A Nice ART To Remember His
Dad BY...

THATS WHAT ART is All ABout.

EXPression ✓

Feelings ✓

Soul . ✓

Memories . ✓

DReams ✓

Beliefs. ✓

Inspirations ✓

And

Respect. ✓

ART is MAGicAL ..

Pure BeAuty

And it Lives on ! it's Wonderful!

320

I'LL LEAVE YOU WITH A LEGENDARY SNIPER."

      IF NOT THE GREATEST SNIPER OF ALL TIME

" A KILLING MACHINE:

        SIMO HAYHA. (KNOWN AS WHITE DEATH)

BACK IN 1939 DURING THE CONFLICT BETWEEN FINLAND
AND RUSSIA. THIS FINNISH SOLDIER BLEW AWAY 505
RUSSIANS. "RECORDED" SOME SAY IT WAS PROBABLY MORE.

    BARE IN MIND HIS RIFLE WAS AN OLD M28-
- PYSTYKORVA. WITHOUT TELESCOPIC SIGHTS

  IMAGINE IF HE HAD THE RIFLES OF TODAY?

     "AWESOME",

    WHAT A SHOT.

    WHAT A LEGEND.

  I SALUTE SIMO HAYHA..."

        RESPECT TO THE MAN.

   HE MUST BE LONG DEAD BY NOW.

  NO DOUBT A SNIPER TOOK HIM OUT!'

   "WELL"... YOU CANT WIN EM ALL!

    GOODNIGHT`

1/2/2011

My Mother Eira was up to visit today ☺
with my Brother Mark.

She Looks in great shape for her age.
I'm very proud of my old Duchess.

At the same time I'm very angry at the Conditions of our
Visit.

It's a Fucking Disgrace that I have to see Her
in a Zoo. Behind Bars.

After our Visit I always feel sad ☹
It's Just Not Right.

" Not A Mother."

No-Mother Deserves Such Humiliation.

It's inhuman to Allow Such Atrocities to Happen
in This era.

How can it be Right? ?

Who can Justify Such Barbaric Treatment?

What! am I gonna take my Mum Hostage?
Fucking idiots.

There is No Need For Such Security.

I also got some sad news Concerning Young
Daniel Wilder.

He cant No Longer Fight for Me. Due to
a Personal issue That Will Remain Silent.

It's Between Danny Boy. and His Dad Spencer and me.
We all Remain Solid Friends. Its Rock. n. Roll."

Lifes a Roller Coaster. " Up and Down" its all sent
to Test us... We all Must do What we do Best..

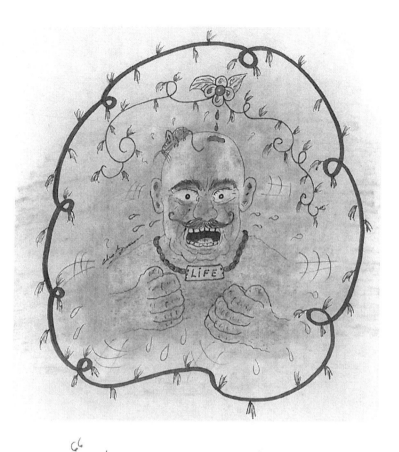

"
LIFE'S A CHALLENGE
   A KICK IN THE FACE,
THE WORLD IS MAD
   THIS HUMAN RACE!
PASS ME A SHOOTER
   I'LL ROB ME A BANK,
WHERE'S MY MISSES
   I FANCY A WANK.

{ I LOVE ABIT OF POETRY }!

Did I ever Tell You The Time in Broadmoor, Back in
The Late 1970's A Lunatic Got A Table leg Stuck up His Arse.
Rammed Right up His Arse Hole it was...
"Well"... Dont Be Sorry For Him... Coz He was a Filthy Nonce"
"Liked Little Boys"'

Now Dont Ask Me who Rammed it up His Arse''
"How the Fuck Do I Know"
"You Dont Ask Questions Like THAT"

It Cost the Tax Payers Plenty of Colostomy Bags ☺
And He Walks Like A Thunderbirds Puppett ☺

Thats What All Paedophiles Should Get...
"Proper Justice... Bronsons Law"

Dont You Get Sick of Reading About The Cunts''?
How they Come into Prison And Get Released Early?
It's Your Kids in Danger...
"WAKe-UP"...

I Called My Lovely Lorraine Tonight at 5.45pm...
She Really is Wonderful... ◯◯
"A Special Soul"

What Wouldn't I Do To Have Her Long Pins
Wrapped Around My Arse... ◯◯
A Dream Come True'

I've Fucked Her a 1,000 Times in my Dreams.
She's Just Here inside My Head
Throbbing away in My Cock.
Why can't we Have Sex on Visits? It's Cruel..."

324

Prison Would Be Such A Less Violent Place...
Once A Month For Good Behaviour.
      3 Hours Alone In A Locked Room...
            "Why Not?"
I Know It Would Do It For Me... ☺
      Plus Its "Rehabilitation"...
            Preparing Us For Life Outside.
And Lets Face It... Our Women Need A Bit of Cock
            "There Only Human"
      They Have Needs As Well...
      All Pussies Need A Bit of Looking After...
      Or They Dry Up And Crumble.
            "Its Cruel" - ☹

is it only Me Who Raises This Problem? ?
      "Our Cocks Need Sucking"
            Cant You Fucking Understand This.
The Gay Convicts Are Having A Ball"
      So Why Not Us Hetro Guys?
            Its Fucking Cruel...

Liver and Onions For Tea. Mashed Spuds and Swede
Fuck All On The Telly...
            "Radio Night"
      I'm Still On My Detox... All I Had On Visit Was
Bottled Water... "Will Power". Its All About Inner Strength.
      "Dig Deep" And Overcome.

I Got A Letter From Paul Howey
      I'll Share It With You All...

325

24/1/11

Paul, ██████
H.M.prison
FRANKLAND
We stgate unit-3
BRASSIDE/DURHAM
DH1-5YD

D.S.P.D
██████████

+Hello Charlie
            Ive Just been Reading your Book. It
WAS Brilliant AND you Just Say It hAS It is. AND
For all those SO HARD con's who Slag you OFF. I'd Like
to See them go In that cage your In and Say It too your
Face. I Dont think they would AND If they DID they
would have to be Insane. Fuck them. Remember when
we were In the Block In white-moore. Me you, warren,
Spanky and Glen wright. you Send those pickure's too
my Nephew's. They've Still Got them In a Frame In our
House. Remember I told you I came In serving
"8" year's for "3" stabbing's In Liverpool and then
I got two LiFe Sentence's For doing Two paedophile's
In this GAFF "11" year's ago. I also done mick stone
but I never got charged with that TWAT. well Since
I Left you in white-moore. Ive been to Rampten "3"
time's and kicked out "3" time's. The LAST time I was
there. I done "4" neurses in. Got Sent back to Full
Sutton and they charged me with the "4" Assault's.
I WAS not even allowed to go up In the dock AND
I had to speak to my solicifor through the DOOR. They
Found me guilty. BASTARD's. AS you Said, you can't
be Insaine one day and Saine the next to get charged
with "4" Assault's. anyway how are you? ok I hope.

326

your book made me laugh. But It also made a lot of sense and opened my eye's. Why do these psychologists support these paedophile's and rap ists so much? If I had It my way I would weld theirk door's up and glue them peanut's every "3" day's. As you said, It's no good killing the cunt's. They deserve to suffer for what they done to those poor Innocent kid's and women. In "8" year's over my TARE If been kicked out of the Funny FARM "3" time's and It's Like the psychologist's are making me out to be worse than those Evil paedo's. I've only been here "3" month's but I don't think Ill ever get out Just because I done "2" paedophile's. But that's the PRISON System For you. Remember when I told you on the yard How I got a Slip out From ALBANY Block to parkHurst Just to get some tobacco and came back the next day to ALBANY Block With 3 OZ OF Tobacco ☺ Well charlie Thank's for the book and the drawing's. Hope your Fit and Well. keep Smiling charlie.

        Take care mate

            Paul

IT's ABOUT 8 YeARS SINCE I see THIS GUY. He's SERVING 2 LIFe SENTENCES FOR CHOPPING UP 2 PAEDOS.
"PERSONALLY I THINK He DESERVES A MEDAL."
ANY OF YOU GIRLS OUT THERE WHO WANT A PEN FRIEND.. DROP HIM A LINE. "He's A TOP GEEZER IN MY BOOK.
"PITY THERE WASN'T A FEW MORE LIKE PAUL.
    THERE Be LESS FLASH PAEDOS ABOUT ☺

3. 2. 2011

$\overset{\frown}{90}$ " Benvenuti Nel. Interno "

YODAY JUST HAD TO BE A LOVELLY DAY!
WHY?

SIMPLE - COZ MY BEAUTIFUL LORRAINE WAS UP TO
SEE HER OLD CHAP.

To GET To THE ZOO ROOM MY VISITORS HAVE To GO
THROUGH ABOUT A DOZEN ELECTRIC DOORS ALL ON CC.T.V
I CAN ACTUALLY SEE THEM COMING THROUGH THE FINAL
DOOR.

She Looked So HOT. Set on Legs'
I STARTED SINGING THE OLD 'Peters and lee Song'
Welcome Home'

As She enteRed The ROOM - it LIT UP'
'WHAT A SMILE .☺

I SAID.. "AS THAT SILLY SCREW BEEN Looking AFTER You"
We HAD A Quick KISS THROUGH THE BARS AND GOT
ON WITH OUR CHAT. 'ALL THE NEWS' ☺

I LOVE TO BE FILLED IN ON ALL THE LATEST
GOINGS ON.

I LIKE TO KEEP MY FINGER ON THE PULSE OF
LIFE OUTSIDE.

I STILL HAVE A LITTLE BIT OF PULL HERE AND THERE.
"You BETTER BELIEVE It"

Hey! MY LORRAINE CAN LICK THE BOTTOM OF THE
INSIDE OF A YOGURT POT.
    "THATS A TONGUE"
    A PROPER TONGUE..
You LESBO's WOULD LOVE ABIT OF THAT EH?
    "WELL". FUCK OFF..... "SHE'S MINE" ☺
AND SHE HAD MY RING ON.. "WHITE GOLD"..

Hey! WHO
SAID ANGELS DON'T
    EXIST?

THIS IS MY
    BEAUTIFUL
    GOD DAUGHTER
        "SAHARA".

WHAT A STAR!
HOW BLESSED AM I?
SHE'S A RAINBOW
    OF LOVE ..

I ALWAYS WANTED A DAUGHTER.
    "GOT A SON". WHY NOT A DAUGHTER?
        "MAYBE LATER.
NEVER DOUBT NOTHING WITH ME!
    "COZ NOTHING IS IMPOSSIBLE".. "NOTHING"

How nice is this?

<u>Dear Charles, and the soon to be Mrs Charles Bronson</u>

A new beginning for you both and I really wish you the very best for your future.

The stars will be shining so brightly at night. The comfort and joy you both bring to each other is so heartfelt I am happy for you Charles that you have found someone to love you for you☺.

I have been here in a mental hospital for nearly three years after 10 months in H.M.P Bronzefield for Arson. I was very depressed and wanted to kill myself! But I am glad now that I didn't as my three lovely children have made me a granny I am 40☺. The system here sucks but I suppose they now have to make sure I am well enough to leave as before the other hospital I was in didn't listen to my fears☹. I have made the enclosed card myself and I hope you like it. Well I wish you both happy ever after and hope we can stay in touch.

Tracey

Mr & Mrs Charles Bronson

"THANKYOU TRACEY'.
   VERY KIND OF YOU.
   IT MEANT ALOT TO ME THIS. CUZ I KNOW
YOUR HAVING A TOUGH TIME OF LIFE
      STAY STRONG MY FRIEND.
   LORRAINE SENDS HER LOVE x
               ADIOS SENORETA

IT REALLY WAS A HEART FELT VISIT TODAY
    VERY CLOSE.
        TOGETHERNESS.
            SOUL DEEP.
I WISH I COULD PAINT HER NUDE...
THEN GIVE HER A GOOD SEEING TO.
    IM DYING FOR A GOOD OLD FASHION FUCK.
    ITS BEEN 18 YRS SINCE I SLIPPED IT IN.
        HOW INHUMAN IS THAT?
    ITS FUCKING CRUEL...
            NASTY. FUCKERS....

Inside Time, February 2011 Issue:

If this Mirror story had any truth in it ...

Charles Bronson – HMP Wakefield CSU

If this Mirror (6 December 2010) story had any truth in it, then why am I not nicked? Or in patches? Or in the same cell? These mad stories are fed to the media every time I'm close to a parole hearing. Some screw is getting a nice few quid out of this crap – and burying me at the same time. I'm banned from talking or seeing the media because the system is afraid of me exposing them for what they are ... parasites.
So how can I get my side heard? 'The Butter Riot' ... I have no excuse, it's just a build up of madness. My visitors have been banned, I'm in solitary, no progression, my mail is stopped, they've set dogs on me, starved me, stopped my art, they tape my phone calls, do me with nerve gas and pepper spray, and they keep me in a cage! What's next??? Add it all up and ask yourself what would you do? How would your head be? Could you cope with so much hopelessness?
I've had 36 years of this bollocks and I'm really getting tired of it now. Hopefully one day they will kick me to death, problem solved. Even the old screws say what has been done to me is wrong, they even tell my brother and mother that I should be freed. This evil corrupt system has created me, de-humanised me, and now they are ashamed and embarrassed of their creation. It's a bloody disgrace. Amen.

Daily Mirror

Charles Bronson in prison 'escape bid' scare

A top security jail has been placed on high alert over a birthday escape plot by Charles Bronson – dubbed Britain's most dangerous convict. A recent search by officers at Wakefield prison found that the window in his cell was unsecured.
A special staff meeting at the West Yorkshire facility heard the opening could lead him to an exercise yard
And though superfit Bronson, who does 2,500 press-ups a day, would need to scale a wall to get his first taste of freedom since 1974, an insider said: "We know the significance of the window being disconnected. He remains very dangerous despite his age and could easily take out the watch in the yard before getting over the wall."
Warders were also placed on alert over a possible kidnap attempt three weeks ago when he took on 12 of them in the gym after covering himself with butter.
An insider said: "There are concerns about Charlie's state of mind. He is again finding it difficult to get his head around being locked up for life. He's been co-operative during searches but his behaviour has changed since the gym incident. He's a bomb waiting to go off."

FEB EDITION
OF INSIDE TIMES

NOW HERE IS A
CLASSIC EXAMPLE
OF HOW STORIES
GET STOLEN AND
EXAGERATED BY
REPORTERS

ON THE NEXT PAGE
YOU WILL SEE
HOW THE MEDIA
WORK...
THEY STEAL MY WORDS
AND TWIST IT.
NOW SEE WHY YOU
SHOULD NEVER EVER
BELIEVE THE PRESS.

331

Daily Mail, 4 February 2011:

PRISON LIFE IS SO HARD IT'S DEHUMANISED ME, WHINGES BRITAIN'S MOST VIOLENT INMATE CHARLES BRONSON

By Jack Doyle, Home Affairs Correspondent

Having taken a string of hostages and attacked many wardens while behind bars, he is the most notorious inmate in Britain.

But now Charles Bronson has had the gall to blame prison for making him the man he is.

The 58-year-old said his behaviour was the fault of the 'evil corrupt system' which had 'dehumanised' him.

Bronson, a former bare-knuckle fighter who was first jailed aged 22, has spent just 121 days as a free man in 36 years

It is thought he has single-handedly caused half a million pounds of damage from rooftop protests.

But in a letter to prisoner newspaper Inside Time, he accused prison officers of setting dogs on him, attacking him with pepper spray and even stopping him painting.

He described his incarceration at HMP Wakefield in Yorkshire as a 'disgrace' and demanded his freedom. He wrote: 'My visitors have been banned. I'm in solitary, my mail is stopped, they've set dogs on me, starved me, stopped my art, they tape my phone calls, do me with nerve gas and pepper spray, and they keep me in a cage!

'What's next? Add it all up and ask yourself what would you do? How would your head be? Could you cope with so much hopelessness? I've had 36 years of this b******* and I'm really getting tired of it now. Hopefully one day they will kick me to death, problem solved.'

Bronson added: 'Even the old screws say that what has been done to me is wrong, they even tell my brother and mother that I should be freed. This evil corrupt system has created me, dehumanised me, and now they are ashamed and embarrassed of their creation. It's a bloody disgrace.'

The 18-stone hardman wrote the letter in response to newspaper reports suggesting he had covered himself in butter before attacking 12 prison staff.

Hard man: Bronson is a former bare-knuckle fighter who was first jailed aged 22 for armed robbery in 1974

He wrote: 'If this story had any truth in it, then why am I not nicked? These mad stories are fed to the media every time I'm close to a parole hearing.

'Some screw is getting a nice few quid out of this c*** and burying me at the same time.

'I'm banned from talking or seeing the media because the system is afraid of me exposing them for what they are, parasites.'

Bronson has been involved in at least ten jail sieges.

His sentences have been repeatedly extended for attacks on prison guards and hostage-taking.

The outbursts have seen him moved 150 times, and he has spent more than 22 years in solitary confinement in total. He has been released twice but quickly returned after committing robbery.

Born Michael Peterson, he changed his name while in prison to that of the actor who starred in The Magnificent Seven and The Great Escape.

He was given a life sentence in 1999 for holding a prison art teacher hostage for 44 hours for criticising some of his sketches.

CCTV footage showed him leading his victim around like a dog with a rope around his neck.

During a later siege Bronson demanded a helicopter so he could fly to Cuba and compare his beard with Fidel Castro's. He also asked for a cheese sandwich in case he got hungry on the flight.

He once boasted: 'I've had more hostages than Saddam Hussein' and reportedly ate a budgie after he became annoyed by its singing.

A Ministry of Justice spokesman said: 'We do not comment on individual prisoners.'

CHARLES BRONSON: A LIFE ON THE INSIDE

1974: First jailed, aged 22, for armed robbery.

1983: Stages two-day siege on roof of Broadmoor after taking hostages.

1994: Holds prison librarian hostage, demanding inflatable doll, helicopter and cup of tea.

1994: Holds deputy governor of Hull prison hostage for five hours.

1998: Takes three inmates hostage at Belmarsh. Insists they call him 'General' and threatens to eat one of them unless demands are met.

1999: Given life sentence for kidnapping prison teacher Phil Danielson at Hull jail

"These Vultures"
Thats Not Journalism...
    It's Theft of A Real Story
Get Your own Stories.
    Do Your own Investigations..
Get The True Facts ..

Contact my Brother .. He will Give You A Box
    of Documents. You can Write A Book on The
Injustices of it All..

    You want Facts.. You're Come To The Right
Place.

' Clock This Next one ..
    It Might Sound Insane.
    It Probally is To The Real World
But To me.. It's Deadly serious ..
Coz it's my Life.
            My World
            My Existance.

 And Nobody Fuckts with my Space ..

Plus Your Note .... There is No Answer To it
' They cant Answer it "

    I've Fucked em. Again.

    It's Another Discrimnational Prison Rule
' Bronson exposes Again "
            " Check Mate "   tt

333

FORM COMP 1
PRISONER'S FORMAL COMPLAINT

Establishment WDCM
Serial N° WD/47/11/F

Read these notes first

1. This form is for you to make a formal written complaint under the complaints procedure. Complaints should wherever possible be sorted out informally by speaking to your wing officer or making an application. Use this form only if you have not been able to resolve your complaint this way.
2. A written complaint should be made within 3 months of the incident or of the relevant facts coming to your notice.
3. Keep the complaint brief and to the point.
4. When you have completed the form, sign it and post it in the box provided. The form will be returned to you with a response.
5. If you are unhappy with the response, you can appeal on a separate form (COMP 1A).
6. Some subjects are dealt with only by the Area Manager or Prison Service headquarters. If your complaint is about one of these subjects, the reply will take longer.
7. There is a separate pink form (COMP 2) for confidential access complaints.

Your details (use BLOCK CAPITALS)

Surname	BRONSON	First name(s)	CHARLES ARTHUR
Prison number	A8076AG	Location	C.S.C. UNIT.

Have you spoken to anyone about your complaint? Yes ✓ No ☐
If so, who did you speak to? S/o STAFF

Your complaint

WHY AM I BEING DISCRIMINATED?
I AM ON PUNISHMENT WHAT I Deserve. BUT OTHERS ON PUNISHMENT
CAN SMOKE AND BUY TOBACCO.
SMOKERS ARE Allowed TO SMOKE ON PUNISHMENT.
So WHY CANT I HAVE MY SWEETS?
You CANT HAVE IT BOTH WAYS.. "PUNISHMENT is PUNISHMENT."
YOUR DISCRIMINATING ALL NON-SMOKERS.
IT'S OBVIOUS TO ME YOUR BEING SYMPATHETIC TO THEM.
BUT YOU DONT GIVE A TOSS ABOUT US SWEET CONS..
We WANT OUR SWEETS AND CHOCS.
WHAT ABOUT OUR HUMAN RIGHTS?

Does your complaint have a racial aspect? Yes ✓ ☐ No ☐
Is your complaint about bullying? Yes ☐ No ☐

What would you like to see done about your complaint?

HAVE A NATIONAL GOVERNOR'S EMERGENCY MEETING.
BEFORE I TAKE THIS CASE TO THE EUROPEAN COURTS FOR
ALL NON-SMOKERS ON PUNISHMENT Denied SWEETS "!"
TOBACCO is A PRIVILGE.. So ARE SWEETS "!"
"We MUST ALL BE TREAT THE SAME". (COLOUR. CREED OR RACE.)

Signed _____ Date ~4/1/2011

VF 011 Printed at HMP Kingston 4334 03/2003

Response to the complaint (*including any action taken*)

Mr Bronson,

I HAVE PASSED YOUR CONCERNS ONTO GOVERNOR PARRY, HEAD OF FUNCTION, FOR HIM TO ADVISE YOU FURTHER. AS YOU WILL BE AWARE PSO 2000 - ADJUDICATIONS, ONLY ALLOWS FOR THE PURCHASE OF TOBACCO ONCE MR PARRY ADVISES ME FURTHER I WILL REPORT BACK TO YOU.

"AS IT HAPPENS GOVERNOR PARRY IS A DECENT CHAP. WHOSE GOT 30 YRS SERVICE BEHIND HIM. BUT I'VE FUCKED HIM ON THIS ONE AND HE KNOWS IT" ILL SETTLE FOR A TIN OF QUALITY STREET FOR CHRISTMAS ☺

Name in block capitals ▨▨▨▨▨▨▨▨   Position S/O

Signed ▨▨▨▨▨▨▨▨   Date 1/2/11

This section for official use only		
Sentence	Category	Status
Release date	Ethnicity	Location

Date received by complaints clerk	Date received by responding member of staff	Passed to RRLO on (date)	Date of interim reply

Reserved subject ? (tick box) ☐	Referred to	On (date)	Date received by Area Manager or HQ

Outcome of complaint		Reserved Subject	
Upheld ☐ Rejected ☐		Upheld ☐ Rejected ☐	

Action taken (where complaint upheld)

335

PROTECT

| Prisoner's Name: Charles BRONSON |
| Prisoner's Number: A8076AG / BT1314 |
| Wing: CSC Unit, HM Prison Wakefield |

Section 3 Date reports due for completion 14/02/2011 **SENTENCE PLAN:** Please attach a copy of the most recent Sentence Plan and comment of the prisoner's level of compliance with that plan. Also include comments on any other activities which evidence self-improvement and sustained examples of changes in lifestyle.	Source of Information and Date
Mr Bronson was sentenced to Life Imprisonment in February 2000 for the offence of False Imprisonment. His tariff was initially set at 4 years but later reduced on appeal to 3 years in 2001. The offence was committed when Mr Bronson was located at HM Prison Hull; he took an Art Teacher hostage. Records inform that Mr Bronson imprisoned the victim for approximately 44 hours and tied him up, initially to himself but then to a chair; there was a rope around his neck with the other end being attached to Mr Bronson who had a homemade spear which he had made from securing a knife to a snooker cue.	Reference to Prison Service/Probation Service files
I have interviewed Mr Bronson on one occasion on 04/02/2011 in direct preparation for this report. This was not my first meeting with him, having met with him several times previously within my role as a part of the Close Supervision Centre (CSC) Unit Multi Disciplinary Team (MDT). During this interaction he engaged well and answered all questions put to him in a polite and appropriate manner.	
In preparation for this submission I have consulted prison records and Probation Service files as well as discussing Mr Bronson's progress with members of staff within the CSC Unit and the Unit Psychologist. I have also attended monthly case reviews pertaining to Mr Bronson.	
Mr Bronson's most recent Sentence Planning Meeting, which he declined to attend, was held at HM Prison Wakefield on 27/09/2010. At this meeting a number of objectives were set as follows:	Sentence Planning Meeting minutes dated 27/09/2010

Short Term Objectives
- Work within structured regime and rules – to comply with the unit regimes and adhere to rules, ensuring you remain adjudication free. To ensure that you engage appropriately with all staff, including the MDT and visitors.
- Maintain health and wellbeing – to meet with a member of

PROTECT

1

336

staff from the Humber Centre, in order to discuss whether there are any psychological wellbeing or mental health concerns.

- Work towards reducing your risks – meet with Kat Matthews to discuss your Sentence Plan.
- To learn to manage your emotional response to situations and appropriately interact with others maintaining stable, consistent behaviour on the unit – to meet weekly with your Personal Officers and discuss any concerns that you may have with them.
- To interact/engage with the Assessments and Interventions Centre to discuss assessment needs – to meet with Lucie Homer to talk about the next steps in terms of psychological involvement.
- To demonstrate a stable period of appropriate behaviour and endeavour to remain adjudication free throughout the next reporting period – to refrain from exchanging insults or anti social comments with other residents on the unit, in particular Bob Mawdsley.
- Continue to attend CSC Reviews – input to the objectives set at CSC Reviews.
- Continue to increase awareness of problems related to previous behaviour and lifestyle – reengage with Psychology to explore previous behaviour and develop insight into risk factors.

Long Term Objectives
- Engage in assessments with different members of the MDT in order to identify appropriate intervention needs

I can confirm that, for the most part, Mr Bronson complies with the unit rules and regime. He interacts well with unit staff and visitors to the wing although there have been recent incidents when he has not done so during the most recent reporting period.	P-Nomis records
12/11/2010 National Resources had to be deployed following an incident that occurred with Mr Bronson in the CSC Unit gym area. He went to the gym area as he would normally do but when there he refused to leave and smashed equipment up. It was reported that he stripped some of his clothes off and greased himself in butter, shouting and refusing to comply or return to his cell. The incident was concluded when Mr Bronson was removed from the gym area under restraint to special accommodation. He was then returned to his cell a couple of days later and resumed the usual regime.	CSC records

On 13/01/2011 Mr Bronson was adjudicated against for an assault. The details are that he spat at the Director General when he came

round the unit; he pleaded guilty to this offence and received a punishment of 7 days loss of earning and 7 days loss of privileges. During interview I discussed this incident with Mr Bronson. He informed me that he does not like Mr McAlister and was derogatory in his description of him and the reasons why he dislikes him. Mr Bronson blames Mr McAlister for the problems and issues that he feels he has had recently and told me that 'he had no right to be in my space'. When challenged about his reaction and offering alternative ways in which he could have reacted Mr Bronson informed me that he maintains that his behaviour was justified and does not regret his actions but was equally happy to take the punishment which was given to him in relation to this instance.	CSC Records P-Nomis Interview with Mr Bronson
Until recently Mr Bronson has been meeting with Dr Kasmi from the Humber Centre. Records inform that Mr Bronson was engaging in discussions with him regarding psychological and mental well being issues but this contact has recently ceased following Mr Bronson deciding that he no longer wanted to engage. When discussing this with Mr Bronson he informed me that he no longer wants to engage with the Doctor as he believes that he can no longer trust him following submission of a report by Dr Kasmi into his Parole Dossier that he believes should not be included. It was clear during interview that Mr Bronson feels anger and frustration regarding this matter. Mr Bronson explained that he felt it was unfair for a report from Dr Kasmi to be included in his Parole Dossier without it having previously been discussed with him; he feels that as the Doctor does not work directly for the Prison Service then his reports should not be automatically included. I advised Mr Bronson to discuss his concerns with Dr Kasmi but the impression he gave was that he would not be doing this.	CSC records Interview with Mr Bronson
In relation to Mr Bronson's third objective I can confirm that our meeting in preparation for this report was the first we have had since September 2010. During this interaction, as previous meetings, Mr Bronson has been open to discussing the issues and his current situation as well as listening to my opinions and perceptions and feeding back to me in an appropriate way. Since September 2010 it has been Mr Bronson's choice not to engage in meetings with me. During the most recent interaction, when asked why he has now decided to engage again, he informed me that he feels he has 'got to do it to progress' and understands that if he wants to move on, which he does, then he will need to get involved in interviews and assessments. Mr Bronson will continue to be encouraged to engage with me and other members of the MDT in order for him to work towards identifying and managing the risks that are present.	Interview with Mr Bronson
In relation to the objectives that are Psychology related I can confirm, following consultation with the CSC Psychologist, that Mr	Discussion with Psychology

PROTECT

Bronson has disengaged from them for the last few months but has now stated that he is willing to start to work with her. During interview Mr Bronson informed me that he finds talking about thoughts and feelings difficult and is not sure to what level he will engage in assessments but maintains that he will certainly engage in discussions with the Psychologist.	Department
From consultation of Mr Bronson's case notes it can be seen that he meets with his Case Officers on a regular basis. When talking about the staff on the unit, Mr Bronson informs that he trusts them and feels 'relaxed and chilled out' at the current time with his situation.	P-Nomis records
I encouraged Mr Bronson to start to attend his monthly CSC Reviews but he informed me that 'there is no point' and he does not want to attend as he feels that there is little value in him doing so.	
Mr Bronson's long term objective remains outstanding at the current time while he continues to work towards addressing the short term targets.	
I can confirm that Mr Bronson continues to engage with the wing regime in that he goes to the gym and exercises on a regular basis; he also receives regular visits and correspondence and informed me that he has recently started a relationship with a friend of his who visits him. He spoke with enthusiasm about this relationship informing me that since she has been in his life he is a better person and he feels that being with her is increasing his motivation to move forward and progress.	CSC records
During interview we talked about progress in general and where Mr Bronson sees himself in the future. He was open in discussion with me regarding this matter and informed that he wants to move on and progress. He explained that he knows that the most likely next step for him would be to the CSC Unit at HM Prison Woodhill which he told me he is 'not looking forward to' but will do what is necessary. He told me that he does not like the regime or building at HM Prison Woodhill and feels that his most recent period there and the incidents that occurred are 'still fresh in their minds' after he attacked a prison dog and hit a Governor. Throughout our discussion I worked towards structuring the expectations that Mr Bronson has in terms of progression. He believes that he presents no risk to the public and should be allowed release so that he can prove that to everyone. When talking about risk management and the inappropriate behaviour he continues to exhibit he was open to listen but I am not sure as to what level he fully understands and takes on board the risk that he continues to present.	Interview with Mr Bronson

Mr Bronson will continue to be encouraged to discuss all aspects of

PROTECT   4

339

his offending behaviour and ongoing progress through his sentence with an aim of addressing the specific risk factors that are present in his case.

Completed by:
Grade/Title: **Probation Officer**
Date: 07/02/2011

Signed: ....

" I GET REPORTS LIKE THIS EVERY YEAR FOR THE CATEGORY A STATUS...
NEARLY 4 DECADES I'VE BEEN CAT A
I'VE GOT MORE CHANCE OF LAYING A GOLDEN
EGG. THAN BEING De-CATEGORISED TO B

THAT'S HOW IT IS.... ☹

List and number attachments:
Sentence Planning Meeting minutes dated 27/09/2010

Are there any other throughcare resettlement/vocational or educational matters which should be taken into account when reviewing this prisoner's progress?
Please give details below

Nothing further to add to the above information

Completed by:
Grade/Title: **Probation Officer**
Date: 07/02/2011

Signed: ....

People outside just can't relate to all this prison rules..
But take it from me.. it can be very stressful ..(if) you
allow it to be. and dwell upon it

What upsets me.. I know alot of killers, and drug barons
who are never on Cat 'A'..

So my argument is ..... "Why am I still on it?
When I'm not a danger to the public or the state?

How the fuck can I ever get parole (if) they wont even
trust me to come off Cat.A.?

It's mind boggling at times.
Lets move on .... Before I get nasty again!

My wonderful Lorraine had on a 3/4 grey shirt.
And a black blouse..
She looks like a very prominent barrister.''
I'm guilty for loving the woman..
Lord have mercy upon my soul..

Oh yeh! An exclusive.... The Crossbow Cannibal
Is hanging on.. 'out just' oo

He's now well and truly fucked.
Almost on the way to hell..
A screw was telling me..(who will remain unnamed).
He has not eaten in 72 days.. he weighs 6½ stone
And he's prolonging his death by drinking orange juice
"You gotta give it to the loony.. he means bizz.
"Hurry up and die you evil cunt..

Oh! There's a dirty protest going on in the seg part..
Thank fuck its not over on our part..
Thats all we need more shit 😖 I think not..

I Remember When "Victor Miller" Was Here A Couple
Of Years Back.

He Actually Smells Of SHIT.

One Dirty Stinking Toe Rag

He Goes Months And Months Without A Shower
What He Needs Is A Good Hosing Down Once A Day
And Scrubbed With A Hard Broom

Then A Good Kicking ...

There Was One Lunatic In Rampton Who Used To Shit In
A Pint Plastic Mug And Stir It Up And Recycle It
Yeh ... Drink His Own Shit.

Well ... It Is An "Astlum". What Did You Expect?

I Could Tell You Stories That Would Turn Your
Hair Grey! OO

You Just Couldn't Relate To My World
My World Is Beyond Your Brain Function.
"Believe You Me".

Yes That Was A Very Special Visit Today With
My Beautiful Lady

I Can Honestly Say, With My Hand On My Heart
"Ill Be A Lost Soul Without Her"
Fuck Knows What She Sees In Me. I'm Baffled By It.
"But I Must Have Something".
It Can't Be My Cock Coz She Hasn't Seen It (Yet)
So It Must Be My Tackle?

What Else Can It Be? ...

342

OH WELL... THATS MY LOT. I'M OFF TO BED FOR A GOOD KIP!
FRIDAY TOMORROW ~ 'FISH-N-CHIPS DAY. ☺

IT SHOULD BE A CRIME TO BE SO HAPPY IN PRISON
      'I CANT FUCKING HELP MYSELF.

"Non_est_excusatio_offensia"

REMEMBER ME TO SANTA

NOT REALLY BEEN UP TO MUCH.
  SORT OF CHILLING.
      HIBERNATING.
      RESEARCHING MYSELF
      DEEP THOUGHTS
      DIGGING INTO MY SOUL.
          SOUL DEEP.

"TRY IT SOMETIME"

I HAD A LITTLE TICKLE WEDS NIGHT.
      "A PREMONITION
      ARSNEL TO BEAT BARCELONA. 2/1

      SO I CALLED MY BROTHER TO PUT A BULLSEYE ON!
          (HE ONLY GOT ME 12/1) 😏
              PICKED ME UP 6 TON.
              NICE DAYS WORST 😊

-- ELECTRIC-SHOCK-TREATMENT --

BROADMOOR

"We CALL IT TORTURE."

⟵ DON'T IT MAKE YOU FUCKING SICK..
      PISS TAKING CUNTS.
          "TREATMENT. DO ME A FAVOUR
      THE S/S DONE THAT IN THE WAR.
          "THEY GOT HUNG FOR IT"
              "WAR CRIMES"

= RIGHT SOMETHING'S GOTTA BE PUT RIGHT
So here it is.

'Big FAT GYPSY WEDDING'
The COUNTRY'S BEEN WATCHING IT '. ' ME TOO"
Yeh I'M A SAD OLD GIT. BUT I SEE SOMETHING THATS MADE
ME MAD. So IM GONNA EXPOSE THE CUNT FOR WHAT HE IS.

IT'S No SECRET IM WELL KNOWN TO THE GYPSY FRATERNITY
(MORE FOR MY LEGENDARY FIGHTS). PLUS THAT STOOD LOYAL TO ME ONCE.
THERE GOOD LOYAL PEOPLE.
APART FROM THIS CUNT IM ABOUT TO EXPOSE.

PADDY DOHERTY

He's GIVING IT ALL THE LARGE ON TELLY
BIT NOSES OFF. BIT THROATS OUT. He's A TOP BARE FIST
FIGHTER. BLAH. BLAH. BLAH..

He GOT A GOOD HIDING IN 2010...
AND He WENT TO THE POLICE AND MADE A STATEMENT.

He's A FILTHY FUCKING GRASS..
AND ANY DECENT GYPSY SHOULD KICK HIM OFF THE SITE

He's ALRIGHT LASHING IT OUT.. BUT AS SOON AS He GETS A BIT
He RUNS TO THE POLICE..

He WENT INTO THE WITNESS BOX.
AS A PROSECUTION WITNESS.

So WHAT MORE PROOF DOES ANYBODY NEED?

'A GRASS IS A GRASS IN MY BOOK'.
DIE OF CANCER YOU RAT.. (SOONER THE BETTER)

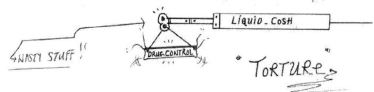

Liquid - COSH

"NASTY STUFF!"

DRUG. CONTROL

"TORTURE"

I JUST HATE A GRASS. EVEN MORE SO WHEN THERE ON
THE TELLY GIVING IT THE LARGE.
  THERE HE IS   SO I'M OLD. ALL THE TATTOOS AND BICEPS
    LOOK AT ME .. "I'M ROCK HARD"
AND ALL THE TIME HE'S A BLOODY DISGRACE TO THE GYPSIES!
    "FUCK OFF AND DIE YOU CUNT.
  IT'S REALLY WOUND ME UP THIS ---
AND I'M SHOCKED HOW THE GYPSY LADS HAVE ALLOWED IT TO
HAPPEN: "YOU HAVE A GRASS IN THE CAMP"

HEY,   GUESS WHOSE WON A BAFTA?
 A GOOD LOOKING GUT. SOLID. STRONG. RESPECTFUL.
 A GREAT ACTOR --
           COME ON GUESS?
   A LONDONER!
     IN LAYER CAKE - ROCK N ROLLA. OLIVER TWIST.

  BRONSON
  YEH .. HE PLAYED ME...
        TOM HARDY'S ONLY WON A FUCKING BAFTA.
          "CONGRATULATIONS TOM."
           "PROUD OF YOU SON.
       WELL DONE ☺
      BUZZING FOR YOU.... ...

ORANGE WEDNESDAYS RISING STAR AWARD 2011

06 January 11

The Orange Wednesdays Rising Star Award in 2011 was won by Tom Hardy as voted by the public.

The final five nominees were voted for by Orange Wednesdays customers from a longlist of eight. Tom Hardy was announced as the winner at the Orange British Academy Film Awards on 13 February 2011 have received the highest number of votes.

WINNER: TOM HARDY

Hardy first rose to fame thanks to his impressive performance in Spielberg's television series Band of Brothers, closely followed by his film debut in Star Trek: Nemesis. His other films include Black Hawk Down, Warrior, Bronson, RocknRolla and most recently Inception.

- Read Tom Hardy's acceptance speech transcript (13 KB)

"Thank you very much. This is very kind of you and much appreciated. I genuinely am grateful just to be working at all. I'd like to thank everyone who voted, everyone who loves a good story and every artist in the house tonight for the work they do." Tom Hardy

THAT'S OUR TOM .... ☺

BIGGER AND BETTER THINGS AHEAD.

BET YOUR ARSES ON THAT .

NO SURER BET .

RESTRICTED

SECURITY REPORT FOR
SENTENCE PLANNING BOARD
C.S.C. WOODHILL . 2010

NAME BRONSON	NUMBER A8076AG	DATE FROM: SEPT 2009 DATE TO: SEPT 2010

Significant Issues   *(handwritten doodle)*   *(handwritten) WATCH WHA[T] You SAY ON The PHONE .*

21.11.2009

Intel suggests that BRONSON A8076AG is unhappy about his numbers for
friends and family being removed from his pin account and also does not think
he will be here long as the prison are playing games with him.

WHO WOULDN'T BE UNHAPPY HAVING THERE NUMBERS TAKEN OFF ?

08.12.2009

BRONSON A8076AG has spoken to a ███████ and has asked for them to
contact IRA so they could both be involved in a project that Robin has put
together, go fifty fifty and be on the set. *BIZZ BEFORE PLEASURE . :)*

14.12.2009

Note handed to a member of staff from Mr. Bronson A8076AG accusing
management of not treating him as other prisoners.

WELL ITS A FACT . DEAL WITH IT .

14.12.2009

During a telephone conversation A8076AG Bronson is making arrangements for
a demonstration outside the prison. *WHO ME ? :(*

21.01.2010

Mr BRONSON A8076AG approached the R/O in an extremely aggressive
manner, believing he was responsible for prossessing his application regarding
photos being taken on a visit. R/o states his manner was extremely aggressive
throughout. *(doodle)*

27.01.2010

In an outgoing call BRONSON A8076AG states he will make out someone is his
cousin so they can have their photographs taken together. *"OKAY" . BANG TO RIGHTS*

03.02.2010

A8076AG Mr Bronson assaulted Gov Smith during Governors Rounds.

ITS A PRISONER'S DUTY AND RIGHT TO CHIN A GOVERNOR .
is it NOT ? :)

348

19.02.2010

A8076AG Mr Bronson writes in a letter that the doctor has told him he will have a scan at MKGH soon but cant say when.

"PARANOID FUCKERS". 😊

21.04.2010

A8676AG Mr. Bronson was in the CV room as part of his normal regime when he started to smash up the room and equipment stating he is doing this for his dad. Substantial damage was caused to both doors and frames within the room and on exit attacked a dog prior to being restrained. Mr. Bronson was located in a special accommadation cell.

" FARE COP GOV".

22.04.2010

Whilst talking to The RO, BRONSON A8076AG said he did not like seeing staff in kit as it made him want to fight.

So WHAT ?

23.04.2010

Bronson A8076AG asked the R/O if they knew what death by cop meant. He then went on to explain that he would take one of the governors hostage and force the cops to kill him as he has nothing left. Once he finished talking he did not give staff a chance to respond and he began running around the exercise yard. Bronson also stated he felt insulted by having been removed from his cell to talk about his intentions to <u>commit suicide.</u>

LYING BASTARD. NEVER IN A MILLION
YEARS WOULD I SNUFF MYSELF OUT
" NEVER ".

28.04.2010

A8076AG Mr. Bronson was abusive and made threats to a member of staff.

(So WHAT DID HE DO TO DESERVE IT) 😊

28.04.2010

Bronson A8076AG informed the R/O that he would take the governors eyes out, it may not be today, or tomorrow, next year or ten years time but he will loose them and never see his children again.

I CAN GET NASTY AT TIMES . "
" Well".. You CANT GET ON WITH EVERYBODY "

19.05.2010

A conversation was heard between Bronson A8076AG and another offender Bronson was explaining the CSC system to Jones and how to work the system. He explained how he could go about getting a move elsewhere and told him what facilities each place had.

I WAS GIVING Good ADVICE TO A YOUNG LAD OUT
OF MY WINDOW.. (So SORRY) I WONT DO IT
AGAIN ..

10.06.2010

BRONSON MADE A CALL TO A MALE 18:41 10/06/10. DURING THIS CALL HE MENTIONED THINGS TO DO WITH HIS BUISNESS AND HOW THEY WOULD MAKE MONEY.

GUILTY YOUR LORDSHIP..
" BIRCH ME ".

24.07.2010

BRONSON 314 EXPRESSED FEELINGS ABOUT V/O'S AND LETTERS, IT MADE HIM FEEL WOUND UP AND STATES HE WAS GOING TO HAVE A RUMBLE.

FUCK WITH MY MAIL AND V/o' AND ILL RUMBLE WITH You CUNTS ALL DAY Long' (Do Your JoB)

30.07.2010

BRONSON 314 IS AGITATED ABOUT HIS V/O'S AND MAIL, STATING STAFF ARE NOT PROCESSING THEM IN TIME AND HAS WRITTEN AND DRAWN PICTURES OF THREATS AND OTHER ISSUES RELATING TO THESE, CONTENTS INCLUDE NEGATIVITY, HOSTAGES, VIOLENCE AND ROOFS IN REVENGE, ALSO STATES IF HE GETS HOLD OF THE EVIL SWINE THEY WOULD BEG FOR MERCY.

"So He Would .... IF THey Done it outside in An office THey Would Be SAcked"

17.08.2010

ANOTHER OFFENDER BECAME ARGUMENTATIVE AND INTIMIDATING REGARDING THE WAY HE WAS SEARCHED PRIOR TO HIS VISIT. HE THEN ATTEMPTED TO INCITE BRONSON A8076AG 314 WHO WAS TRAINING IN THE CSC GYM. MR BRONSON BECAME QUITE IRATE AND HAD TO BE CALMED BY STAFF.

I DoNT Need INCITING BY ANY CONVICT. IF I See A LIBERTY. THeN I SHALL STAND BY MY BROther IN ARMS. (UNLess Hes A Nonce or A GRASS). Amen †

PRINT	SIGNATURE	DATE OF REPORT

THis is RestRicted Security CRAP FRom WoodHill. it sHows How PAtHetic it All is ....

BUT STUFF Like THis FeeDs THe BRonson MYTH.

I DoNT Need it .. BUT THe SysTem Does.

SHit Likes THis .. Helps To BURY me DeePeR.

MUGGY LittLe RePoRTs. BUT WHAT it Does Tell You'!

THink BeFore You TALk on A PHone" I TRY To Keep it iN A RiddLe .. PRivAte Bizz ... ITs BLooDy HARd AT Times. ... I Guess THATs SHow Bizz FoR You

MY STATEMENT FOR THE CAT 'A' REVIEW TO DE-GRADE ME TO B

OFFENDER'S REPRESENTATIONS

OFFENDER'S NAME: Mr Bronson   NUMBER: A8076AG BT1314   WING: S

Charles

CATEGORY 'A' is Supposed To Be For TERRORISTS. SPies. GANGSTERS: DRUG BARONS. SERIAL KILLERS AND MEN WHO ARE A THREAT To The PUBLIC AND STATE.

So HOW DO YOU JUSTIFY ME BEING oN CAT 'A' FOR OVER 30 YEARS?

WHAT EXACTLY HAVE I DONE SO BAD?

PUT YOUR DECISION iN WRITING. SO WE CAN ALL HAVE A GOOD LAUGH AT YOU CRANK POTS..

I'M CHARLIE BRONSON —
— NOT CHARLES FUCKING MANSON.

Give ME A BREAK WILL YOU.
AND STOP BEING A BUNCH OF IDIOTS

I'M NOT A DANGER To ANYBODY.

ASK MY MUM.

OFFENDER'S SIGNATURE: ....

DATE: 18/2/2011

351

" MY OLD Duchess AND Me." 😊
MUMS THE SAME AGE AS MY (AND(AOJ (THE QUEEN)
    BUT ...
The QUEENS NOT GOT A SPARKLE ON MY OLD Duchess.'
    " You BETTER believe it
Everyone Loves MY MUM...
        SHE'S A SPECIAL OLD LADY.
    SORRY QUEEN...... You COME 2ND HERE..
        ALL It's Time You GAVE ME A FREE PARDON So Z CAN
Go HOME AND Look AFTER MY MUM.
        " WHY NOT "?
WHAT ABOUT MY MOTHERS HUMAN RICHTS?
    People FORGET How HARD it is FOR PRISONERS MUMS.
MY OLD GIRLS HAD ENOUGH OF VISITING ME IN A CAGE
    SHE DESERVES BETTER ',
Like ME VISITING HER.'
    " SORT it QUEENIE ".
    I'LL BUNG You A NICE FEW QUID ... " PROMISE " x

352

CHRIS COWLIN AND ME DECIDED
NOT TO PUT TO MANY PHOTOS
IN THIS BOOK ....
COZ ALL MY OTHER BOOKS ARE
FULL OF THEM —

   BUT I JUST HAD TO
PUT DEAN SHEPHERDS IN.

   THIS GUY IS A LEGEND.
HE IS ONE OF THE TRUE
   BRONSON SUPPORTERS. WHO
NEVER GIVE UP ON ME.

I ADMIRE AND RESPECT HIM.

HE'S HAD ALOT OF BAD SHIT
IN HIS LIFE. "REAL BAD LUCK".

   HE ALMOST GAVE UP ON LIFE
IN 2008.
OVER FAMILY ISSUES.
" PERSONAL PROBLEMS "
I WONT GO INTO

   BUT THIS GUYS CRAWLED BACK.
HE'S A FUCKING WINNER IN MY BOOK.'

" RESPECT TO YOU BUDDY.

" LOVE THE SCOOTER ".'
BRINGS BACK MEMORIES TO THE 1960'
   MY MOD DAYS
WHAT A GREAT ERA THAT WAS.'
   " FANTASTICAL "

353

STU CHESHIRES UP THIS SUNDAY WITH HIS OLD MAN HENRY.
" TWO DIAMONDS "
ALWAYS A TREAT FOR ME TO SEE THEM.
HENRY'S OFF TO AUSTRALIA NEXT MONTH TO SEE HIS DAUGHTER.

I'VE ALSO GOT ANOTHER VISIT ON THURSDAY FROM MY LORRAINE : ☺
(THAT WILL BE TWICE THIS MONTH FOR US)
ONLY WISH I COULD SEE HER EVERY DAY ... " BRIGHTENS MY LIFE UP ".
I'VE HAVE A GOOD LAUGH ... ☺
BELIEVE IT ..
SHE'S OFF TO LITTLEDEAN JAIL TUESDAY, ☺ !
IT'S A CRIME THROUGH TIME MUSEUM .
A REAL OLD PLACE ... HAUNTED ... SPOOKY.
SHE'S GOING WITH THE ACTOR " LOUIS MURRALL
LOUIS AS RECENTLY PLAYED ME IN A T.V DOCUMENTARY ...
(BY ALL ACCOUNTS HE'S DONE ME PROUD)

I CAN'T SAY TO MUCH ON WHY THERE BOTH VISITING
LITTLEDEAN JAIL ... (JUST WATCH THIS SPACE)
" IT'S WICKED .
AWESOME . . . . . ☺
GONNA BE MASSIVE . . . . . ☺

" FUCK ALL TO DO WITH ME "
SO DON'T FUCKING ASK ......

OH. I SEE " REBECCA BEACH " ON TUESDAY
SHE WORKS FOR MY BRIEF HARRIETT .
THINGS ARE MOVING " SLOWLY BUT SURELY "
I'M IN THE PROCESS OF ANOTHER APPEAL ....
IF DREAMS COME TRUE .... I'LL SEE YOU ALL AT MY PARTY ☺

I GOT A CRAZY "EQUALITY IMPACT ASSESSMENT" QUESTIONAIRE
SLIPPED THROUGH MY DOOR HATCH LAST WEEK

NOTE DATE "JAN 2011 ✓

ITS FEB 18TH 2011 ✓

WHOS PLAYING GAMES HERE....

OR DONT BRONSON COUNT IN THIS ?

ALL REPLIES ARE ANONYMOUS ....

WELL MINE AINT !

HERES MINE FOR ALL TO SEE ..

ITS FUCK ALL TO HIDE FROM NOBODY !

I CAN TAKE THE PISS TOO

ITS EASY '

GET ON THIS

EQUALITY IMPACT ASSESSMENT

QUESTIONNAIRE

POLICY AREA – CLOSE SUPERVISION CENTRES (*Isolation·Unit*)

JANUARY 2011

We want to find out if prisoners think they are being unfairly affected/treated because of their:

Race/Ethnicity
Gender (including Gender Identity)
Religion or beliefs
Sexuality
Disability
Age

Your opinions and knowledge about this are very important, so we would be grateful if you could spare a few minutes to complete this form.

The responses you give will be used to help develop strategies with the policy area named above.

All replies are anonymous and as such there is no need to tell us your name or prisoner number. You will not be identified and your responses will not be linked to you. When you have completed the questionnaire please seal in the envelope provided and hand to the nominated member of staff. (*No envelope with it*)

Please try to answer all of the questions as honestly as possible. If you do not wish to answer a particular question please leave the answer blank.

If you need help to complete this please tell the person distributing it and a member of the research team will assist you.

Then your No with He is

Age range:

21-25	
26-35	
36-45	
46-55	
56+	✓

1. What was your stated religion on reception into custody?
(Please, tick the appropriate box)

Roman Catholic		Church of England	
Hindu		Muslim	
Jehovah's Witness		Mormon	
Buddhist		Pagan	
None		Other (please specify): *SATANIST.*	✓

2. Have you changed your religion whilst in custody?

Yes		No	✓

If yes, please state which religion(s) you changed from and to and approximate dates:

X

If you **have** changed your religion whilst in custody, please explain the reasons why:

X

3. What is your ethnic origin?
(Please, tick the appropriate box)

White

W1 British	✓
W2 Irish	
W9 Any other White background (please specify):	

Black or Black British

B1 Caribbean	
B2 African	X
B9 Any other Black background (please specify):	

Asian or Asian British

A1 Indian	X
A2 Pakistani	
A3 Bangladeshi	
A9 Any other Asian background (please specify):	

Mixed

M1 White and Caribbean	X
M2 White and African	
M3 White and Asian	
M9 Any other Mixed background (please specify):	

Chinese or Other Ethnic Group

O1 Chinese	X
O9 Any other Oriental (please specify)	

4. Do you consider yourself to have a disability?
(Please, tick the appropriate box)

Yes ✓   No

5. If 'YES', have you had your disability diagnosed by a medical professional?
(Please, tick the appropriate box)

Yes ✓   No

6. If 'YES', do you need any adjustments in order to help you to live such as equipment, help with reading, walking etc?
(Please, tick the appropriate box)

Yes ✓   No

If Yes, please detail:

A COCKTAIL BAR IN MY CELL
A ROCKING CHAIR
AND A DAILY MASSAGE · (COCKT INCLUDED)

7. If 'YES', have the necessary adjustments been made?   No ⌣

Yes	No	

If 'NO' what needs to be done?

ABit of SWeet AND TenDerness
AND PleNTY of Food.

8. How would you describe your sexuality?
(Please, tick the appropriate box)

Heterosexual	✓	
Homosexual	Fuck oFF	Y
Bi-sexual	Be HAre	Y
Trans-sexual	cHeeRY Sdd ..	Y

9. Has your sexuality changed whilst in prison?
(Please, tick the appropriate box)

Yes	No ✓	

10. Have you ever sought gender reassignment?
(Please tick the appropriate box)

Yes	No ✓	cHeeRY Sdd

11. If Yes, are you currently undergoing assessment or treatment?
(Please tick the appropriate box)

Yes	No X	

If 'YES', please detail:

You BuNcH oF PeRvs . ..

Please proceed to Section 2 below.

SECTION 2

359

Referral to the CSC

12. Do you think any of the following played a part in your <u>referral</u> to the CSC system? (Please tick any that apply):

Race/Ethnicity	
Gender (including gender identity)	
Religion or beliefs	✓
Sexuality	
Disability	✓
Age	✓

13. If you have ticked any of the boxes, please explain why or how you think your <u>referral</u> was affected:

THEY DONT LIKE US SATANISTS :
THEY LAUGH AT MY HUMP ON MY BACK.
THERE JEALOUS OF MY BIG COCK.
THEY HATE US OLD FOLK.

14. If you have ticked Yes in question 10, regarding gender reassignment, please explain if and how your needs were catered for during the referral process:

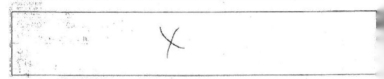

Selection to the CSC

15. Do you think any of the following played a part in your <u>selection</u> into the CSC system (for either assessment, or full selection after assessment)? (Please tick any that apply)

Race/Ethnicity	
Gender (including gender identity	
Religion or beliefs	✓
Sexuality	
Disability	✓
Age	✓

16. If you have ticked any of the boxes, please explain why or how you think the decision to <u>select</u> you was affected:

COZ THERE Wicked CRuel Bastards.

17. Do you think your continued placement within the CSC is affected by any of the following areas? (Please tick any that apply)

Race/Ethnicity	
Gender (including gender identity	✓
Religion or beliefs	✓
Sexuality	
Disability	✓
Age	✓

If 'YES' – in what way?

FUCKING WORK IT OUT You MUPPETS
IT's NOT Rocket SCIENSE..!

Movement

18. Have you been provided with the opportunity to practise your religion when located within;

a) A main CSC unit (i.e. Woodhill, Wakefield, Whitemoor)? If no religion observed, write N/A in the box.

Yes		No	✓

If 'NO' – please explain why/how not:

US SATANIST ARE VICTIMIZED.
DEVIL WORSHIPPERS ARe PERSECUTED BEYOND BelieF.

If **Yes,** how and how often do you practise your religion?

EVERY DAY IN MY FLOWERY DELL

b) A designated CSC cell in a segregation unit?

Yes	No	✓

If 'NO' – please explain why not:

NO. COMMENT

If Yes, how and how often?

No. COMMENT.

19. Has your movement between CSC units and/or designated cells affected you based on any of the equality strands listed below?

Race/Ethnicity	
Gender (including gender identity	
Religion or beliefs	✓
Sexuality	
Disability	✓
Age	✓

Yes	No

If 'YES' – in what way?

COZ THEY TAKE THE PISS OUT OF MY HUMP. AGE. AND RELIGION..
I GET A GOOD KICKING EVERY SUNDAY.

20. Do you think decisions about your location are made for genuine reasons i.e. progression, visits etc?

Yes	No	✓

If 'NO' – what is your opinion regarding your location?

Well.. I'M NOT HAPPY WITH IT
IN MY Cell I've Got Mice. RATS. CockRoaches. ANTS.
SiLver FiSH. WORMS. SCORPIONS. SPiders..
IT's Like LONDON Zoo...

21. Have you spent some time in a designated CSC cell in a segregation unit?

Yes ✓   No

22. If 'YES' – For how long?

Fucking YeARS......
YeARS AND YeARS OF SoLiTARY..

23. If 'YES' - Do you think your stay within a designated cell was due to any bias on the diversity grounds listed at question 19?

Yes ✓   No

If 'Yes' –please explain how and why you think that way

Coz I'm A FReAK-
THeY CALL Me THe C.S.C. FReAKY FuckeR.

Regime

24. Were you made aware of your entitlements with regards to religious observance, activities, and artefacts, following transfer into the CSC system?

Yes   No ✓

25. Are you aware of your entitlements with regards to religious observance, activities and artefacts, disability adjustments, age specific matters?

Yes   No ✓

If 'YES' - please provide a brief explanation of your understanding of your entitlements:

NO COMMENT.. (I'M UNDER THREAT)

26. If you required any changes due to disability adjustments or matters regarding your age, were these addressed following transfer into the CSC? (If this is not relevant write N/A in the boxes):

Yes	✓	No	

27. Have you been provided with the opportunity to meet with the relevant member of chaplaincy for your religion? (If no religion observed please write N/A)

Yes		No	✓

If 'NO' – why not?

BECAUSE WE ARE DENIED ANY CONTACT WITH THE DEVIL OR THE SATANIST HIGH PRIEST...

28. How often do you see your own faith chaplain?
(Please, tick the appropriate box)

Daily		Weekly	
Monthly		Never	✓
Other (describe):			

29. Do staff take into consideration your religious needs when operating the regime?

Yes		No	✓

If 'No' - Please explain how or why not:

THEY CALL MY GOD A NASTY BASTARD AND HIT ME WITH BIG WOODEN CROSSES AND CALL ME AN ARSE WIPE...

30. Are you provided with adequate facilities to practise your religion?

Yes		No	✓

```
ARe You ALL SILLY
       I'm Told You  WHY..
```

31. Do you require specially prepared meals or alternative drinks in accordance to your faith?

Yes ✓   No

32. Do you think your requirement for particular food provisions is sufficiently met?

Yes   No ✓

If 'NO' – Please explain;

```
I NeeD ALoT of STeAk. CHops. AND FRuiT CAke
   AlSo PlenTY of  VUoDkA  AND  ALe .
        (ALL PART oF MY ReligioN)
```

33. Are Racial Incident Report forms freely available on the wing?

Yes   No ✓

34. Would/do you use the Racial Incident Report procedures?

Yes   No ✓

If 'NO' – why not?

```
Coz LAST Time I DiD THAT .  1o GuARDs Come INTo MY
Cell AT 3 AM AND kicked SHiT ouT oF Me ...
```

35. Are you aware of the normal complaints procedure?

Yes   No ✓

36. Would/do you use the normal complaints procedures?

Yes   No ✓

If 'NO' – why not?

```
Coz THe GuARDs WiLL  HANg me FRom MY  BARS
```

37. Are the details of the Race Equality Officer and Management Team advertised on your unit?

Yes [ ]   No [✓]

Care and Management Planning

38. Do you think that your care and management within the CSC system is influenced by any of the following that may apply to you? (Please tick)

Race/Ethnicity	
Gender (including gender identity	
Religion or beliefs ✓	
Sexuality	
Disability ✓	
Age ✓	

39. If you have ticked any of the boxes please explain why or how you think your care and management is being affected, either positively or negatively:

The GUARDS Tell Me I'LL DIe IN THe C-S-C SYSTEM IF I CONTINUE To WORSHIP LUCIFeR.

40. Do you think your religions needs should be taken into consideration when the Care and Management Plan targets are set?

Yes [✓]   No [ ]

If 'YES' – in what way?

Give Me ALL MY FOOD AND DRINKS AND A 19 YR OLD VIRGIN GIRL eveRY 13TH OF THe MONTH " We DO NEeD FRESH MeAT"...

41. If applicable, does your faith chaplain attend or have input into your Care and Management Plan reviews?

Yes		No ✓

If 'NO' – are you aware of the reasons why not?

> COZ WE ARE NOT ALLOWED TO See HIM.

42. Have you experienced targets set at your Care and Management Plan review that conflict with your religion or beliefs?

Yes ✓		No

If 'Yes' – please explain

> THEY WANT Me TO KISS THE PRISON CHAPLAINS BOOTS
> AND LeT HIM Bugger Me –

General questions

43. Have you personally experienced any discrimination since being held within the CSC system?

Yes ✓		No

44. If 'YES' – what type of discrimination? (Please tick)

Race/Ethnicity	
Gender (including gender identity	
Religion or beliefs ✓	
Sexuality	
Disability ✓	
Age ✓	

45. If 'YES' – from whom, i.e. prisoners, staff, policies?

> GUARDS. DOCTORS. CHAPLAINS. GOVERNORS. PROBATION.
> PSYchologists
>   (THEY ALL SHIT IN THE SAME POT)

46. If 'YES' – how were you discriminated?

They ABUse MY BeLiefs ..
AND De-Humanize Me ..

47. If 'YES' – what did you do about it?

I CUT AND STABBED A FeW .
TooK some Hostages
AND Tore off ½ A Dozen RooFs .

48. Were you satisfied with the outcome?

Yes ✓   No

If **NO** – please explain why not:

49. If you have been discriminated against, do you think it is because of a lack of understanding regarding your sex/race/ethnicity/religion/disability?

If **YES** – how?

FUcK Me ... I GiVe up ...
I Feel Like A PARRot Now +.×

Thank you for taking the time to complete this questionnaire. Please now seal in an envelope and return to the staff who issued the questionnaire.

I HAve No eNVeLope .. ✓
I DoNT No WHo STUck IT UNDeR MY Door.
AND MY NAMe is ...
MR IAN HUNTLey !

← Lets Hope ANOTHer Kictraining

368

I See The Godfather of Fitness Passed Away Last Month.
The Great "Jact LaLanne"
96 Years of Age... What a Strong Man He Was.
Even in His 60' + 70' He was Smashing out World Records.
A True Legend.   R.I.P.

Another Great Strong-Man who Died of 104 was The Legendary
Joe Rollino. He Passed on Last Year.
Joe once Picked up 635lb with one Finger.
He was only 5 Feet 5 inches and 150lbs
Born in Brooklyn, New York
Joe was a Serious Brave Man
He was Awarded 3 Purple Hearts in The 2nd World War.
Most will Remember Him as a Travelling Boxer under The Name
of Kid Dundee
They Dont Make Them Like Joe Rollino Anymore.
One Hard Nut Geezer.
I Salute You Joe.
R.I.P

Well The Crossbow Lunatic is Still Breathing +
Alive But Not Kicking.
He is Living on Orange Juice.
What a way To Die .... A Lingering Death.
Would It not Be Better To Slice Your Throat.
Oh well ...... All To Their own ..

I Keep Asking These Screws if I can Have His Food.
Waste Not .. Want Not I Say ..

I Remember a Guy in Rampton Asylum who was on a
½ a Hunger Strike. 00
He Just ate His Lunch and Left His Deserts "
"Fucking idiot"

My old Buddy Ronnie Easterbrook Died of a Hunger Strike
in Gartree Prison, its a Terrible ending.

369

I was chatting to one of the old screws yesterday, he was telling me about when Bamber was here.
You know the one. He killed 5 members of his family.
Two of them were small kids.

Anyway. This screw was on duty on association time when he piped into the showers to check it was all okay.

Bamber had a big black cock up his arse.
And another one in his mouth

You cant make this shit up ...

Bare in mind this prison was the 1st in the U.K to hand out condoms.

This place is full of shirt lifters.

Men serving life with no hope.
It pushes alot of them over the edge
They become prison poofs.
Suck my cock for ½ oz of bacca.
Give us a wank I'll give you my rice pudding Sunday

Some just weaken ...
They lose there way in life.

But cunts like Bamber. Become rent boys and enjoy it.
Sick fuckers...

Oh well ... it is Monster Mansion ..
If there not shagging. There killing.
Peace and love man ....

Bamber is in Fullsutton now. Still sucking
Bell ends. (till the day he dies)
What a fucked up life ...
Why dont he just follow the crossbow killer and call it a day .. Amen ...

I had curry and chips for tea.
And 8 bread rolls.
washed down with a pint of orange squash.

370

Fills me up I can tell you.

I was gonna stick along more letters in so you can read.
But I thought.. 'Fuck it ...
    I CAN'T keep spoiling you guys.

OH Yeh.. One nutter posted me in a surf board
    Why? Fuck knows.
  This How crazy life is..
You just would not believe the shit I get sent in.
    These are serious nutters out there amongst you lot.
I'm safe in here ☺

    Right... I'm gonna call it a day.
And it Has Been a nice Day.

    I Bid You Farewell.
      Be safe.

        PS. if I'm not back I died
          Peacefully in my sleep.
            Amen.

  P.P.S

    OH and don't you gypsies forget.
    You have a filthy Grass in the camp
      "Paddy Doherty".
    Hid the cunt out..
  (Big Tough guy Runs to the Police)
    Your a disgrace to the whole Gypsy community
      Fuck off and Die.
                          Amen.

371

IAN HUNTLY.

THIS IS HOW YOU DO IT.
it's simple.

STOP PRETENDING —
— CUNTLY.

OOPS SORRY —
HUNTLY.

JUST DO IT AND
FUCK OFF.

BE A MAN.
ACCEPT IT.
YOUR A CUNT

Bie Bie
WORLD.
KISS MY
RING.

HMP

28-2-2011

CAN You BeLieve iT?
  MARCH TOMORROW.
   A BRAND New MONTH.
  Time is FLYiNG
   LiFe's GeTTiNG SHORT...
  MY PAROLe ReView is CReePiNG UP.
     VeRY CLose..
    SooNeR THe FucKiNG BeTTeR I SAY.

I See THe NoTORiOUS PaeDoPHiLe COLiN HATCH
 GoT SNuFFeD ouT iN A CeLL AT FuLL SuTTON JAiL
LAST WeeK ☺
I RememBeR His CASe BAcK iN 1993. He SeXuALLY
 ABuseD 7YeAR oLD SeAN WiLLiAMS iN His NONCe
FLAT iN NORTH LONDON. THeN KiLLeD THe BoY
AND STucK THe BoDY iN BiN LiNeRS.
  I WAS iN BeLMARSH AT THe TiMe oF
THe CuNTS ARReST.
   ONe eViL BASTARD.. AND He WAS
ReLeaseD eARLY ON A PReViOUS SeNTeNCe
FoR ABuSiNG LiTTLe BoYs.
   (WHY DONT THese PRiSON oFFiCiALs
   NeVeR LeARN) ?
ALL THeY eVeR Do is PARoLe MoNSTeRS
AND PuT THe PuBLiC iN DANGeR.
  THis eViL CuNT HATCH SHouLD

BRONSON
A8076AG
C.S.C. CAGe
MONSTER MANSiON
WAKeFieLD
W. YORKS
WF2 9AG

By ReAsoN oF iNSANiTY...

373

Never oi' Been Set Free."

Would You Want The Cunt Living Next Door To You?
This Penal System Should Be Held Responsible every time
They Parole A Nonce, And He Commits Another Sex-Crime.

Anyway Hatch is Dead... Murdered

Damien Fowltes is Charged With It.

He's The Same Convict Whose Also Charged With Cutting
Ian Cuntley's Throat...

This Guy Should Get A Medal... :)

Atleast An O.B.e. Surely.

Fowltes Will Be Here Any Day...

His Cell Awaits In The Belly of The Beast.

Only The Best Come Here :) or The Worst...

"Whatever way You Look At it"

Last Week Was A Cracker For Me. :) Sunday 20th z Ha
A Great Visit With Stu Cheshire And His Old Man Henry. And Stu
Lady Nicity. We Had A Good Laugh..

Then on Weds. (oops sorry) z Mean Tuesday. How Could I
Forget! My Beautiful Partner Lorraine Paid A Visit To Littled
Jails Museum. Run By Andy Jones.

The Actor Louis Murray Went With Her To Research
A Film Project

It Was A Magical Day For Them Both.

She Was Put In A
Strait Jackett. And Locked In
A cell.

Spooky Stuff

I Called Her The Night Before To
Prepare Her For It.. All Good Stuff.

"Forever Lost. Forever In A Bubble. Hurry up And Burst".

374

Its No-Good Fucking About with These Sort of Projects.
You've Got To Face Reality. Littledean Jail is Historical.
Those Cells Hold Nightmares Behind every Door

Rapes... Yes. Mens Arses... Plenty of Them.
Murders... Suicides... Brutality. Insanity. Pain. Torture.
That Place is Hell on earth.

Cold Cells... No Heating. Vermin.
We Are Talking Pure Old Fashion Misery

It May Be A Museum Now......
But it was once A Hell on earth.

It's Well Worth A Visit ... "Forest of Dean". "Gloucester".
Lorraine is Working on A Movie (I Cant Say Alot)
But Louis will Be Playing The Lead Character

Watch out For it Later
It will Blow Your Panties Clean off 😊

Lorraine was up To See me on Thursday To Tell me How
The Day Went ... "Brilliant"

Fudt Me. She Looked A Million Dollars on The Visit
even in Jeans she Looks Classy.

First Time I Have Seen Her in Jeans in Person
A Nice Brown Leather Jacket and Black Top.
She's Just A Very Special Lady To Me
Who Lights up My World.

Thank You
Who Said Mad-Men Dont Fall in Love? 😊
Let me Tell You Now... Love will See me Through All This
Bollocks... You Mark My Words...
Love Can Change A Man... And Save Him. It's True.

I Guess I'm Just A Lucky Guy To Find Somebody
So Special At My Time of Life...
How Does A Guy Like Me Do It From Inside A Coffin?

"Fuck Knows... Who Cares?
But I've Achieved The Impossible....
That's My Woman. I'm So Proud!
<u>Cheers!</u> ☺

Hey. Get on This Amazing Letter I Received Last Week.
It Just Had To Go Into This Book.
"Enjoy".

Dear Mr Bronson,

Congratulations on your engagement, it's great news and is another example of how you have managed to overcome your situation, many people don't ever find love and you've done it whilst living in solitary confinement.

 I am currently reading 'Solitary Fitness' and am very impressed with the amount of topics you cover. When I picked it up in the shop I thought it would just be a guide on how to exercise with access to no equipment and in a confined space, but in fact the book is so much more than that, it is in my opinion a book on fitness philosophy and the amount of detailed information contained puts every other fitness book I've read to shame.

I have already began to share your views on diet and cancer reducing techniques with family and work colleagues, and when I say they came from Charlie Bronson people are bowled over, as many people who have not read your books believe you to be a dangerously strong and aggressive madman.

 So keep up the good work, keep sharing your knowledge of health & fitness and at the same time prove to people that you are so much more than a circus strongman. You are an educated and informative fitness expert.

I have been to the shops to buy a selection of seeds and nuts, this is to get some of the beneficial vitamins and nutrients you highlighted into my system. I have not yet managed to buy the Flaxseed oil you talk about but that is definitely on the shopping list.

Probably the most inspiring part of your book is the fact that at 58 years of age you can still perform feats of strength and fitness that would leave most 20 year olds lying in a heap.

One topic that you didn't mention was dental hygiene, this isn't a criticism because I appreciate that you couldn't include everything, but I have read recently that poor dental hygiene can lead to many illnesses because you are constantly swallowing the bacteria growing in your mouth and also these toxins can enter your blood stream through your gums.

I originally learnt about you and your love of fitness

training after reading your book

and watching the film 'Bronson'.

I thought the book was great especially the bits focussing on your boxing/bare knuckle fights, even Roy Shaw and Lenny Mclean never fought savage dogs!

Whilst on the topic do you have any opinion about their fighting ability? Many people seem to think Roy was better, even though Lenny won 2 out of their 3 fights.

That is another reason I bought 'Solitary Fitness' because I thought that if I put in the effort to follow it I would gain a level of strength and fitness that would be beneficial to me in a self defence situation. I have also started ~~to doing~~ boxing, so if I combine the two I hope to see results soon.

Seeing that you are known for your fighting ability I was wondering if you always aim for the head/jaw or if you think a good placed body shot could be just as effective in a self defence situation. If you have any advice on boxing or self defence it would be greatly appreciated.

I've been watching lots of old Boxing matches on 'youtube' and the best have been the Muhammad Ali vs Joe Frazier 'Thrilla in Manila'

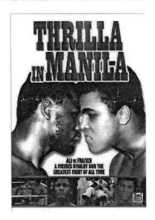

Ali won after 'Smoken' Joe Frazier's corner threw the towel in at the start of the 12th round. Both fighters could barely stand and experts say that if Frazier's corner hadn't quit Ali wouldn't have come out for round 12 anyway. Someone heard Ali asking for his gloves to be cut off.

Nigel Benn vs Gerald McClellan

McClellan had totally dominated the early rounds, sending Benn flying through the ropes, but as the fight went on is was obvious McClellan was suffering from a problem and dropped to his knee in the final round and refused to get up. Benn won after McClellan was counted out in the final round, McClellan later fell into a comma and lost most of his hearing & sight, he now needs round the clock care. Lots of people think he had received a brain injury months before the fight but had been told by Donn King to keep it quite or jeopardize his boxing career.

Which boxers do you admire? Are there any that you would have liked to spare with?

If you find the time to write back that would be great, it would be fantastic to have a letter from Charlie Bronson, even just a line or two.

Good luck Charlie, thanks for all the information you have provided in your books and don't let the system get you down, though you've already proved they can't break you.

Cheers Danny.

Nice one DANNY BoY..
Respect To Jim.

ALSO A FEW SNAPS OF SOME OF THE BRONSON SUPPORTERS OUTSIDE OF
MONSTER MANSION ON 30TH JAN 2011 "RESPECT TO YOU ALL.

IF YOUR WANTING TO JOIN THESE PROTESTS. THERE HELD EVERY 2 MONTHS,
AND WILL CONTINUE UNTIL IM SET FREE... IF THEY DECIDE NEVER TO FREE
THEN MORE SHAME THE SYSTEM. BUT YOUR NEVER STOP MY SUPPORTERS. (EVER
CALL IFTY UP FOR DETAILS - 07976579483.

CLOUT THE BEER BARRELS!
MONSTER MANSION is THE ONLY JAIL iN U.K WITH
A FUCKING BREWERY NEXT DOOR!
"PISS TAKING FUCKERS"

"ANYWAY". THANK'S GUYS FOR ALL YOUR FANTASTIC
SUPPORT. COZ WITHOUT YOU.... THE SYSTEM WOULD OF
KILLED ME YEARS AGO.
       AND THAT'S A FACT.
WHAT YOU GUYS DO IS "EXPOSE THEM FOR WHAT THEY DO"

    WITHOUT YOU.. THEY WOULD DO SO MUCH MORE.

LET THE WORLD KNOW THE TRUTH..

       OPEN THERE EYES..

              THANK'S GUYS..

DID YOU HEAR ABOUT THE BOSNIAN SERB WAR CRIMINA
       "RADISLAV KRISTIC"
HE GOT ATTACKED IN HIS CELL HERE LAST YEAR.
BY 3 MUSLIMS IN A REVENGE ATTACT OVER HIS CASE.
       RADISLAV WAS CONVICTED OF 8,000 MUSLIM DEATHS IN SREB.
HE WAS A GENERAL IN THE BOSNIA ARMY.

THE GENERAL IS 63 YRS OLD. WITH A LEG MISSING.
AND THESE 3 GUYS STEAM INTO HIS CELL TO SERVE HIM UP
        BUT GET ON THIS "
  2 OF THEM ARE NONCES!

  BOTH INDRIT KRASNIQI AND ILIYAS KHALID ARE IN FOR KILLING
    WOMEN.
CAN YOU MAKE THIS SHIT UP?
                                                    ''
            NONCES ATTACKING A ONE LEGGED WAR GENERAL!
  ALL 3 RECEIVED AN EXTRA LIFE SENTENCE FOR ATTEMPTED MURDER!

        WHAT A FUCKING CARRY ON...
                                                        ''
                OH WELL IT IS MONSTER MANSION "

  WHAT IS A FACT IN PRISON... THE MUSLIM LADS ACCEPT
  MUSLIM NONCES... WHY? FUCK KNOWS... BUT THEY DO...
  IF YOUR A MUSLIM. THEN YOUR A BROTHER... NO MATTER WHAT
  CRIME YOUR IN FOR...

      THAT DONT WORK FOR ME...
                                                    (
              A NONCE IS A FILTHY NONCE TO ME.
        '   (
        NO FUCKING BROTHER OF MINE'

              THATS WHAT RELIGION DOES FOR YOU.
                    " BRAINWASHES "
      THEY BECAME SHEEP ..... " PASS THE MINT SAUCE " ☺

  I SUPPOSE THE BIGGEST JOKE OF THIS STORY IS ...
          3 YOUNG MEN IN THERE PRIME, ALL SUPER FIT
  CANT EVEN TAKE OUT A ONE LEGGED OLD MAN! ☺
                                                    ''
                FUCKING HELL... I NEED A LAY DOWN!
                THE WORLDS GONE CRAZY...   😊

I REMEMBER AN OLD CON IN PARKHURST IN 1976.
He MUST HAVE BEEN A GOOD SEVENTY. WHITE HAIR, AND VERY
CRINKLED FACE WITH SUNKEN EYES.
A YOUNG CON WAS TAKING THE PISS OUT OF HIM ONCE TO OFTEN.
The OLD CHAP STABBED HIM IN THE EYE WITH A 6 INCH NAIL.
    The LAD LOST HIS EYE...

  YOU JUST DONT FUCK WITH THE UNKNOWN...
SOME OF THOSE OLD GUTS ARE WALKING BOMBS JUST WAITING
  TO EXPLODE...   BELIEVE IT
  ONE LAST FIGHT IN THEM...
        GO OUT WITH A BANG.
    A LIFE TIME OF MADNESS BOTTLED UP
    ALL READY TO EXPLODE.

LOOK AT 82 YEAR OLD   BERNAARD INGLEBY, HE WAS UP
ON TRIAL AT BIRMINGHAM CROWN COURT LAST DECEMBER
    FOR KILLING HIS 77 YEAR OLD GIRLFRIEND MARY FORD.
He SLIT HER THROAT AND SHOVED HER DOWN STAIRS.
    He GOT SENTENCED TO LIFE!
  AT 82. He WONT BE SERVING TO LONG WILL He.
      The OLD FELLA WILL BE LEAVING JAIL IN A BODY BAG.

SO WHY DID He KILL MARY?
        WHO WILL EVER KNOW?
  IT TOOK HIM 82 YRS TO KILL ANYBODY.
        SOME OLD FOLK JUST WAKE UP ONE DAY AND FEEL THE NEED
  TO KILL.   SAD BUT TRUE.

ANOTHER OLD CHAP IN SANTIAGO - CHILE. IN DECEMBER LAST YEAR STABBED
  HIS WIFE TO DEATH. SHE WAS 90 YRS OLD... He WAS 87.
  He CAUGHT HER WITH A TOYBOY WHO WAS 84 YRS OLD ☺
      YOU CANT MAKE THIS SHIT UP
  OLD JOSE RAMIREZ WILL NOW DIE IN A JAIL. FOR WHAT?

Killing His old lady For Betraying Him?
87 yrs on the Planet And He Becomes A Killer.
That sums life up in a Nut Shell To me

"Anybody can Snap" at any Time
You Could Be Next.
So Watch out.

OO
Lu

If Your on The edge. And About To Snap.
Make it Spectacular." A one off.
Go Down in The Criminal History Books.
The Madder The Better OO

Taken Through A Judas Hole
in the Prison Door

Hey!
This is Lou Murrall.
With My Shades on.
With My Prison cat A Suit on
in Littledean Jail.

Watch out For This Guy.

He's Gonna Become Britains
Top Actor.

If You Dont Believe it.
You Wait And See... ♥

_ Welcome To A Fellow Loon!

387

I ONCE GOT A NONCE IN THE EYE THROUGH A SPY HOLE IN
A CELL DOOR IN WANDSWORTH JAIL IN THE 70'
                    ABOUT 1975 ... MAYBE 76
    ABT OF THE JUDAS HOLES WERE EMPTY. (GLASS KNOCKED OUT)
IT WAS HANDY FOR PASSING ITEMS THROUGH.
            PAPERS. MAGS. MATCHES. TOBACO. ECT

THIS CUNT HAD JUST CAME IN FOR RAPE ON AN OLD LADY.
    SO I SHARPENED A BROOM HANDLE UP LIKE A SPEAR.
I BANGED HIS DOOR AND WAITED ...
            SECONDS LATER HIS EYE APPEARD .. BOSH

                AARgghhhhhhh.
THATS HOW TO DEAL WITH A NONCE.
        POETIC JUSTICE I CALL IT.

    Lovely Memories.

    AND THE TRUTH IS .... I DONT KNOW ANYBODY FROM MY
WALK OF LIFE WHO WOULD NOT WANT TO STAB A NONCE UP
    THATS WHAT NONCES ARE FOR !!!
IF WE CANT HAVE A PUNCH BAG .. THEN WE SHOULD BE
ALLOWED A NONCE TO SMASH UP..
                (AT LEAST ONCE A WEEK)

OH YEH!.. THE CROSSBOW CANNIBAL IS STILL KICKING
    LINGERING ON. LIKE A RATTLING SKELETON..
I STILL ASK FOR HIS FOOD ... WHAT A WASTE!

        OH WELL ... 1ST MARCH TOMORROW ..
    EARLY NIGHT FOR ME.
        ADIOS AMIGOS.

        STAY SAFE

When writing to Members of Parliament please give your previous home address in order to avoid delay in your case being taken up by the M.P.

In replying to this letter, please write on the envelope:

Number A8076AG   Name CHARLie BRONSON

Wing C.S.C. UNIT Special-Cage

F WING
HM PRISON
5 LOVE LANE
WAKEFIELD
WES ... G

1. 3. 2011

"RIGHT" .. THis is iT .. THe eND To MY FiNAL BooT iN PRisoN..

THere Be No-MoRe. ...

SiMPLY Because iTs Bloody HARD WoRK GeTTiNg iT SeNT To MY PubLisHeRs Desk..

"ALMosT ImPossiBLe"

AND iF iT WASNT FoR A BeNT GuARD, WHo GeTs A Nice Few QuiD ouT oF DoiNG THe HoNouRs FoR Me, THeN THis BooT WouLD NoT Be PossiBLe

PLus I HATe HAViNG To FoRK ouT CASH To A CoRRuPT TuRN Key.

He CouLD oF ATLeAST THRoWN iN A BoTTLe oF BRANDY FoR Me..

"TigHT FucKer"

ANYWAY Here iT iS. (oN THe PubLisHeRs Desk)

THere Be HeLL To PLAY WHeN THis is PubLisHeD —

BY PRISON H/Q.

How THE FUCK AS BRONSON DONE ANOTHER BOOK?
WHEN WE HAVE HIM IN A SECURE CAGE. ON A MAX
SECURE UNIT, AND WE HAVE SECURITY TO CENSOR
ALL HIS MAIL. OUTGOING AND INCOMING.

WELL. LETS SAY. ITS YOU PRATTS WHO EMPLOY
CORRUPT SCREWS. YOU DEAL WITH IT
                    BUT
    YOUR NEVER FIND OUT WHO IT WAS BY ME.
            SO FUCK OFF.

COZ IM PROUD OF ALL MY BOOKS.
        EVERY ONE IS A GREAT ACHIEVMENT.
        EVEN MORE SO WHEN THE SYSTEM TRIES
EVERYTHING TO STOP IT.

    IVE ACTUALLY CHOSE TODAY TO END IT.
SO AS TO LEAVE A BIG QUESTION UNANSWERED

        DID BRONSON WIN HIS PAROLE?
        DID HE EVER GET HIS APPEAL HEARD.
            IS HE STILL INSIDE?
            IS HE DEAD OR ALIVE!

    IM A CRUEL BASTARD.
    I LIKE TO KEEP YOU IN SUSPENSE.
        BETTER STILL SUSPENDERS.

TODAY I RECEIVED A BAG LOAD OF MAIL
MOST FROM WELL WISHERS
   TO NAME A FEW..
        Mickey MCLERNIN   HOLME HOUSE JAIL
        ANTHONY OBRIEN   STRANGEWAYS JAIL
        MICHAEL LONERGAN   OUTSIDE
        BEN KIDD   ALTCOURSE JAIL
        PAUL ELLIS   DARTMOOR JAIL
        DALE SMITH   WETHEROY JAIL
        KERRY   OUTSIDE
        JAMES ELPHICK   OUTSIDE
        TONY CONAGHAN   OUTSIDE
        TEEJAY WALTON   WETHERBY JAIL
        GEORGE SALMON   OUTSIDE
        JENNY THOMPSON   OUTSIDE

PLUS A PILE FROM MY FAMILY + FRIENDS
MY SON / DAVE TAYLOR / LORRAINE / AL RAYMENT / JOHN GRIFFITHS /
SANDRA GARDNER / HARRIETT MATHER (LAWYER) AND GAVIN MEEN FOR
POSTING ME IN A BULLSEYE. "CHEERS GAVIN"   7 (ILL BUY SAID CANTEEN) ☺
        NOT BAD FOR A MONDAY EH
           THATS 18 LETTERS.
   E NOW SEE WHERE MY TIME GOES ?

IF IM NOT DOING ART. IM READING. OR REPLYING LETTERS.
        MY WEEKS FLY..
        SOMETIMES TO FAST..
        LIFES A FAST TRACK.. WITHOUT STOPS.

I REALLY WANT TO THANK YOU ALL FOR
HELPING ME ALONG... YOUR ALL STARS TO ME.
I LOVE AND RESPECT YOU ALL.
WHO CAN KNOW WHAT MAY HAPPEN TOMORROW?
    WITH THE WAY MY LIFE IS --- "ANYTHING"
        GOOD OR BAD

FIGHT TILL
You Die.

ALL I CAN
REALLY PROMISE
YOU ALL .. I WILL
DIE FIGHTING.
NO MAN WILL
EVER ABUSE ME
AND LIVE TO GET
AWAY WITH IT
'NEVER'
ITS BETTER TO
DIE THAN LIVE
AS A SLUG.

HOPEFULLY
LOVE WILL NOW
SEE ME THROUGH
WHATS LEFT.
IT WOULD BE SO
NICE TO LIVE IT
REST OF MY DA
BEING LOVED.

When writing to Members of Parliament please give your previous home
address in order to avoid delay in your case being taken up by the M.P.

In replying to this letter, please write on the envelope:

Number A8076AG   Name CHARLie BRoNSoN

Wing C.S.C. UNIT. Special Cage.

F WING
HM PRISON
5 LOVE LANE
WAKEFIELD
WF2 9AG

"

FIGHT TiLL You Die.
BY
Himself.

"Keep on PuNcHiNg TiLL THe LigHTs go ouT.
The HeART WiLL see You THRough.
Never give iN, Never BAck oFF
THe WiNNeR cAN oNLy Be You.
Your BoRN To FIGHT uNTiL You Die
DREAMS WoNT SHoW THe WAY.
Look THe FuTuRe iN THe eye
Live FRom DAY To DAY.
Keep Your MoRALS AND SeLF-RespecT
PRide is A PoWeRFuL THiNG.
A SoLiTARY LiFe. A BuLLeT PRooF SouL
iN THe DARkNess TEARS WiLL STiNg

1-3 2011

So WHAT HAPPENS IF I DU WIN MY
FREEDOM?
THE MILLION DOLLAR QUESTION

MARRY MY LORRAINE!
CREATE MY ART.
WRITE SOME NOVELS.
TRAVEL.
DO MY AFTER DINNER SPEECH.
DO A BRONSON TOUR.
TRY MY LUCK AT ACTING
A COME BACK FIGHT.
DO A FITNESS D·V·D.
STOP THE YOUTH FROM GOING INTO CRIME.

So-So. MUCH I NEED TO DO.
AND MY LORRAINE BACKS ME ALL THE WAY.
WIN OR LOSE SHE'S THERE WITH ME.

OUR FUTURE CAN BE WONDERFUL.

CRIME AND CRIMINALS... FUCK OFF.
I'M SICK OF IT
I DONT NEED IT

GUNS. DRUGS. MUGS. GANGSTERS.
PLEASE JUST GO AWAY.

MY LIFE IS SO MUCH BETTER.
"SAFER TOO"

WE ALL GOTTA GROW UP SOMETIME!
IT TOOK ME NEARLY 6 DECADES.

HEY!
DONT THINK I'VE GONE SOFT IN THE CRUST.
I WILL STILL KNOCK TEN BELLS OF SHIT OUT
OF ANY FUCKER WHO GETS MY BACK UP.

OLD FIGHTERS NEVER DIE PUSSIES.

I'VE NOT SURVIVED ALL MY ADULT LIFE IN
HELL TO BECOME A PUSSY.

SOMETIMES A DARK ALLEY IS THE BEST JUSTICE.
THE ONLY WAY TO PROVE A POINT.

STAY CLEAR OF ME.
LET ME LIVE MY LIFE AS I WISH,
AND THERE'S NO REASON TO STEP INTO THE
DARKNESS..
LIVE FREE AND HAPPY I SAY.

THE GREAT POWER I DO HAVE IS MY LOYAL
FAMILY AND FRIENDS..

THROUGH THEM I SHALL BECOME THE WINNER.

"BET AGAINST IT AND YOUR LOSE."

THANKS TO MY LOVELY MOTHER FOR A LIFETIME OF CONFUSION I'VE GIVEN HER. SORRY MUM xx

THANKS TO MY LOYAL BROTHER MARK "BE LOST WITHOUT YOU"

MIKE KEEP YOUR CHIN UP SON. LOVE YOU TO BITS x

LORRAINE. THANKS FOR HELPING ME TO FIND LOVE ITS WONDERFUL. x

AND A SPECIAL WORD FOR "DANIEL WILDER" YOUR GO ON TO BE A GREAT TRAINER LIKE ANGELO DUNDEE. A LEGEND.

PEACE LOVE AND MADNESS. THE WORLDS A BIG ASYLUM

THE END.

Me with my mother, Eira, 2000

Me with my brother, Mark, June 2010

Top of the rock - Gibraltar, October 2010. From left to right: Wayne Andrews, Graham Ormesher, Paul Mead, Gordon Murphy, my brother Mark Peterson, Tony Leach, Stuart Godfrey, Jason Murphy and Adie Perry

Irish Town, Gibraltar, October 2010 - my brother's 50th birthday. From left to right: Stuart Godfrey, Paul Mead, my brother Mark Peterson, a friendly Gibraltar old bill, Jason Murphy, Gordon Murphy, Tony Leach and Adie Perry